ADVENTURES ON THE
INFINITE HIGHWAY

First published in 2004 by

WOODFIELD PUBLISHING
Bognor Regis, West Sussex, England
www.woodfieldpublishing.com

© Peter Rivington, 2004

The right of Peter Rivington
to be identified as Author of this work
has been asserted in accordance with
the Copyright, Designs and Patents Act 1988

ISBN 1-903953-56-1

Adventures on the Infinite Highway

*A Pilot's Experiences
in Peace and War 1938-62*

PETER RIVINGTON

EDITED BY ROD PRIDDLE

Woodfield

"The desire to fly is an idea handed down to us by our ancestors who, in their gruelling travels across trackless deserts, looked enviously on the birds soaring through space, at full speed, above all obstacles on the infinite highway of the air."
Wilbur Wright

Contents

Preface

Peter Rivington was born in 1920, with his twin brother Paul, at Ivy House Nursing Home in Devizes, Wiltshire. Their parents, Charles and Frances Rivington, had met at the Bristol Royal Infirmary where she was a nursing sister and he a trainee doctor. The father of Charles was a naval captain and he allowed his son to enter the medical profession on the understanding that he would become a missionary. After their marriage Frances gave birth to a son Francis who they took with them to Peking in 1912 where Charles headed a mission hospital.

During the years in China, Frances had four more children. A daughter and a set of twins died but another daughter survived. The family returned to England in 1915 when Charles enlisted in the R.A.M.C. The family home at that time was in Combe Down, Bath. Frances had now become frail and was advised not to have any more children but despite the advice had a daughter Kathleen in 1916.

Charles was later invalided out of the Army and entered private practice with a Doctor Raby at Sandcliff, Devizes, Wiltshire in 1920, the year that Peter and Paul were born.

The family moved from Bath to Craven House in Station Road, Devizes and lived there until Dr. Raby retired, when they moved into Sandcliff. Doctor Rivington employed two nurses, a cook and housekeeper to assist his wife with the children and the up-keep of the house.

Peter and Paul started their schooling in Lansdown House in Long Street and then at Braeside in Bath Road. When they were

10 years old they were amongst the first boys of primary school age to attend the old and well-established private Dauntsey's School. Entries at this level commenced in 1930 in the school occupying The Manor at West Lavington on the A360 Devizes to Salisbury road. The boys' mother had died in 1929 and shortly after they started school at Dauntsey's, the Doctor re-married. As is so often the case, the step-mother was despised by all the children of the house.

Tragedy struck the family again in 1933 when Francis the first born died just as he had qualified in medicine.

Peter and Paul made their mark at Dauntsey's but in very different fields. Peter's interest and participation was in sport and Paul's in acting. Peter commenced a life-long love of cricket and captained the school team. He also played rugby, hockey and soccer for the school teams. Peter was influenced considerably by Norman Creek, his sport's master at Dauntsey's. He had played amateur soccer for 'Corinthians' and had represented England at both amateur and full international level. He also played Minor Counties cricket for Wiltshire. He flew with the RFC during the First World War and had been awarded the Military Cross. Listening to the stories of Norman Creek's flying experiences influenced Peter considerably and was instrumental in his pursuance of a flying career.

Doctor Rivington died in 1938. The twins who had left school before war broke out; both joined the RAF to serve their country, as their father had done during World War 1. The clouds of war were forming when Peter joined in 1938 on a Short Service Commission. Paul, who had taken up a Scholarship at RADA, entered the RAF in 1939. It was no surprise that Peter would qualify for his pilot's wings, but Paul who was drawn to the Arts and to religion and did not have the same mechanical and engineering aptitude as his brother, failed his training course.

Undeterred however, he went on to train as a W.Op/AG at RAF Cranwell. It was while still under training that he was killed when the Proctor aircraft in which he was flying crashed on Thursday 10th July 1941. Low cloud unexpectedly rolled in over the airfield at Cranwell, and his Polish pilot, in trying to get beneath it, crashed into some treetops. Paul Rivington is buried at Cranwell (St. Andrew) Church.

The poem *Retrospective* refers to Llwyngwril on the coast of North Wales where the two brothers as young boys, regularly spent family holidays.

Retrospective

I know a little garden
Sloping steeply to the sea,
And there above all others
Is the place I long to be.
These mountains rise up all around
A mighty sweep of bay,
And plunging breakers pound the cliffs
Unceasing night and day.
Yet there is peace and rest and ease
In that fair happy land
And simple pleasures that all men
Can love and understand!

Paul Rivington, 1st September 1940, RAF Benson

These pages tell a story, not of a pilot with one of the more glamorous Fighter or Bomber squadrons but one of a young man who served with the Royal Air Force through the years of the Second World War and, on more than one occasion, faced death in a different form than at the end of a gun.

Peter Rivington tells of pre-war RAF discipline, Messroom customs and of Britain's vunerability at the time war was declared. He tells of his training as a pilot and of early flying experiences where good fortune was sometimes the difference between possible death and survival. The occasion of another survival, unrelated to flying, was his rescue from a ship sunk in a torpedo attack.

During his career as a pilot he flew many kinds of aircraft and the reader will learn from his explanations some of the characteristics, good and bad, of the various types he flew.

When the war ended and he left the RAF, he pursued his love of flying but with civilian airlines. Initially this involved flying passengers and cargo to and from Europe and the Middle East and later equally precious cargo in the 'Berlin Airlift'. At the conclusion of this Russian seige, Peter joined Short Brothers for whom he flew many types of Royal Navy aircraft from piston engine types, to jets, to helicopters.

In addition he gave flying and navigation instruction to the post war pilots of the Royal Navy.

Squadron Leader Peter Rivington was awarded the 1939-45 Star, Atlantic Star, Africa Star, Burma Star, 1939-45 War Medal and the Defence Medal 1939-45.

Rod Priddle

About the Editor

Rod Priddle was an officer with Bristol and Wiltshire Fire Brigades and took up writing following his retirement in 1991. His subject matter has been confined mainly to local history in Wiltshire, where he lives on the edge of Salisbury Plain. The majority of his books are associated with the Royal Air Force and his mammoth 400-page tome *Wings over Wiltshire*, published recently, was the culmination of six years of research and writing.

Rod was drawn to Peter Rivington's *Adventures on the Infinite Highway* because it features the wartime flying activities of a branch of the RAF about which little has been written previously. The tasks faced by Peter and his colleagues posed a unique set of challenges which called for skill, courage and stamina. Peter's postwar flying exploits were also very varied and make for interesting reading.

Also by Rod Priddle:

GWR to Devizes (with D. Hyde), Millstream Books, Bath 1996
Wings of the Brave, Wilbek & Lewbar, Devizes 1998
Bombers' Moon, Wilbek & Lewbar, Devizes 1999
On a Wing and a Prayer Wilbek & Lewbar, Devizes 2000
One Step to Heaven Wilbek & Lewbar, Devizes 2001
Flying without Wings Wilbek & Lewbar, Devizes 2002
Shades of Blue Wilbek & Lewbar, Devizes 2003
Wings over Wiltshire, ALD Design & Print, Sheffield 2003

Peter Rivington in RAF uniform, 1943.

1. *The Seeds are Sown*

The Wessex Helicopter droned steadily over the misty Dorset countryside, cutting through drooping wisps of cloud hanging from an 800ft base. The visibility was a bare mile. Not ideal weather for a last flight, for that's what it was. The Group Captain at the Central Air Medical Board had been quite explicit: "Certain irregularities in the electrocardiogram – unfit for further flying until a Harley Street Cardiologist of the standing of Dr Evan 'B' pronounces on his fitness".

Well, Dr Evan 'B' had said that although he was prepared to give the OK, the blood pressure was a little high and the CAMB-wallahs would be on the warpath from now on, so as there was a question of loss of licence insurance. His advice was to bow out now rather than hang on for another few years. After all, 42 was quite an advanced age for a pilot.

So, I shouldn't really be doing this flight, but I couldn't resist the temptation to have just one more go. Looking back over the mists of 24 flying years, how had it all begun? With that first flight at Gatwick on 6th October 1938 (some dates one never forgets)?

No. Probably four or five years before that, at school…

The Games Master at Dauntsey's – my school in Wiltshire in the 1930s – was Norman Creek, best known as a Cambridge University, Corinthians and England (full international) inside forward. He was also a fine minor counties cricketer: an attacking middle order batsman and as a bowler was quick by club standards. It was he more than anyone else who aroused by second great interest in life, cricket. But more important for this story, he had a great interest in flying.

Norman had served in the R.F.C. in what we knew then as the Great War, when, flying as an Observer he had won the Military Cross. At school his classroom subject was geography, but we would at every opportunity side-track him into talking of his flying experiences. This interest fitted in well with his subject, and I well remember the huge chart he pinned to his Geography Room wall at the time of the McRobertson Air Race from England to Australia in the autumn of 1934. Little flags were moved every few hours as news of the competitors' progress came over the wireless. Sometimes, when he was on evening duty, he would come to our dormitory before lights out and talk of the war, of flying and of aeroplanes.

It was about this time that I decided that I too would become a flyer. Copies of 'The Aeroplane' and 'Flight' were eagerly scanned in the school Reading Room and scrap- books made, listing all the modern aeroplanes with photos and drawings. Bulldog, Hart, Hind, Siskin, Sidestrand, Overstrand, Heyford, Grebe, Gamecock and Gauntlet, they were all there with details of performance, sometimes very sketchy. "The maximum speed of this new aircraft has not been released, but it is known to be in excess of 200 mph" etc, etc.

I remember our "Old Boys' Day", an O.D. arriving from Brooklands (I think) in a red and black Tiger Moth, landing in one of the school farm fields. We stood around this machine with awe, wondering that something looking so small in the sky could be so big on the ground. We peered into the cockpit and imagined ourselves controlling this marvellous machine in the air.

There was, it seemed to me, only one possible way to fly and that was with the Royal Air Force and the way into the RAF was through the college at Cranwell. So, in the summer of 1938, I found myself in London, with several days off school, taking the exams, the interview and the medical, for a cadetship at the Royal Air Force College. Unfortunately, although the last two hurdles were surmounted, the first was not. This, I imagine, was no great surprise to my schoolmasters (I had left before the results were out), as I had, I'm afraid, done little in my last year but play games and enjoy myself. I had thought, however, that as I was young enough to have another try at the Cranwell exam, I might go to a 'crammer' and get through in the following year. In the event this proved impossible, as my father, a hard working country G.P., died suddenly that August, making it imperative for me to earn my own living. There would be no money for 'crammers' or for Cranwell. (Yes, everyone paid in those days). But there was an alternative. The RAF was expanding rapidly and needed a large number of officer pilots under the Short Service Commission scheme. This provided for four years regular and six years reserve service. I applied for one of these Commissions as soon as the Cranwell results were out and was accepted without more ado.

Early in September my instructions arrived. I was to report to No.19 E & R.F.T.S., Gatwick Airport, Surrey, on the 5th October 1938. So I really was to become a pilot.

2. No.19 E & R.F.T.S Gatwick

My train arrived at the Airport Station at around 4 o'clock and, following my joining instructions, I carried my suitcase through the subway from the station to come up in the white airport building. The modern traveller would not recognise the Gatwick of 1938. The present airport terminal and the runway are built over the old Gatwick racecourse and the technical and office buildings to the south of the runway over the old aerodrome. The old terminal building and hangars are now cut off from the new airfield by the loop of the diverted A23 London-Brighton road.[1]

The present Gatwick Airport Railway Station is on the site of the old Gatwick Racecourse station. The old Gatwick Airport station is long gone.

The Airport Terminal I entered that October afternoon was the pride of its designers in the mid-1930s. Circular in shape, it had a number of exits radiating like the spokes of a wheel through which passengers could reach the aircraft. Telescopic covered walkways could be extended to afford sheltered access right up to an aircraft's door. In the main ground floor concourse were bays for customs, immigration, health-control and so on. On the first floor was a restaurant and bar and above that, a

---

[1] The terminal building was re-furbished and re-opened on 1st December 2000 by HRH The Duke of Edinburgh. Gibraltar Airways leased the Grade II listed building for 25 years from British Airports Authority to accommodate GA's administration staff and cabin crews.

purpose-built Air Traffic Control with a view over the landing and take-off area.

The circular airport terminal building at Gatwick in 1938 with Tiger Moths in evidence. The terminal, known as the 'Beehive' because of its shape, had been opened in 1936.

Lockheed Electrix G-AESY of British Airways Ltd. preparing for take-off at Gatwick in 1938. The covered footbridge of Gatwick Airport railway station is seen above the tailfin.

The first thing I noticed when I climbed the stairs of the subway into the terminal building were a number of exits; 'gates' in modern parlance marked BERLIN, PARIS, BRUSSELS etc. The surprising thing was that everything was deserted. Then a notice on an office door caught my eye: 'PUPIL PILOTS REPORT

HERE'. I correctly assumed that this meant me. Inside a friendly secretary ticked my name off a list and said there was no accommodation on the aerodrome. All Pupil Pilots (this was to be our title while at EFTS) were to be billeted out for bed and breakfast, but lunch and high tea would be provided in the airport restaurant. Tea was now available if I liked to go up. Upstairs I met some of the young men who were to be my colleagues for the next year.

It appeared that the modern airport building in which we were sitting had been built in 1936 to serve the new Gatwick Airport, hence all the signs and trappings below. Unfortunately the powers that be did not relish a competitor for the long established airport at Croydon, and in any case, the aerodrome was low lying and badly drained. This was, of course, before the days of runways. For much of the year it had proved itself to be unsuitable for heavy aircraft and the owners, Airports Ltd., had abandoned attempts to attract airline traffic, and had opened an Elementary and Reserve Flying Training School under contract from the Air Ministry. The Reserve section operated mainly at weekends and provided flying for RAF Reservists from the South London and Surrey areas. We were the Elementary part, the first such course, in fact.

We learnt that in these schools, and there were a number dotted around the country, that civilian firms provided the airfield and staff (mainly ex RAF) while the Air Ministry provided the aircraft. It was, it seemed, cheaper to do it that way than for the Service to carry out the whole operation.

Of course everyone wanted to know what aircraft we were to fly. The probable answer could be seen through the restaurant windows. Dotted around a hangar in the middle distance were a number of bright yellow low wing monoplanes with tandem cockpits and engine cowlings of bright un-painted metal. It looked as if we were to use Miles Magisters.

Two Miles Magisters with N5814 in the foreground.

Soon transport was provided to take us with our luggage to our 'digs'. I was to be billeted in a small guesthouse with two others. It was about a mile from the aerodrome on the Horley-Three Bridges road and as may be imagined, we had plenty to talk about that evening.

In the morning, after a 20 minutes walk to the airfield, no time was lost in getting down to business. Flying kit was issued, Sidcot suit with 'teddy-bear' lining, flying helmet with goggles and 'Gosport' tubes, gauntlet gloves and sheepskin-lined suede leather flying boots, all to be stowed away in tall lockers.

Then came an introductory talk from the C.O. (Although they were civilian units it was the custom at an E & R.F.T.S. to use Service terms and he was, in fact, the Manager, Flt/Lt Bennett, RAFO).

Our course was to last until early December. During this time we would get about 50 hours flying, roughly half of them solo. A proportion of our time would be spent in the classroom studying theory of flight, navigation, airmanship and armaments. We would have our meals in the airport restaurant, but the bar was out of bounds to pupil pilots at all times. Although this was not said directly, we understood that if anyone should fail to make the grade in the air or on the ground, he would be packed off home with a minimum of formality. This was, of course, one of the advantages of our being given civilian, not service, status.

Students and Instructors of No.1 Course at No.19 E&RFTS Gatwick in 1938.

We were then introduced to our instructors. Mine was Flt.Lt. Leigh-Smith. If I ever knew his Christian name I can't recall it and I certainly had no occasion to use it. An urbane relaxed character with a wry sense of humour, he possessed a delightful white bull terrier that he nicknamed "Dr Williams". He would patiently remind the enquirer of the well known 'cure all' of the time, "Dr Williams Pink Pills"!

I still think of Leigh-Smith as the best pilot I ever flew with. I realise that this is most unlikely to be the case, but it is natural to think of one's first instructor in this way.

We had been correct in surmising that our aircraft would be Miles Magisters, though a small group was to be on Tiger Moths.

The Magister, built at Reading by Phillips and Powis, had been developed from the Hawk two-seater monoplane that first flew in 1934. Early models had a 90 hp Cirrus 111 engine. Later, as the Hawk Major with a 130 h.p. Gipsy Major, it set up a number of long distance records in the mid 1930's. Ordered in quantity by the RAF and named Magister, it became the Service's first monoplane ab-initio trainer.

The 'Maggie', (no political connotation in those days), was a wooden framed ply wood covered aircraft, with fabric covered control surfaces. The fixed undercarriage consisted of two separate main-wheel struts with neat metal fairings and wheel spats (many wartime pilots will remember the aircraft without these), and a sprung fully castoring tail-wheel. Wheel brakes were fitted to the main wheels operated by a motor car like lever in the cockpit. When applied they worked differentially with the rudder bar, as was the British fashion at the time. The aircraft was finished in RAF training yellow, with the very smart bright metal engine cowling already noted. This also disappeared when the war came. A novel feature for the time was the fitting of split trailing edge flaps to the wings, inboard of the ailerons. These were needed because the comparatively clean monoplane lines gave far less drag (air resistance) than the then more usual bi-plane. This gave a very flat engine-off gliding angle making the approach to land difficult to judge. When the flaps were lowered the extra drag gave a much steeper gliding angle with the additional bonus of increasing the lift and lowering the stalling speed.

No time was lost in getting us into the air. I don't remember that we were ever formally 'shown around' the aircraft, but were simply bundled into the rear cockpit (from which the aircraft was always flown solo) and taken off for 'air experience'.

This was the first time I had flown, and my most vivid memory is of the aircraft hitting what the layman would call "airpockets" and we came to know as 'bumps'. The effect seemingly, was to leave a large part of my insides several feet above my head as the aircraft dropped out of the sky. I was taken up on this occasion by the Chief Flying Instructor, Flt.Lt. Kingswell, a very experienced pilot of the old school who was later to do the test flying on the General Aircraft Owlet nose wheel aircraft, a novel departure at that time.

Peter Rivington in the rear cockpit of a Magister preparing for take-off.

Peter Rivington with the Instructor in the front cockpit of Magister L8350 starting-up in preparation for take-off from Gatwick.

I have said that no explanation of the controls or instruments was given before that first flight and this lack of discussion on the ground was a continuing feature of our course, whereas pre-flight briefing is a vital part of modern flying instruction. To give just one example: one of the first lessons in flying, is to be shown, and to experience, the effect of the controls. The instructor proceeds like this:

"Put your hands and feet on the controls. Now you feel me moving the control column to the left and the left wing goes down. Now to the right and the right wing goes down. The aircraft is now moving in the rolling plane. Now I ease the control column forward and the nose falls below the horizon, now back and it rises. The aircraft is now moving in the pitching plane. Now feel me push my left foot forward on the rudder bar and the aircraft's nose swings to the left, now the right rudder and the nose swings to the right. The aircraft is now moving in the yawing plane". At this point I interrupted:

"The what sir?"

"The yawing plane."

"What plane?"

"Yawing, Y-A-W-I-N-G, Yawing!

Now the point of this is that if you haven't heard the word 'Yawing' before, in a noisy aircraft, under the stress of an early flying lesson, you are unlikely to have the faintest idea of what the man is talking about. Two minutes explanation on the ground before the flight would have made everything clear and saved a lot of frustration.

A further example of this lack of preparation on the ground came quite soon. I was having some trouble learning the 'simple' art of flying straight and level. The novice imagines that he has to fight to hold the aircraft steady and will sometimes find himself gripping the 'stick' with whitened knuckles, when only gentle guidance is needed. Anyway, after a not very successful lesson in rather rough conditions, Leigh-Smith said to me as we walked away from the aircraft:

"By the way, how do you hold the controls?"

"Both hands on the stick and feet on the rudder" said I.

"Both hands on the stick? He exclaimed. "Why?"

"I don't know", I replied, "Isn't that the way?"

Of course it wasn't. Right hand gently on the stick and left hand on the throttle was the way. That made it much easier, but I should have been shown that on the ground before my first flight. This type of mistake would not be made by modern instructors.

By now a few days had gone by and we were getting to know our fellow pupils. We ranged from 18 year olds just out of school, to 26 year old 'men of the world'. One of the most senior in age was Charles Green, a Rhodesian, he had worked for Imperial Airways as a Station Manager in Africa and, tiring of watching others fly, had decided to have a go himself. Chosen as our Senior Course pupil, he was outstanding both as a pilot and as a man, and was destined to survive the war, reaching the rank of Group Captain.

Another of the older pupils was 'Tolly' Rothwell, chosen as Charles' number two. He also survived the war after being shot down and taken prisoner. In the prison camp he displayed a talent for script writing and produced several shows. On his return after the war one of these was put on in the West End, 'Cage Birds'. Afterwards Talbot Rothwell wrote scripts for a string of successful television and film comedies including the 'Carry On' series and Frankie Howard's 'Up Pompei'.

Then there was Walker, a bluff Canadian with previous flying experience, including some solo time, and George Petit, who had gone solo on Autogyros under the guidance of that doyen of rotary wing pilots, Alan Marsh. In all there were 22 of us including 4 regular RAF airmen (a corporal and 3 L.A.C's). These had been selected for training as N.C.O. pilots. All were a grand lot to be with, but sadly, a high proportion, something over half I think, failed to survive the war.

Peter Rivington on the right with a fellow student on a Thompson 500 gallon refueller at Gatwick.

In such a diverse group there was bound to be the odd 'bad egg'. One character lasted about a week, nothing to do with flying, I think, but he hardly seemed what would later be called 'Officer Material', and one wondered how he had got through the selection procedure. Another, whose name I shall conveniently forget, was the typical 'bang on old boy' cartoon RAF Officer. Unfortunately, his tastes in women and general living were incompatible with his income. Thus he was in the habit of borrowing money from unsuspecting colleagues who were very lucky if they were repaid. I got off comparatively lightly and finished only 10/- worse off. I met him in London after the war in Sheppards pub (wearing what he asserted was a Free Forrester's tie, but was nothing of the sort) and asked him how he had got on. "Oh I was in the jolly old Battle of B. Old Boy" he said and carried on in like vein. I afterwards learnt that he had in fact been court-martialled and dismissed the service early in 1940 for bouncing cheques. A few weeks later I saw a paragraph in the evening paper concerning a man of his rather unusual name who had been in court accused of stealing £20 from the girl with whom he was living. I suppose the Selection Board could not be expected to win them all.

Once the course got underway we flew for about 90 minutes a day, 45 minutes in the morning and the same in the afternoon. The time taken to 'go solo' varied with each individual, from a minimum of about 6 hours to a maximum of about 12. If a pupil had not gone solo by this time he was in danger of rejection. I can't exactly remember the time I took to go solo but I know it was over 10, perhaps 11 hours. I have to rely on my memory for this and all other facts of my early flying career, as my first log book was deposited on the floor of the Atlantic Ocean in 1941 by an unfriendly U-boat Commander. Its owner was lucky not to go with it but more of that later.

The reason for the variation in times to solo is mainly that every individual takes a different time to get the hang of landing, a tricky procedure, unlike taking off, which is quite simple.

For the take off the aircraft stands across wind, while the pre take-off drill is carried out. Older pilots will remember the mnemonic T.M.P.F.F.G. (Trim, mixture, pitch, fuel, flaps, gills). On the Magister, of course, there was no pitch control and no gills. Then when the take-off path is clear and the other aircraft coming in to land will not be baulked, the aircraft can be turned into wind and taken off without delay. We had no Air Traffic Control and on the grass airfield there might be three or four aircraft making their final approaches at the same time. As long as they are all into wind this is perfectly safe as parallel lines do not meet, but no doubt a modern Controller would consider this a nightmare.

Returning to the take-off, once lined up, the throttle is opened smoothly and fully and the aircraft kept straight by coarse use of the rudder. Without the benefit of a runway one has to pick a tree or building on or beyond the aerodrome boundary to keep straight on. As the speed increases a slight forward movement of the stick brings the tail up and the aircraft into flying attitude. The rudder is now very effective. As flying speed is approached, forward pressure on the stick is maintained so that undulations on the aerodrome surface do not throw the aircraft prematurely into the air. When full flying speed is reached a slight backward pressure takes the aircraft into the air and it is then held in level flight for a few seconds until the correct climbing speed has been reached. Few pupils have any problems in mastering this technique, but the landing is a different kettle of fish.

This can be divided into two stages, the approach to land and the actual landing itself. In a power off glide approach (normal in the old days) the pupil is expected to fly across wind (later called 'base leg') at 1,000ft. He has to judge the point at which to close the throttle and glide, lowering the nose to maintain the correct speed and correcting with rudder the tendency to yaw as the power comes off. At 500ft, a 90 degree turn is made to line the aircraft up with the chosen landing path. As circuits are normally left hand, all turns will be to port. When it is clear that the aerodrome can be reached, the flaps (if any) are lowered, considerably steepening the glide. The airspeed all this time is held (in a Magister) at 65 mph. It was not, bye the way, until after the war that we started talking of all aircraft speeds in knots. At this stage two things can go wrong, either an overshoot or an under-shoot. In the first case the aircraft is too high and will either miss the aerodrome or land so far in that it is in danger of running into the up wind boundary. In the second the approach is too low and there is a danger of the aircraft finishing up in an untidy heap short of the aerodrome. In an overshoot, the pilot must swallow his pride, open up to full power, climb away and make another circuit. In an under-shoot he must use his engine to get himself to within gliding distance of the aerodrome. In the old days, before modern aircraft called for power on approaches at all times, it was considered infra dig to resort to engine power on the approach, with the consequent temptation to 'stretch the glide' often with disastrous results. If the approach has been correctly judged, the next problem is the landing itself. In theory this is quite simple. As the aircraft approaches the ground the stick is eased back to flatten the glide. Instructors have various ways of telling pupils when to do this. To delay too long means flying into the ground and bouncing back into the air again. To act too soon may mean flattening out too high and a possible heavy landing. Some instructors would say "at about 10 feet" (though research indicates that it is, in fact, more like 20 or 30 feet). Others "about the height of a double-decker bus" or at about this height. Each pupil has to sort out his own method. Anyway the object is to get the aircraft flying level about 5 feet above the ground. As the speed drops off the aircraft starts to sink and this is checked by further backward movement of the stick until it is flying about a foot above the ground in landing position with the stick fully back. Overdo the backward move-ment and the aircraft will 'balloon' back into the air again, delay it and the main wheels will strike first, with a resultant bounce. The apogee of the instructor's art is to talk through (patter is the word used) this procedure until he comes to "....until with the stick held fully back the aircraft lands gently on 3 points", this accompanied by the gentle rumble as the wheels touch the ground, heard rather than felt. Some people learn to land without trouble, most after going through various stages of despair, and a few never learn.

I have, of course, been talking of tail wheel aircraft. Most modern aircraft have a nose wheel placed in front of the main wheels. As will be readily seen, a tail wheel aircraft must have it's main wheels placed well forward of the centre of gravity to ensure stability on the ground, while with a nose wheel, the reverse is the case. So if the main wheels of a tail wheel aircraft contact the ground before flying speed is lost, the aircraft may be thrown back into the air in a dangerously nose up attitude, whereas with a nose wheel the effect will be to pitch the aircraft forward firmly onto the ground. This greatly simplifies the landing process. There is a further point in favour of the nose wheel layout. Once the pilot has landed his task has not ended, he must keep the aircraft running straight until normal taxiing speed is reached, any "swing" must be corrected at once. This is much easier with a nose wheel as when the cause of the swing is removed, the aircraft tends to run on in a straight line. This is not so with a tail wheel, where once a swing has started it tends to increase until, if uncorrected, will turn the aircraft through 180 degrees and, supposing the undercarriage stands up to it, finish its landing run backwards! In motor car parlance the nose-wheel causes 'under-steer' and the tail wheel 'over-steer'. The racing driver who 'loses it' on a bend is in exactly the same position as the pilot of a tail-wheel aircraft swinging on take-off or landing, once past a certain point nothing will control the swing.

From the foregoing it will be seen that the pupil pilot has his hands full during the first few weeks of his training. Before solo he has to be able to take off, fly round the circuit, judge his approach, and to land. He has to know what action to take in the event of a bad or baulked landing and he must have some experience of stalling, or losing flying speed when airborne. Regulations also stated that he should be able to recover from a special kind of stalled condition, the spin.

In a normal stall the aircraft is held in level flight with the power off. As the speed drops off the stick is moved progressively back to increase the angle of attack (the angle at which the wings meet the airflow) and so maintain the lift. There comes a point when the smooth airflow over the wings on which lift depends, breaks down. Almost all the lift is then lost and the result is a stall. This is a gentle process in any aircraft suitable for *ab initio* pupils, and is easily corrected. In fact, it corrects itself providing the stick is centralised, the nose falling, thus restoring the airspeed and the lift. On some aircraft one wing will drop at the stall but this is easily corrected. More advanced aircraft sometimes have a pronounced even vicious, wing drop at the point of stall. The North American Harvard, being bought at this time (1938) for advanced training in the RAF, was said to be one such and for this reason its use was opposed by C.G. Grey (doyen of pre World War 2 aviation journalists) and some others – but more of that later.

Obviously a pupil must experience stall and recovery before going solo. Whether he should also be able to recover from a spin is a matter of some controversy. A spin is a special type of stall in which a yawing moment is introduced at the point of stall, by say, applying rudder. This causes the inner slower moving wing to stall, causing the aircraft to lose height while rotating round its fore and aft axis in a more or less nose down attitude. Recovery is effected by correcting the yaw with application of opposite rudder, and the stalled condition by moving the stick forward. The spin will then stop and the aircraft can be eased out of the resultant dive. A pupil would have to be incredibly ham-fisted to get into an inadvertent spin while flying a circuit of the airfield. If he did he would be more likely to survive by allowing the aircraft to spin into the ground (he would be in the rear cockpit in the sort of aircraft we are dealing with) than by trying to recover. When spinning the forward (downward) speed of about 45 mph, while on recovery the speed rapidly builds up with the risk of a far more serious crash. As I have said, a pupil is most unlikely to get into a spin during normal flight, but I have seen a very fine Indian Air Force instructor actually allow his pupil to spin off a gliding turn when coming in to land. More of that in due course.

For me the day of my first solo came quite unexpectedly, as is often the case. We had been slogging away at circuits and landings for several hours without, it seemed to me, much progress being made. Then Leigh-Smith suggested that I should have a ride with the C.F.I. I thought that this was a progress check, but after a couple of circuits Kingswell said, "Well, I expect you would like to go solo". Before I could reply he had unplugged his voice tube and was climbing out of the front cockpit. After securing his straps (as I recall the control column was not detachable in the Magister, although it was in the Tiger Moth) he was standing on the wing shouting the usual advice against the slipstream of the idling propeller. "Just one circuit and landing, don't forget she'll climb more quickly without my weight. Come back and pick me up after you've landed".

So this was it! The front cockpit looked so very empty without that reassuring black helmeted head. (The black helmet was a kind of instructor's status symbol. Ours were the more usual RAF tan). I carried out the well remembered drill - stand across wind, facing the direction of the circuit. Carry out cockpit checks. Trim set for take-off, mixture rich, fuel on and sufficient in tanks, flaps up, then, with no aircraft coming in to land and a clear take-off path, turn into wind and slowly open up to full throttle. Keep straight, tail up, now the view's better. Hold her down until she really wants to fly, then climb away at 70 mph.

Nobody ever forgets their first solo. I recall a sensation of terrific happiness. I think I was singing at the top of my voice. But there was serious business to attend to. Level off at 1,000 ft, turn 90 degrees left and then left again, down wind. Unusually the wind that day was from the East so I had taken off over the railway line and was now heading westwards parallel to North Downs which stood out a few miles to the north. As the airfield's western boundary came into view behind the trailing edge of the port wing, it was time to turn across wind to close the throttle and glide. 65 mph was the speed, no more, no less. Opposite my chosen landing path, turn another 90 degrees towards the aerodrome. Flaps down, nose down to maintain the speed and there was Kingswell's tiny figure, looking up, no doubt anxiously. Instructors will know the feeling! Across the boundary at a respectable 50 ft and down. I think the landing was quite respectable, at any rate I landed first time. Some first soloists go round several times before getting it right. Of course they have it drummed into them "If in doubt go round again", but it doesn't help their instructor's nerves. I do remember that after landing I started to turn back to pick up Kingswell at rather too high a speed and was worried in case I had strained the undercarriage, but he didn't seem to notice.

Now that the solo hurdle had been surmounted, the business of learning to fly and enjoying it could begin. The pre solo hours were far too busy for me to take in the full flavour of being airborne and to wonder at the complete absence of any sensation of height. Also to savour the beauty of the Surrey countryside with the line of the downs to the north and the fields and farmhouses which we flew over every day. The small towns of Horley,

Three Bridges, Crawley (yes Crawley was small in those days) and the rather larger Horsham at the end of its long straight railway line, became well known landmarks and very important ones too. For his first solo hours the pilot clings to these things as a duckling clings to its mother. Stories were rife of the over confident pupil who tried "just a few more steep turns" and then found to his dismay that he could recognise nothing on the ground around him. "Getting lost" was a fate to be avoided at all costs and although it seems ridiculous to the experienced pilot, it is very easily achieved by the tyro. Woe to the unwary is the motto of one of my wartime squadrons. This applies in very great degree to the learner pilot. Much of our time on the ground was spent in the lecture room. As I recall we had two main lecturers; one the Chief Ground Instructor, dealt with theory of flight, airmanship and navigation. I don't remember a great deal about these lectures, except that we were introduced to a little instrument called a Course and Distance Calculator (no not the C.S.C. that many later pilots will recall). This C.D.C. had little arms on a dial like the hands of a clock and pointers that moved up and down the arms. The instrument was designed to solve a problem common to navigation both on sea and in the air. The element through which the craft is moving may also be moving in relation to the ground, and therefore the craft will not always travel in the direction in which it is pointing.

Anyway we did not have this first C.G.I for long. There was this question of the bar in the airport building. This gentleman found time lying heavily on his hands, and where better to while it away than in the bar? Thus there were times in his lectures when he was not, so to speak, at his best. I think the Management decided that it would be better for all concerned if he went to work where temptation was not quite so near at hand.

The other main lecturer dealt with armament and, I think, signals. He was, I suspect, an ex N.C.O. or Warrant Officer Armour, possibly of R.F.C. vintage. To say that he was not a born lecturer would hardly do justice to the situation. He had a not very up to date copy of A.P. something or other, the R.A.F.'s armaments bible. From this he would dictate and we would write down in our notebooks.

"The Course setting Bomb sight..." pages and pages of it. "The Vicker's machine gun" (what did the rear sear retainer keeper do?) "The 112 lb General Purpose bomb - detailed description". This bomb was in use during the 1914/18 war and for a time afterwards: we were never likely to see one and I never did. On and on and on it went, futile and time wasting. We did, however, do a little pistol and machine gun firing on a 25 yard range that backed onto the main London-Brighton railway embankment, and that was rather fun.

If much of the ground instruction was a bore, the flying certainly was not. As the Course progressed the rate of solo to dual changed from about 1:1 to 2:1 and later to 3:1. The object was that by the end of the Course we should be able to handle our aircraft with confidence under all reasonable conditions.

One of our most practiced manoeuvres was 'the forced landing', although the chance of our Gipsy Major engines failing was very remote. We had to be able to cope with this misfortune should it occur. The drill was this:

If the engine fails assume the correct gliding angle and look for a suitable field or area in which to land. Glide towards the down wind side of this. (The alert pilot will have no problem here as he will have been monitoring the surface wind strength and direction continuously during his flight, using smoke, flags, waving grass or crops etc. as indicators).

After settling into this glide, check the cockpit for obvious causes of engine failure, ignition switches accidentally knocked off, empty fuel tank selected and so on. If it is clear that the engine failure cannot be rectified concentrate on the landing. On reaching a down wind position the pilot keeps the proposed landing area in view and within gliding distance, by flying a series of cross wind legs, turning always towards the field. A final turn is made into wind and when it is certain the field can be reached the flaps are lowered and the landing made.

During dual instruction, instructors would sometimes close the throttle, announcing "Engine failure, force land." We would go through the drill, remembering to keep the engine warm with an occasional burst of throttle on the way down. Not doing this could result in the engine failing to respond on abandoning the exercise. Result, a real forced landing instead of a practice one.

Another regular exercise was 'steep turns'. We had, of course, learnt to do 'medium turns' at the pre-solo stage and had discovered the need to 'balance' the turn accurately, that is, to match the rate of turn to the angle of bank. Too little bank and the aircraft will skid outwards, too much and it will slip inwards. A correct turn can be judged by an experienced pilot flying by 'the seat of his pants', but we had a very useful instrument to help us. The 'Turn and Bank' had two needles, one pointing upwards the other downwards. The top needle was linked to a simple pendulum. In a correctly balanced turn it remained in the central position. It indicated slip or skid by an inward or outward movement. The bottom needle was linked to a gyroscope, and under the laws of precession indicated both the direction and rate of turn. In practice the rate of turn was dictated by the bank, and slip or skid corrected by the rudder.

In turns with a moderate angle of bank the controls act much as in level flight, but it will be seen that, as the angle of bank increases, the elevators increasingly control the rate of turn, and the rudder the position of the nose on the horizon, until at a 90 degree angle of bank this change over is complete, and a backward movement of the stick has the sole effect of increasing the rate of turn. Any turn in which the reversal of control function becomes noticeable, say 45 degree angle of bank or more, is called a 'steep turn'.

Aerobatics were another important part of our Course. The loop, the stall turn, the slow roll and the roll off the top (of a loop), we learnt them all.

The loop was simple. In training aircraft of those days it was necessary to lower the nose slightly to gain speed (to about 140 mph in a Magister). The stick was then eased back and the throttle opened fully. The horizon would disappear under the nose and the world would be full of sky. With the aircraft fully inverted the horizon would appear again but the land would be where the sky should be. The loop was completed by allowing the aircraft to dive out with a closed throttle. It was advisable to close the throttle in the inverted position to prevent the speed building up too quickly in the dive and the engine over revving (no C.S. airscrews on the Maggie). In a correctly executed loop the loading on the aircraft remains positive (as in level flight) throughout, so that even if the pilot were not strapped in he would remain in his seat.

This is not the case in the slow roll, where the aircraft is rotated 360 degrees round its longitudinal axis. A Magister needed a little extra speed, picked up in a shallow dive; the nose was then raised just above the horizon and full aileron applied in the direction of the roll. As the aircraft rolled on its side a little top rudder was needed to hold the nose up, and in the inverted position, firm forward movement of the stick prevented the nose from falling. Top rudder was needed again on recovery. It was not possible to slow roll without losing some height and a perfect roll really was a work of art, unknown to the modern jet pilot, whose aircraft will roll at the touch of a finger, gaining height all the while. In our Magisters, as in most aircraft with normal carburettors, the fuel supply to the engine was cut off under negative 'G' so it was advisable to close the throttle when the aircraft was inverted, opening up once the loading became normal again. (This fact was to give the German fighters with fuel injection engines an advantage over our Hurricanes and Spitfires in the years to come).

In the 'roll off the top' the first half of a loop was completed and when the aircraft was inverted it was rolled onto an even keel, thus reversing its original direction of flight.

For the unaccustomed stomach we found the stall turn a most disturbing manoeuvre. Here the aircraft was pulled up from level flight into an almost vertical climb. Just before all speed was lost, full rudder was applied causing the aircraft to fall over sideways, pivoting on one wing. The resultant dive with closed throttle would quickly restore the airspeed and the aircraft would have turned through 180 degrees. It was common to hear one pilot ask another; "Have you done stall turns yet?", and if the answer was "No" to regale his colleague with all the gruesome details. For the student who was inclined to be airsick, and we had one or two, the stall turn was probably the last straw.

One of the first things we learnt before going solo was that man does not possess any in-built directional sense when in the air. As a pigeon he is a complete dead loss. He needs to keep a continual check on his position and to know how to use his compass. Until he has considerable experience he can all too easily become completely lost, even when quite close to his own airfield. In fact, what instinct he has will almost certainly be misleading and if followed blindly will lead him into deep trouble.

I remember on one of my first solo flights being detailed to practice some simple manoeuvres; medium turns perhaps. I aimed to stay within sight of the aerodrome but carelessly failed to keep a check on my position. After a few minutes I looked round to see where I was and to my dismay could recognise nothing. Panic was not far away, but never fear, I 'knew' that the airfield was over to starboard. How did I know? I knew by instinct that I had not learned to suppress. As I started to turn right, a glint of light way over to the left caught my eye. It was the reflection of the light sky on the wet tarmac apron at Gatwick. I had been about to turn and fly in exactly the wrong direction. Two or three minutes and I would have been well and truly lost. This seems ridiculous to the experienced pilot but to the pupil the danger is very real, as many have found out.

We soon learned to keep a prominent landmark in view during our local flying. I used to fly up and down the Three Bridges-Horsham railway, and do many of my practices over Christ's Hospital School.

The days of October and November 1938 passed happily away. There can be few more enjoyable experiences for a young man than learning to fly in the company of a group of like-minded companions. We soon became, as we thought, expert pilots. There are several danger points in a pilot's career. One of these comes when he has done about 50 hours flying. He thinks he knows it all, when in fact he knows almost nothing. Luckily, perhaps, we all survived this phase and I cannot remember an aircraft being so much as scratched let alone a pilot injured.

We were allowed Wednesday afternoon off for sports, and organised a rugby team, using the Reigate R.F.C. ground, kindly lent to us by the club. No doubt we showed more enthusiasm than skill, and I remember we enjoyed the traditional pints of shandy after the games. At 18 I had not yet cultivated a taste for beer, or for that matter alcohol of any sort. Eighteen year olds in 1938 lacked the sophistication of modern youth.

It was towards the end of the course that I gained a nick-name that was to stay with me throughout my training. As I have said, the Magister was equipped with flaps for use on the approach and landing. These should be raised at the end of the landing run before taxiing to avoid the risk of damage by stones or water kicked up by the wheels or propeller. They should certainly not be left down for take off (these flaps were either 'up' or 'down' with no intermediate position).

One afternoon I was sent solo to practice circuits and land-ings. The wind was unusually from the north so we were taking off over the racecourse and landing over the terminal building and aircraft-park. After my first landing I taxied back towards the buildings, turned and took off. Too late I realised that I had left the flaps down. Once committed to take off it was not possible to raise the flaps until a safe height was reached and the climb was painfully slow. On taxiing back for another take off I saw Leigh-Smith waiting to 'tear me off a strip'. He threatened dire penalties if I did such a thing again, but I did, twice that after-noon. From then on it was "Flaps Rivington"!

Before the end of our course we had to carry out a cross-country flight, landing away and returning to Gatwick. Our route was to be Gatwick-Hamble-Gatwick. There could hardly have been an easier route as one 'ran out of land' on arriving at Hamble but I'm sure everyone felt as relieved as I when the Solent and the Hamble river appeared over the nose. We carried a certificate to be signed by the 'away' timekeeper saying that we had arrived and that the landing was "good/fair/poor" (delete as required).

This was the part of the course called 'Pilot Navigation', and the two essentials were a map and a compass. The compass was fixed in the aircraft just below the instrument panel, between the pilot's knees and within easy reach. The needle with its magnets was immersed in alcohol to damp unwanted oscillation and the whole system sealed by two glass covers. The lower cover was fixed but the upper was able to rotate, and the compass rose, with n/s grid wires, was marked on this. A lever clamped the 'grid ring' in any desired position. There was a lubber line fixed parallel to the aircraft's fore and aft axis. If the grid ring was rotated until the required course was against the lubber line and the aircraft was then turned to line up the needle with the grid wires, then the aircraft was heading in the required direction.

Two traps lay in wait for the unwary pilot when using this excellent instrument. He could fail to lock the grid ring, thus allowing it to vibrate round, causing the aircraft to wander off course, or instead of lining up the needle 'red on red' he could put 'red on blue' and fly in the opposite direction to that required. Both mistakes have often been made and result in a red faced pilot arriving at a wholly unexpected destination. I have described the simple magnetic compass in some detail as it was a first class instrument, not found in modern aircraft. Any pilot who persuaded himself that "there was something wrong with the compass" was heading for deep trouble.

Another important facit of our training was 'blind flying', that is controlling the aircraft solely by reference to instruments. This is practiced by pulling a canvas hood over the pupil's cockpit. We soon learnt that any instinctive reaction under these conditions was almost certainly to be misleading. Man has balancing equipment in his inner ear that enables him to remain upright in the dark or when blindfold. This relates to the normal gravitational forces that apply on the ground. His senses when 'on

instruments' in the air will feed in a series of completely misleading messages. He must learn to rely implicitly on the evidence
provided by the aircraft instruments and ignore all other sensa-
tions. This takes some doing as it goes against every natural
instinct.

The Magister, in common with most elementary aircraft of its
day, was equipped with primary instruments. These were an
airspeed indicator (A.S.I.) an altimeter and the 'turn and bank'
already described. The aircraft is controlled in the pitching plan
(flown level or made to climb or descend) with reference to the
airspeed or altimeter. It is kept on course or turned as required
with reference to the turn and bank indicator. This is something
of a tight rope act, as there is no direct indicator of the aircraft's
attitude as provided by the actual horizon in visual flight, or the
artificial horizon in instrument flying on a full panel.

However we were not expected to do anything except fly
straight and level, perform gentle 'rate one' turns and to turn on
to and hold given compass courses. When using the magnetic
compass we had already been introduced to one of its idiosyncrasies 'northerly turning error'. Very briefly this means that the
compass is lively when steering N/S courses and stable on E/W
courses. The reason for this is that the compass magnets try to
line themselves up with the line of force of the earth's magnetic
field. These lines run parallel to the earth's surface at the Equator
and directly down-wards at the Poles. At our latitude they point
down-wards towards the north magnetic Pole at an angle of
roughly 20 degrees (called dip). As it would not be convenient to
have the compass needle at this attitude, the magnet system in
the compass is suspended well below the pivot on which it
swings, and gravity keeps the system on a nearly horizontal plane.
This applies as long as the aircraft is on an even keel. But if bank
is applied on a northerly or southerly course, the magnets are

freed to line up with the lines of force, until at 90 degrees of bank, on north or south they will have been freed to swing down to their full angle of dip and the compass reading will be 20 degrees out. It was for this reason we were instructed that the compass would be very lively when turning through north and sluggish when turning through south. "Northerly Turning Error". Just another thorn in our flesh.

Towards the end of the course we all underwent a C.F.I. test as a final check that our flying was up to scratch. The only thing that I remember about my test was that after I had taken off and was climbing away, at about 400 ft., I felt the throttle close under my hand. Thinking that Kingswell had taken over, I left the controls and put my hands on the cockpit rim where he could see them in his mirror. The nose of the aircraft dropped and we did a steepish gliding turn, heading straight for the ground. At about 100 ft. the aircraft righted itself, the throttle came on and we climbed away once more.

"Is that what you would do if you had an engine failure on take off," came the calm voice from the front cockpit.

"Sorry Sir," said I. "I felt the throttle close and I thought you had taken over."

"Well I hadn't," said he, and we carried on with the test. I felt a bit of a fool, but I don't think he held the incident against me.

One or two of us were tested by a very grand RAF Flight Lieutenant from the Training Group, I suppose to check on the general standard of the course. I was not so honoured, and as the November days shortened into December, our course came to an end.

It had been a grand experience, with a fine set of companions, and although I was sorry to leave Gatwick, it was good to know that we would all go on together to the next phase of our training and that meant joining the RAF proper.

7 Hawker Hinds with L7200 in the foreground and a Whitley bomber, photographed at Gatwick by Peter Rivington during his period of training.

3. *No.12 S.F.T.S. Grantham*

On the 12th December 1938 those of us who were travelling by train left Gatwick for our first RAF posting to No.12 Service Flying Training School, Grantham. On that day the Short Service entrants became Acting Pilot Officers on Probation, A.P.O's, just about the lowest form of animal life in the service.

From Grantham L.N.E.R. Station we were taken by service bus up the hill to the RAF camp. We found comfortably mature buildings, solidly brick built, mostly dating back to the 1914/18 war. The Officers' Mess, which was to be our home for the next eight months, was an imposing two-story building. It comprised a central block and four wings, the whole making up the shape of a double-ended 'Y'. The central spine was made up of the public rooms with sleeping quarters in the wings. One of the north wings housed H.Q. No.23 Training Group, to which No.12 S.F.T.S. belonged.

We were met at the main entrance by a bevy of batmen (if that is the correct collective noun) each of who claimed his two or three 'gentlemen', and led off to our quarters in the south wings. We discovered that even as A.P.O's we were to have individual rooms and batman service, albeit shared. These batmen were Air Ministry civilians (wearing the dark blue serge uniform with the golden crown on the jacket lapels). As they were mostly ex-servicemen and knew the routine of mess life like the back of their hands, during these strange early days we came to rely on their advice on many matters.

We knew before we left Gatwick that normally pupil pilots from civil schools went to Uxbridge for two or three weeks before going on to their S.F.T.S. This was for a Disciplinary Course, square bashing and a general introduction to service and mess life. In our case, however, this Course was to be carried out at our S.F.T.S. owing to lack of space at Uxbridge, and we found a Flight Lieutenant and a Flight Sergeant from the RAF Depot awaiting us at Grantham, ready to turn us into RAF 'Gentlemen'. The Flight Lieutenant, one 'Granny' Westmorland, was to initiate us into the customs and ways of the service, while the Flight Sergeant's task was to smarten us up on the parade ground.

No.1 Course, No.12 SFTS Grantham 1938/39. Peter Rivington is seen 3rd from the right, back row.

During our last few weeks at Gatwick a number of suave individuals had been in evidence, extolling the virtues of various tailoring firms. We would be needing RAF uniform and the Air Ministry would pay each of us £40 to buy it. We could go to any one of a number of approved suppliers, so the vultures in the guise of firms' reps. were circling, waiting to grab their share of the spoils, so by the time we left Gatwick we had all been 'signed up' by one or other of the well known London Service outfitters, often with assurances that the job would be done for £35 or less. I remember one particularly smooth individual who dropped service officers' names in his conversation like confetti. "I was only saying to Group Captain .... the other day" or "I've been making Air Commodore ....'s uniforms for many years, such a pleasant man", and so on. When we got to Grantham and the work of measuring and fitting had to be done, these 'front' men were nowhere to be seen, clearly more adept with the tongue than with the tape measure. Thus, after a surprisingly short time we exchanged our mufti for Air Force blue, with the thin Pilot Officer's stripe but no wings; they would come later, we hoped. For our £40 (or £35 if we were lucky) we got:

- 1 Service Dress uniform
- 1 Greatcoat with 2 sets of epaulettes, (one normal and one in gold with eagle for wear with mess kit)
- 2 Caps, one round, peaked and one forage (the 'side' cap known vulgarly by what Sir Alan Herbert described as a short and unattractive word)
- 1 Mess Kit with 'bum freezer' jacket, tight trousers (known for some obscure reason as overalls) worn over patent leather boots (known more understandably as 'Wellingtons')
- 2 waistcoats, one blue, one white
- various blue shirts with collars detached, stiff fronted evening shirts (with starched wing collars), socks, shoes, gloves and ties. One couldn't buy the greatcoat these days for the sort of money we paid for all this. Anyway we were now equipped to give a passable imitation of a RAF Officer.

On our 'Dicip' course, Westmorland lectured us on the minutia of Service and Mess life. "You will need visiting cards, two of which should be left at the Station Commander's residence within a week of joining the station. The cards will be made from an engraved plate with the wording embossed - not cheap and nasty printed things like this." I can still picture 'Granny' holding up the 'nasty' visiting card between finger and thumb, as if unclean, and to this day I still run my finger over the writing on a card to see if he would approve. Mostly he would not. "Officers do not wear made-up evening ties. If you don't know how to tie an evening bow then you'd better learn quickly".

Here's where one's batman's help was invaluable.

We were told of Guest Nights, of Dining in Nights, of "Mr Vice, the King", and so many more things that were to become part and parcel of our, lives.

On the parade ground we suffered endless "To the front salute!" (up one two down), "To the left salute!" (up one two down) "Not like that, you look as if you're waving goodbye to your old granny at King's Cross - Sir"! The 'sir' very much in parenthesis, was an acknowledgement of that thin stripe but was added in such a way as to be more of an insult than anything else. Later when we were being drilled by our own Station Warrant Officer (still at that time known more often as 'Sar'nt Major'), we found that he could pack as much meaning into that short title as into the stream of invective he was apt to direct at his actual subordinates.

At 6.30 in the morning we were roused by a batman with a cup of tea. We then formed up in a squad outside the mess and ran the few hundred yards to an empty hangar for P.T. Then back to the mess for a shower and breakfast. Anyone who remembers those days in the run-up to Christmas 1938 will recall that the weather was unusually cold. This did not make our early morning P.T. sorties any more comfortable.

Our Course from Gatwick was joined by one from the E.F.T.S. at Prestwick run by Scottish Aviation. They had flown Tiger Moths, and McIntyre of Everest Flight fame, had been their C.F.I. Charles Green was once again appointed senior pupil, with Tolly Rothwell as his deputy. We had joined an old established Mess, with an unusually large number of senior officers, due to the pressure of No.23 Group. One can imagine what they thought of the 40 or so A.P.O's who had invaded their domain.

Although we did not know at the time we were to have only a short experience of a peace-time Officers' Mess. It was an experience that I, for one, found most enjoyable. We pupils had our own anti-room, (in a hotel it would be called the lounge), comfortably furnished with deep settees and armchairs and with an open fire at each end. Daily papers were available here with a good selection of periodicals, including, of course, 'Flight' and 'The Aeroplane'. In those days it was against King's Regulations for a Mess to have a bar at which one could buy drinks. To get one you had to ring for a steward who would take down the order and return with the drinks on a tray. Each officer signed for his own drinks in his wine book, there was no treating, and it was not possible to pay by cash. Monthly wine bills were strictly limited; to go over the top meant a carpeting in front of the Station Commander. The figure of £5 sticks in my mind, but I imagine that a lower limit was set for A.P.O's whose pay was something under £20 per month. Mess bills could make quite a hole in this as in addition to a Mess subscription, one had to pay a messing charge of about 2/- a day. These bills were payable by the 10th of the following month by cheque and to default on this was a Court Martial offence. In our case as officers on probation we would simply have been out on our ear.

One facet of Mess life at Grantham that left a lasting impression on me was the excellence of the food. No doubt the fact that this was an old established Mess, with a high proportion of senior officers, helped in this respect and of course my only previous experience of institutional catering was at boarding school where one does not find cordon bleu standards. Nevertheless I still recall the cold table at lunch groaning with meats and salads of every kind as something I never saw equalled in Messes or Wardrooms over the next 24 years.

In the Mess, meals were a most important part of our ceremonial. Dinner was served on four of the weekday nights, the fifth was a 'dining-in' night. On dinner nights the dress was dinner jackets. On the 'dining-in' nights Mess-kit was worn, with a black tie and blue waistcoat. Once a month there was a 'guest night' with full Mess kit, white waistcoat and tie. Flight Lieutenants and above had a rather natty gold stripe down their 'overall' trousers and for full kit, medals in miniature were worn (not that that affected us). At weekends lounge suits or sports jackets were permitted for evening supper. We were expected to 'dine in' unless 'warned out' in the book provided. There was no 'warning out' for pupils on 'dining in' or 'guest nights'.

On these occasions we assembled in our anti-room half an hour before the meal was to be served. Presumably this accounts for the title of our lounge or 'living room', it was quite literally the 'before' room. It was not advisable to take too much drink at this stage as the meal took quite a time and nobody was allowed to leave his seat until the end no matter how pressing his need. When dinner was announced we trooped into the dining room and stood by our places. The President for the evening took his place in the centre of the 'high' table. He was usually a Squadron Leader or perhaps a Flight Lieutenant. The Vice-President, always an A.P.O. (we were detailed for the job in turn) sat at the far end of one of the tables. All the Mess silver would be on display and the station orchestra played in the gallery.

After grace, said by the Padre or the President, the meal proceeded. Waiters came round taking orders for wine and the sherry decanter circulated with the soup, with an eagle-eyed wine steward noting the names of those who partook. Usually four courses were served and when the tables had been cleared the port commenced its rounds. When every glass had been charged (a waiter followed the port around with a water jug for those not taking port) the President would stand: "Mr Vice, the King!" The V.P. would then rise: "Gentlemen, the King!" All would then stand, raise their glasses and drink in silence. There were no murmurs of "God bless him" etc. as one often hears nowadays in less formal circumstances.

After the toast, fruit and nuts were served and the President would light up a cigarette or cigar, or if a non-smoker, indicate that smoking was now permitted. At about this time the band-leader would be invited down to take a glass of port with the President, and nobody was permitted to rise from his seat until the President himself did so. Mr Vice was, by custom, the last to leave - another reason for his going easy on the drinks before or during dinner.

As the whole process was liable to take an hour and a half, those who had not taken the precautions outlined were liable to find themselves in desperate straits before the end. As a last resort it was known for a diner to slide under the table and thence to crawl to a point near an exit from which an escape could be made. Two problems arose here. The first was that because of the tight mess kit 'overalls' already mentioned, it was difficult or impossible to sit with one's knees bent, thus restricting the space available to the escapee. The second arose because his 'friends' were liable to 'help him on his way' with a kick or two. All in all one had to be pretty desperate to attempt this form of escape.

After dinner or 'guest nights' all repaired to the largest ante-room and the tradition of playing boisterous, some would say boyish, games was usually followed. One could see senior and often quite stout officers playing "Are you there Moriarty?" or "High cockaloram' with sweaty intensity. It was on these occa-sions that after the departure of the more senior, though not always the more sober officers, that sooty bare foot prints were liable to appear across the ante-room ceiling. This to the amusement of officers coming down shakily to breakfast in the morning but no doubt to the fury of the Mess cleaning staff.

These were colourful occasions, made more so as the guests would often include army officers from nearby units with the reds and golds and greens of their Mess dress. Some would dismiss many of the goings on as childish behaviour, but I have no doubt that they served a serious purpose in building morale and esprit de corps, in much the same way as the 'Squadron thrash' did in later years. And anyway, under what other circumstances can an A.P.O. hit a Wing Commander across the head with a rolled up newspaper and avoid close arrest?

But important though our introduction to the customs of the service undoubtedly was, the main purpose of No.12 S.F.T.S. was to turn us into service pilots. By the New Year our Uxbridge Course was over and our flying training could proceed. We discovered that we were to be split into two groups; one would fly Avro Ansons and the other a new training aircraft from America, the North American Harvard.

The Anson had been in service for about three years. It was a low wing cabin monoplane, powered by two Armstrong Siddeley Cheetah engines each of 360 h.p. In its primary role it was a reconnaissance bomber and equipped a number of Coastal Command squadrons. When introduced in 1936 it was the first RAF aircraft to have a retractable undercarriage, albeit manually operated, and was in fact faster than many of the fighter aircraft then in first line service. By 1939 it was being replaced in Coastal Command by the Lockheed Hudson, a military version of the very successful Lockheed 14 airliner, and these and the new aircraft already equipping Bomber Command needed a supply of properly trained twin engined pilots. Thus Ansons fitted with dual controls carried out the task, together with the Airspeed Oxford just coming into service.

A Fairey Battle visiting No.12 FTS Grantham in the snow of January 1939.

The North American 'Harvard' as the RAF dubbed it, had been in service with the U.S. Army Air Corps and Navy for some time, where it was known as the A.T.6 (Army) or S.N.J. (Navy). As an advanced trainer it was a new concept for the RAF. Previously pilots had gained their 'wings' flying much the same aircraft as equipped operational squadrons - some fitted with dual controls. Thus whole generations of pilots in the mid '30's were trained on Hawker Harts and many went on to fly these aircraft, or their variations, in squadrons. The Harvard was the first specifically training aircraft on which RAF pilots could qualify for their 'wings'. The Miles Master and the Oxford were to follow a little later. It is perhaps significant in view of the enormously successful expansion of the U.S. Air Force in the early 1940's that, although behind us in operational aircraft (who would have wanted to go into the Battle of Britain flying a P-40?) they led the way in training aircraft, thus providing a sound basis for the future.

Shipped from the United States and assembled at RAF Shawbury, the first of the original batch of 200 Mk.1 Harvards reached the Experimental Establishment at Martlesham Heath early in December 1938, during our last days at Gatwick. It was a metal framed aircraft with fabric covered rear fuselage and tail control surfaces with wings and ailerons of metal. The tandem cockpits (pupils in the front) were covered by a long 'glass house' with sliding hoods. Power was derived from a 550 h.p. Pratt and Witney Supercharged Wasp Junior Radial engine driving an ungeared two bladed Hamilton Constant Speed metal propeller. The high tip speed of this propeller produced the well remembered 'calico tearing' noise which made us so popular with the towns people of Grantham, especially when night flying was carried out. The main undercarriage legs retracted inwards and the fixed tail wheel was steerable by the rudder pedals, within certain limits. Split trailing edge flaps were fitted, operated by the hydraulic system that also retracted the undercarriage. The hydraulic wheel brakes were operated by the rudder pedals after the American fashion, the upper part of the pedal applying the brake to the wheel on that side. With the feet in the normal position, heel on cockpit floor and ball of foot on rudder pedal, rudder alone was applied. This is a sound system but takes some getting used to, as when he wants to apply brake, the pilot has to lift his feet into the higher position, and, if the aircraft is already being held straight with rudder, say in a cross wind, this could be tricky.

The Mark 1 Harvard that we knew was a very different looking aircraft from the Mk. 11 that so many war time pilots encountered. We had the fabric-covered fuselage while theirs was all metal monocoque. Our aircrafts' wingtips and fin and rudder were tastefully rounded while in the Mk.11, I suppose for ease of production, the wingtips were cut off square and the wing and rudder was an ungainly triangular thing. In addition, our aircraft were fitted with fixed slats on the leading edge of the wings near the tips. The function of these was to smooth out the airflow over the wingtips as the stall approached and so minimise the tendency to 'drop a wing' on landing. The manufacturers acknowledged this mildly vicious characteristic by the provision of the slats, and by making the wingtips easily replaceable in the event of damage.

I describe the Harvard in some detail as it was, arguably, the most advanced aircraft in RAF service at that time, for in addition to its retractable undercarriage and flaps, it also had a constant speed propeller. This device enabled the power plant to be operated efficiently throughout the whole speed range of the aircraft. On most British aircraft the propellers were of the fixed pitch type designed to operate efficiently at the aircraft's cruising speed and were inefficient at either end of the speed range. This was not very important when the range was no more than 100 mph - 50 mph stalling, 150 maximum, but when this range increased to something like 300 mph in aircraft like the Hurricane and the Spitfire, it became impossible to design an efficient fixed pitch airscrew for them. Nevertheless the early Hurricanes and Spitfires did have wooden two bladed fixed pitch propellers and anyone who can remember these aircraft taking off with their huge propellers clawing the air at absurdly low r.p.m., must have sensed the need for a change.

The first answer was the variable two-pitch propeller. This had a 'fine pitch' position, enabling the engine to operate efficiently at high r.p.m. on take off, and a coarse pitch position for normal flying. This was a step forward, but the coarse pitch position was a compromise suited to only one condition of flight. The pilot would re-select fine pitch on throttling back for landing, making full power available in the event of an 'overshoot'. As early as

1934 the D.H. Comets in the McRobertson air races to Australia had Ratier two position airscrews, enabling these heavily laden aircraft to give optimum take off performance on the short landing strips then available and to cruise at over 200 mph.[2]

The two-pitch propeller was a step forward, but the coarse position was again a compromise. A solution was the infinitely variable pitch system used by Curtiss and employing electrical power. The Hamilton propeller and most of its successors were operated hydraulically. This allowed the pilot to select the best pitch for any flight conditions, but having done so the propeller was once more in fixed pitch, requiring further adjustment with any change of flight conditions - not ideal for the pilot of a combat aircraft. The answer was the constant speed propeller. This was the equivalent in a motor car of an infinitely variable automatic gearbox combined with a governor controlling engine revolutions adjustable by the driver. With a constant speed propeller the pilot simply set the pitch control to give the desired r.p.m. A governor then took over and held those revolutions irrespective of any change of power and airspeed, within, of course, the limits of travel of the propeller. In fact, in British aircraft the manual infinitely variable pitch propeller was never used. The sequence of development being from fixed pitch to variable two-position, to constant speed propellers.

I have said that the Harvard had a constant pitch propeller and a supercharged engine. There were two main engine controls, a throttle controlling the manifold pressure ('boost' in British aircraft) and a propeller or pitch lever controlling the revs.

---

[2] The airscrews changed automatically into course pitch at 150 mph, at which speed a disc on the spinner was forced back to release the 80lb of internal air pressure, but a return to fine pitch could only be made on the ground before each flight, with the aid of a bicycle pump.[Ed]

The manifold pressure, as in all the American aircraft, was calibrated in inches of mercury. It will be seen that in the case of an unsupercharged (normally aspirated) engine, the manifold pressure is always below atmospheric, even when the engine is operating at full throttle. This is because there is not enough time for the combustion chamber to fill fully in the induction stroke when the mixture has only atmospheric pressure behind it. Thus the manifold pressure of an unsupercharged engine is always below say 30 inches of mercury, although it may approach this figure when running at full throttle and low r.p.m. at sea level. If the engine is supercharged, then the mixture can be forced in at above atmospheric pressure, up to a maximum of 50 or 60 inches of mercury in the most powerful of cases. Around 30 inches was a normal cruising power on supercharged engines, while on a tick-over the manifold pressure would be down to about 15. British engines of the time used a different measuring system. Zero inches boost was roughly atmospheric pressure and the gauge was calibrated upwards to about +20 and downwards to about -5. The Merlin engines fitted to the Hurricanes and Spitfires of the day would cruise comfortably at zero boost with a maximum of about +12.

I have described the Harvard in fair detail, but we had to wait some time before seeing one at Grantham. After finishing our disciplinary course we officially joined No.12 S.F.T.S. and were divided into two groups; one to fly Ansons and the other Harvards. It seemed that, in general, the older, and I suppose more 'responsible' students were chosen for the twin-engine course. Needless to say, I was on Harvards.

The Anson flight could get on with their training straight away, somewhat handicapped by the snow that fell quite heavily in Lincolnshire that year, but we had to twiddle our thumbs — well, not exactly; we were kept very busy on the parade ground and in the lecture room – waiting for our Harvards to arrive from Shawbury.

Then, one cold February morning, with flurries of snow in the air, the sound that was to become all too familiar down in the town was heard for the first time in the Grantham circuit. The attractive yellow aircraft landed, taxied up to the terminal and out climbed a genuine American test pilot. It was with some interest that we all, instructors and pupils, assembled in a lecture room to hear him talk about the aircraft.

The yellow Harvard Mk.1 N7003 at No.12 FTS Grantham in February 1939. No.12 FTS was the first RAF Unit to use the type.

He spoke of the ship's (aircraft's) landing gear (undercarriage), of manifold pressure (boost), of exhaust gas analysers, of carburettor air temperatures, of gas (petrol) and 'wobble pumps' (hand pumps for maintaining full pressure), of inertia starters and of 'flying in the soup' (in cloud). Many of us had seen Clark Gable in the film "Test Pilot" and this cigar chewing character seemed to fit the bill to a tee. He left us with a burning desire to get our hands on this wonderful monster, and in despair, as surely we would never be able to master its complications. Of course, like many other things, the seemingly impossibly intricate became quite straightforward with experience, although we were not helped in our initial efforts by the fact that our instructors were nearly as much in the dark as we.

My instructor was a young Pilot Officer who seemed to me to be a somewhat surly individual, florid of face and not at his best first thing in the morning. I met him much later when we were both Squadron Leaders and found him a pleasant person. I realise now that his ill-temper might well have been caused by his being a reluctant instructor who would have far preferred life on a fighter squadron. At all events, he and I did not hit it off.

As I have indicated, the Harvard was to us a most intricate aircraft with a host of unfamiliar instruments and controls. Our efforts to master these were not helped, as I came to realise later, by the fiddling way we were taught to handle the aircraft. For instance, we were required when flying the aerodrome circuit, to make a number of precise adjustments to boost and r.p.m. settings. Suppose we joined the circuit at 30inches/1900 r.p.m., we were to set 25inches/2000 r.p.m. down wind. After lowering the undercarriage and turning across wind, the settings were to be 20"/2200 r.p.m. On turning into wind the throttle was closed and the pitch control set to 'fully fine'. Most of this was quite superfluous as we discovered for ourselves later. All that was needed was to adjust the power to give the required speed in the circuit, leaving the revs at cruising until 'fully fine' was selected on 'finals', this as a precaution in case full power was needed for an overshoot.

So, in addition to attempting to cope with a new, and to us difficult aircraft using unnecessarily complex procedures, I had a bad tempered instructor, who made it quite clear from early in the course that he thought I was a clot. An indication of his unsuitability as an instructor was his inability to leave the controls completely in the hands of his pupil. Often I did not know who was flying the thing, he or I. I knew when I was supposed to be in control, but the stick and rudder often felt as if he had his hands and feet on them, especially during the more tricky manoeuvres. On one occasion after a more than usually unsatisfactory session of 'circuits and bumps', I was supposed to be doing a final landing. I could feel the control column moving under my hand so took my hands and feet away and just watched. The aircraft flew beautifully down the approach path, levelled off, the stick came gradually back, back and finally fully back, and an excellent three-point landing resulted. "That was good," came the voice from the rear cockpit, "why can't you always do them like that?" There was no answer to that.

The upshot of all this was that I was put up to the Flight Commander as not making satisfactory progress and I suppose unlikely to go solo on the Harvard. In charge of the Harvard flight was Flt/Lt Grindell, a mature, experienced officer and an excellent instructor. Flying with him was a revelation to me. The calm and friendly atmosphere he created made handling the aircraft seem easy and I did a thoroughly good test. In the Flight Office afterwards he told me that it seemed to my instructor that I was not trying, and that I must always fly as I had done with him. I suppose he had to say that, but I'm sure that his experience told him what the situation really was. Anyway, a few flying hours later I went solo on the Harvard and all was well.

Our Course at Grantham was divided into two parts, the first in the Initial Training School and the second in the Advanced Training School. In the I.T.S. we learnt to fly our aircraft and qualified for our pilots' 'wings'. To get these we had to fly a certain minimum number of hours on 'Service Types'. As I have indicated, the Harvard now came into this category. We also had to carry out certain tests satisfactorily such as a 'height climb' to 15,000 ft (no oxygen) and a couple of cross-country flights, landing at a strange aerodrome. Our first attempt at the cross-country test resulted in something of a fiasco. All the available Harvards were to be flown from Grantham to South Cerney in Gloucestershire, about one hour's flying away. We were to leave at five minute intervals so that there could be no 'follow my leader' tactics. Now on the direct route from Grantham to South Cerney lies a very similar airfield, Little Rissington, about 20 miles nearer Grantham. Well the first pupil in the stream wrongly identified Little Rissington as South Cerney and landed there. The next pilot flying over spied the Harvard on the ground and knew that it was one of ours as no one else was using them. He assumed that he had arrived at South Cerney, and landed to join his chum. So we all flopped down like ducks going for a decoy and the exercise was a complete failure - you don't pass a cross-country test by landing at the wrong aerodrome! The upshot was a red-hot telephone line between Little Rissington and Grantham, and an icy reception for us on our return. Of course the exercise had to be repeated and this time we were careful to get it right.

I had another fiasco on a cross-country flight. I forgot the destination but I arrived there safely, had lunch and set off on the return flight. Now there are few more satisfying experiences in flying than navigating an aircraft by map and compass, when all the landmarks come up exactly on time and every small town and village can be pinpointed. Conversely there are few more dismaying experiences than when is the reverse case. With experience one learns not to worry if a few landmarks are missed or if for a few minutes the ground fails to match the map. Provided the compass course is checked carefully it is impossible to get more than a mile or so off course, and in any case an unmistakable landmark is bound to turn up sooner or later, even if, in a small island like ours, its the coastline! But for the very inexperienced, the feeling of being completely lost is most unpleasant, and the temptation to circle hopelessly looking for a landmark is strong.

This was precisely the situation I found myself in on my return flight and I can well remember the mounting panic I experienced as I realised I was completely lost. Eventually I came to an airfield that I couldn't match with anything on my map. After a few minutes circling I landed and walking up to the watch office, admitting to the duty pilot that I was lost. I was at Upwood and I still blush when I look at the map and realise that I must have flown over the main London-Grantham railway line a few moments before arriving there. In the earlier and more carefree days of flying, no doubt a pupil in my position would have landed, taxied up to the tarmac, called out to the nearest airman to find out where he was and shot off into the air again and home. Not so in 1938. If one made an unscheduled landing there were strict orders to ring base for instructions. In this case, as there was very little light left, I was told to stay the night and return in the morning.

I felt very small in the mess that night. Upwood was a Bomber Command airfield and the squadrons were equipped with either Blenheims or Battles, I forget which.[3] Anyway, this wingless A.P.O. who was incapable of following the nearby main railway line back to Grantham must have been an object of some pity to the squadron pilots. I arrived back at Grantham early the next morning via the L.N.E.R. to a rather cool reception.

I refer to the Duty Pilot and not to Air Traffic Control because there was no A.T.C. at that time. In place of the modern 'Control Tower' there was a Watch Office usually situated in a modest hut somewhere near the hangars on the edge of the tarmac. Here resided the 'Duty Pilot', usually an N.C.O. pilot detailed for the

---

[3] 52 & 63 Squadrons were at Upwood in 1938 equipped with Battles [Ed].

duty that day. Mild breaches of flying discipline were liable to result in an informal sentence of so many days duty pilot and it as not a widely sought after job. His main function was to see that aircraft on cross-country flights were booked in and out and to inform destination airfields that aircraft were on their way. He had very little to do with airfield traffic control, and in any case, the view from his hut was often limited. A further task was to send coded weather reports to the nearest Met. Office at regular intervals, there being no weather service actually on the airfield.

We pupils had to act as deputy to the 'Duty Pilot' as part of our course, a task that came round about once a month. During one of my stints, a staff officer from Group elected to land an Avro Tutor in a tree on the airfield boundary. He quickly found that a Tutor was not a rook and finished up sitting in a crumpled mass of fabric and wire in the grass. I have never since seen a man move as fast as that 'duty pilot'. From a somnolent posture, feet on desk to outside, ringing the crash bell and shouting his head off in just one second flat.

On another occasion I witnessed the type of scene one only expects to see on the stage. The characters involved were the 'Duty Pilot', an N.C.O., new to the station, and the No.23 Group Commander, Air Vice Marshal Lawrence Pattinson, a craggy individual, as I recall, with eyebrows of the C. Aubrey Smith variety. Now while the said N.C.O. was away at lunch the A.V.M. had taken the Station Flight Hart for a flip around. On landing he found that due to some slip up, his car was not waiting for him on the tarmac. Somewhat testily and still wearing his Sidcot flying suit, he walked over to the Watch Office to ring for his driver. The Sergeant 'Duty Pilot', being as I said, new, failed to recognise him and being asked for the use of his phone, treated his visitor in a somewhat off hand manner, probably requesting him to "Hang on a bit Squire", or whatever the idiom of the time was, "I'm just on the blower to so-and-so". I can only assume that the Sergeant took the AVM for a rather elderly NCO pilot. He was soon to be disabused, for the AOC started to peel off his flying suit revealing officer's uniform, wings, two rows of medal ribbons and finally, as the arms came clear, the thick and thin stripes of his rank. As the early Punch cartoonists would have put it, 'complete collapse of duty pilot!'

Another non-flying duty we were required to perform was that of Orderly Officer. This entailed remaining on the Station for 24 hours in uniform when not in bed, and in a room with a telephone provided for the purpose. It meant inspecting the airmen at dinner to see if there were any complaints, inspecting the men under punishment (defaulters) at the Guardroom morning and evening, attending flag raising and lowering ceremonies, visiting certain outlying signals stations and checking code books in the safes. In all this, one was assisted by an Orderly Sergeant who acted as 'nursemaid' to very raw APOs. This duty was even more unpopular than that of Duty Pilot, as the latter's stint was over when flying finished for the day.

It was in the I.T.S. that I was involved with my instructor in a somewhat unfortunate incident. We were not at this stage, allowed to take an aircraft up first thing in the morning until it had been flown by an instructor. So a pupil, scheduled for a solo exercise, would have a quick dual circuit before being sent off by himself. This was the plan on the occasion to which I refer. Off we went and my instructor seemed more than usually taciturn. Down wind he closed the throttle prior to lowering the wheels and the warning horn sounded. I should explain here that there were three devices fitted to indicate to the pilot his undercarriage position:

1. Two lights, a red on for 'up' or 'unlocked' and a green for

'down' and 'locked'. (Front cockpit only).

2. Mechanical indicator below the throttle on the left hand side of the cockpit that indicated the undercarriage position. (Both cockpits).

3. A warning horn that sounded when the throttle was closed beyond a given point with the wheels not locked down.

Now, as I have indicated, my instructor was often not at his best first thing in the morning. I discovered later that this was not an uncommon trait, and when we were carrying out exercises that needed a closed throttle, he would shout at me to use a cancelling button, provided in the front cockpit only. Now on this occasion I quickly stabbed the button as the horn sounded, anticipating a bad tempered snarl from the rear cockpit. Unfortunately the horn stopped just as my instructor moved the under carriage lever forward towards the 'down' position. He took this as an indication that the wheels were locked down but he had not moved the lever fully forward and the wheels remained locked up. By this time he had turned into wind and was gliding in to land. Unfortunately he had no need to open the throttle which would have reactivated the horn. I saw the position and called a warning over the electric intercom. I well remember my words:

"Undercarriage Sir! Undercarriage!" Now another bad habit was coming home to roost. There was considerable background noise on the intercom (bad for fragile early morning heads), and he would avoid this by easing his electric plug partly out of the socket, thus cutting out the noise and the intercom. So my words went unheard. There was now I suppose 30 seconds between us and a belly-landing. I could simply have pushed the undercarriage lever fully forward and perhaps the wheels would have locked down in time. I could have turned in my seat and tried to attract his attention by mouthing and waving or I could have taken over control and opened the throttle to climb away.

Thinking it over afterwards I realised that by the time I had discovered that the intercom was cut off, it might have been too late to try to get the wheels down. A landing with the wheels hanging unlocked would have been more damaging to the aircraft, and possibly to us, than if they were fully retracted. Had I tried to attract his attention I might have failed as my instructors head would have been out of the left hand side of the cockpit, and anyway, if he had seen me he would probably have thought I had gone clean off my rocker and landed anyway. The last course of action would have been best, but because of lack of communication between us, might have been risky. So, as we glided down the last hundred feet or so I braced myself, and the landing was really quite smooth. The damage to the aircraft was minimal - a bent propeller and a few buckled panels - and it was flying again within a week. Our problems went on longer.

First there was the accident report, Form 765C, to be filled in. In my report I said that I had cancelled the horn, but that I had not noticed that the wheels were not down until it was too late to do anything. This was not strictly true, but I couldn't say anything else without raising the question of the intercom not working, and that would have dropped my instructor in the cart. So we were both rightly blamed; I because I had cancelled the horn and, as they thought, failed to pay attention to what was going on, and my instructor because he was flying the aircraft and was clearly negligent. In due course we received an official raspberry from the Station Commander and the incident was closed. It did, however, underline the importance of good instructor/pupil relationships. If our partnership had been more satisfactory, I'm sure our accident would not have occurred.

By the time we had finished the I.T.S. part of our course, spring was with us and with it came an international crisis. We had started flying at Gatwick in the aftermath of the Godesbury euphoria and the Munich agreement. Now at the halfway mark of our Grantham Course came the pay off - the final coup de grace for the Czechoslovaks followed closely by the British guarantee to Poland. It would be easy to say that at that time we realised where our training was leading us and that war with Germany could only be months away, but it would not be true. We were young men glorifying in our new found 'mastery' of the air, who left thinking about politics to others. At the breakfast table we were more interested in Jane's latest escapade than in more serious matters. It was just as well we could not see into a future which was to kill half our number in a few short years.

We had now completed all the flying requirements for the award of our wings. There only remained the ground exams in navigation, airmanship, armament, engines and airframes. These completed we went happily on leave to return two weeks later for the second part of our course with the Advanced Training School. When we returned, for me, disaster. No wings yet for I had failed one examination, aural armament. I looked incredulously at the marks on the board: Pass 50%, my marks 49%! How could someone fail by one mark in 50 in an aural exam? Perhaps it was that the sergeant who conducted it was a surly individual who did not have much regard for A.P.O's. Anyway, I had to sit that exam again and then, after about a week's delay, I could look proudly down at the wings on the left breast of my tunic.

We were now the senior course at No.12 S.F.T.S. A junior group had now joined, half of them to fly Ansons and the others, not Harvards, but Hawker Harts. We understood that the reason for this was that the people of Grantham had protested vociferously about the noise of the Harvard, especially when night flying. We could have greatly reduced this by taking the propeller out of 'fine pitch' very soon after take off, and not returning it until the throttle had been cut back for the approach, but as I have said, the aircraft was new to everybody and such measures were not considered. I often wondered if a 'high-up' in the Government or Air Ministry lived in or near Grantham. It seemed unusual that such quick response was made to local complaints. As it happens, I believe a young lady by the name of Margaret Roberts was living in the town at the time, attending the local Girls' Grammar School, but of course she did not then wield the influence she was later to command.

In the A.T.S. we were treated as qualified pilots. It was taken for granted that we could fly the aeroplane and the time was spent in learning to use it as a weapon. More and longer cross county flights, more instrument flying and a fair quota of night flying including a few night cross county flights was our ration. It was a new experience to see the twinkling lights of towns and villages that we were already familiar with in daylight.

In addition to flying at night we took turns in laying out and manning the flare-path. On the grass fields of these days there was no permanent airfield lighting. We used paraffin flares laid out in a line into wind with a 'T' piece at the up wind end. Two types of flare were used: goose necks, which had, as the name implies, long, goose-like necks into which a wick was inserted and 'money flares' – solid lumps of wadding in a wire frame standing in a bath of paraffin. This last type was usually used as the first flare of the line and was useful in keeping the flare-path party warm. Red, battery-powered 'Glim' lamps were positioned at either end of the flare-path to mark the boundaries of the landing area. As there was no radio, the Officer I/C flare-path, controlled the flying with red and green Aldis lamps, and the aircraft communicated with him using key operated recognition lights.

We only flew on clear nights and with all the lights around we really had no problems. Landing was a little tricky but as long as the aircraft was put down on its main wheels and not 'three pointed,' there was no real problem. We also had a 'chance light', an electric floodlight on wheels with its own petrol driven generator which was used to illuminate the landing area for some landings, and a 'glide path indicator'. This was set to show an amber, green or red light to the pilot on the approach, depending whether he was too high on the 'glide path' or too low. The Harvard was fitted with powerful landing lights, and we were allowed to use these for some landings.

The climax of our S.F.T.S. course was our visit to the Armament Training Camp. We went to Penrhos near Pwllheli in North Wales. The plan was for us to fly the Harvards over in two flights, one led by the A.T.S. Commanding Officer and the other by the Harvard Flight Commander. I was in the latter formation with two other pupils. After 24 hours delay due to bad weather we set off under a 1,500' cloud base with enough visibility to enable us to avoid any cloud covered high ground, not that any navigation problems worried me. I simply concentrated on staying close to Grindell. We crossed the Nottingham/Derby built up area, skirted to the South of the Peak District and were soon past the Cheshire Plain and flying up the Dee Estuary. The cloud had now lowered and it became clear as we followed the North Wales coast and the Menai Straights, that the Snowdon Range would be truly 'in the clag'. It was therefore a case of picking up the Caernarvon - Pwllheli railway and we were just able to squeeze through the pass without being forced up into cloud. It was not a happy thought with radio-less aircraft and surrounded by mountains. In any case, although we had practised some formation flying, I don't think we would have been happy trying out our skill in cloud. As it was, at some stage we lost two of our number and I don't suppose the Flight Commander was too happy about that. Anyway, he and I came safely to the South coast of the Llyn Peninsular and on past Pwllheli to Penrhos. We landed in wide formation and I felt very happy when he came over to me and said: "Well done, where the Hell are the other two?" However within a few minutes they turned up to be reminded that they were supposed to be part of a formation, and in future would they kindly remain so until the end of the flight.

Penrhos in 1939, was a small grass airfield just about big enough for a Harvard or an Anson. It had I think, been the site of some sort of Welsh Nationalist protest, but we found the natives very friendly! After the war, I believe it became the site of one of Billy Butlin's Holiday Camps, but we knew it as a small wooden hutted RAF camp.

During our two weeks there, we of the Harvard Flight, were to practice air to air and air to ground firing, and low level and dive bombing. The Harvard was provided with one forward firing fixed Browning .303 machine gun, fitted in the port main plane clear of the airscrew disc. These guns had been fitted to the aircraft before we left Grantham - they were not in place for ordinary training flying. A rack to carry four 11 and a half pound practice bombs had also been fitted under the starboard wing. These bombs had no main explosive charge but carried a chemical that gave out a white smoke puff.

Away from the restrictive atmosphere of Grantham we at last felt like 'real' RAF pilots, and in our off duty hours, enjoyed the holiday atmosphere of this part of the North Wales coast.

The firing and bombing range was at Hells Mouth, a large bay near the tip of the Llyn Peninsular. The bombing target was a few hundred yards out to sea, a triangular wooden platform surmounted by a 'Belisha Beacon' type of marker. The 'air to ground' targets were 10ft squares of canvas on wooden frames, while for air to air firing, flag targets were towed by old Westland Wallace biplanes from a Flight stationed at Penrhos. So that several pilots could fire at one target, coloured paint was applied to the bullets, and this came off when the target was hit, enabling each pilot's score to be counted. Of course those with poor scores always insisted that this caused mistakes to be made, but I believe that in fact the system, though crude, was very reliable.

The high rate of fire of the Browning gun (1200 rounds per minute) caused some trouble at first and one or two pilots came back with reports of jammed guns when, in fact, they had fired off all their ammunition in a couple of bursts. We soon learnt that the way to get good air to ground scores was to fire one short burst at the closest possible range on each pass. We had to bear in mind though that the range safety officer was watching and would quickly report any dangerous flying, after sending the offending aircraft home by firing a red Very cartridge.

Our time at Penrhos passed happily and we felt that at last we were becoming fully trained pilots, capable of a useful job of work.

Back at Grantham towards the end of July 1939 we were busily preparing for our 'passing out' parade, to be taken by the A.O.C. - rifle drill, fixing and unfixing bayonets, the lot. "When I says 'fix' you don't fix, but when I says 'bayonets' you whips 'em out and whops 'em on". I think we attained quite a high standard of drill and found the whole thing quite satisfying.

This was the time of our end of course reports made by the Flight or Squadron Commanders and passed on to the Station Commander for approval. I got the impression that the 'Groupie' did not think a lot of our course, why I'm not sure, but a number of 'blacks' put up at a Mess cocktail party may have had something to do with it. Anyway our assessments were subtly changed on passing through his hands. I can't remember how it came about that we saw the original drafts, but I know we did. For instance, mine "A good average pilot, very reliable in formation" (perhaps the Flight Commander had remembered our flight to Penrhos), became "An average pilot, no special faults", a slight but definite down grading. Most of the others suffered in the same way.

We were now waiting for our end of course postings. Naturally all the 'Harvard boys' confidently expected to be sent to fighter squadrons. In fact, only a handful had this luck; the rest, together with most of the Anson pilots, were to go to Manston on a short Navigation Course. So it was a gloomy group of self styled fighter pilots that went off on end of course leave. We could, quite logically, have been posted to squadrons equipped with the Fairy Battle, the standard single engine bomber of the time. This aircraft as we know, proved wholly inadequate when the shooting war began, suffered very high casualties and was quickly withdrawn from front line service. Anyway, at the beginning of August we were on leave with rumours of imminent war everywhere and a feeling that time was running out. Sure enough before August was done our leave was cut short and we were ordered to report to Manston forthwith.

4. *War*

Manston was at that time a fair sized grass aerodrome with hangars and other buildings dating back to the Great War. It was home for the school of Air Navigation that ran short and long courses and was equipped with Avro Anson aircraft for use as flying classrooms. Air exercises were carried out over the eastern part of the English Channel and the southern part of the North Sea. As war with Germany was clearly imminent it was obvious that the school would have to move and its chosen wartime home was RAF St.Athan near Cardiff. Preparations for the move were well advanced when we arrived and there was little for us to do except help to load equipment and furniture on to lorries and generally get in the way.

By Saturday 2nd September the lorries and the Ansons had all departed for South Wales, and those of us who had cars were organised into a convoy to leave the following morning. I still recall that Saturday night spent in the bright lights of 'Dreamland', the last bright lights we were to see for many years.

Just before 11 o'clock on Sunday 3rd of September we were gathered with our cars on the tarmac at Manston. Someone had a portable wireless set (not all that common in those pre-transistor days) and in silence we listened to Neville Chamberlain, "…I have to tell you that no such undertaking has been received from the German Government… It is evil things we shall be fighting…"and so on. As soon as he had finished we were off to the west, putting as many miles as possible between ourselves and the war which, according to the conventional wisdom of the time was due to burst out over our heads at any moment. Sure enough, we had been going for less than an hour when the sirens were sounding all over the south east of England. It was, of course, a false alarm and, although we did not know it at the time, the country was settling down to the period later dubbed 'the phoney war'.

We spent that night in Cirencester and it is interesting to note that it seemed perfectly reasonable to spread the journey over two days, when with modern motorway travel the journey from East Kent to South Wales would take no more than four hours.

At St Athan there was little indication that war had come to the country for the second time in 25 years. Only the appearance of slightly older than average officers in the mess, recalled for the duration, and the disappearance of branded petrol in the pumps, (replaced by 'Pool', available on coupons only) indicated that things were not normal. Perhaps there was a tendency to listen more carefully than before to wireless news bulletins, exuding confidence which later events were to belie. Of course this over confidence was very general; many will remember the popular song suggesting that certain German fortifications should be used for laundry purposes. I hope the perpetrators of that one had the decency to blush a few months later. Another change was that we were now wearing uniform at all times and not only when on duty and as from 3rd September we were full blown POs, no longer 'Acting'.

The Ansons of the Navigation School now ranged over the Bristol Channel and Exmoor. Flown by staff pilot instructors, we learned to calculate wind by the three drift method, to work out running fixes, interceptions from a moving base, critical points, radii of action and many other calculations that practical navigators soon forget. We learnt to plot these things on Mercator's charts and spent hours in the classroom doing theoretical exercises.

The presence of another unit at St Athan rubbed salt in our wounds. This was before the days of Operational Training Units. Under the peacetime system, pilots joining squadrons received their operational training at the squadron. During the summer of 1939, with the Service being brought to a war footing, this became difficult, so the 'Group Pool' system was instituted. At these 'Pools', pilots were given some experience on the aircraft they were to fly operationally, thus relieving the squadrons of part of the training burden. At St Athan was No.11 Group Pool, where some pilots were being given experience on Harvards before flying Hurricanes. This was an obvious source of irritation to those of us who had been trained on Harvards, especially as we were being flogged round in the back of Ansons drawing silly little lines on paper! I now realise that the 'Pool' may well have been giving experienced pilots quick refreshers, but it seemed unfair to us.

Late summer turned to autumn and our short Navigation course was soon over. On 6th October 1939, just 12 months after the start of my Gatwick course, I, together with two or three others was posted to No.6 Coastal Patrol Flight, St Eval, Cornwall. St Eval was in No.19 Group, Coastal Command, and was on the North Cornish coast not far from Newquay and none of us knew what to expect when we got there. I was pleased to be going to Newquay as my family had spent a number of holidays in the area and I looked forward to exploring old haunts.

It was a full day's drive from St Athan to St Eval via the Aust ferry and it was late evening before we arrived at our new station. The prospect was hardly inviting; no hangars, just unfinished steel skeletons, some wooden huts, plenty of mud and a few Ansons dispersed around the grass aerodrome. At the Guard Room, another wooden hut, we were told that there was no Officers' Mess; officers lived in the Bedruthan Steps Hotel a mile or so down the road at Mawgan Porth. So down we went to find another wooden building perched on the cliff top - this was the Hotel, not quite as grand as its name implied. Naturally, no one knew anything about us, nor had anyone heard of No.6 Coastal Patrol Flight. (This will be no surprise to anyone with Service experience). Nevertheless we were found beds and were made as comfortable as possible.

Over a beer after diner we were told that the hotel was still run by its peacetime owners. Their time seemed to be divided between calculating the financial windfall the war had brought them (in normal circumstances the hotel would have been empty at this time), and protecting their nubile 16 year old daughter from the predatory attentions of a number of young RAF Officers. The Ansons we had seen on the aerodrome belonged to No.217 (G.R.) Squadron whose tasks were escorting convoys and flying anti-submarine patrols over the Western Approaches. Two Flights of the Squadron were at St Eval and the third was across the water in South Wales at Carew Cheriton. Because the hangars at St Eval were unfinished, aircraft had to be flown back to the Squadron's main base at Thorney Island, near Portsmouth, when major maintenance was required. Still no one knew anything about No.6 Coastal Patrol Flight.

Next morning we reported to the Station Adjutant and were told that our C.O. was to be a Flying Officer Cray, that he had been visiting Coastal Command H.Q. and would arrive at St Eval that day. In due course he turned up and we learnt to what sort of Unit we had been posted.

We were to fly Hornet Moths (CPFs mostly flew Tigers) on anti-submarine patrols around the coasts of Cornwall and Devon. We would carry no armament or radio, but if we sighted a submarine, were to fly to the nearest land, locate a house with telephone wires leading to it, land and report, by landline to No.19 H.Q. at Plymouth.

"I've just spotted a German submarine, can I borrow your 'phone". I kid you not. Two factors are relevant here. Firstly, much military thinking in 1939 was, quite understandably, based on theories developed during the Great War. This seemed perfectly reasonable, as all the senior officers running the Services had been juniors in 1914-1918. Conventional thinking then, had it that enemy submarines would take shelter in isolated parts of the British and Irish coastline, to recharge their batteries or effect minor repairs.

These CPFs (there were to be a number of them dotted around the coasts) were to flush out these interlopers. The other factor was that the RAF had at the time, more pilots than could be usefully employed. The influx of reservists had brought about this temporary imbalance, and the CPFs were a method of keeping junior pilots in flying practice.

We were lucky to be flying Hornet Moths - the only CPF to be so equipped. Lucky because two hour patrols in open cockpit aircraft in the winter of 1939-40 was no joke. Our Hornets (a member of the D.H. Moth family developed between the wars) were a two seat, side by side cabin biplanes, the cabin filling the hole centre section between the wings. Although there was no heating, this was an improvement on the open cockpit Tigers. The undercarriage was of course, fixed as in all Moths, but a novel feature was that the farings on the main undercarriage struts could be turned through 90 degrees by a lever in the cockpit. It provided a crude air brake for landing, a system also used on Puss and Leopard Moths.

Within a short time our aircraft started arriving having been commandeered from flying clubs and private owners, looking very smart and quite business like in their new camouflage paint and RAF roundels. So much so in fact that a passing local leaned over the airfield fence and asked: "Are these them there Spitfires?" The vehemence of the reply probably surprised him!

We soon settled into a routine. Four patrols were flown each day; two taking off at first light and two landing at last light. The aircraft departed together, one flying South to strike the coast at St Austell and then coastwise round Land's End and back to St Eval, the second to fly north east up the coast as far as Lundy, circuiting the Island and then returning to base. Needless to say, none of us saw anything remotely resembling a submarine but two sightings by CPFs were reported from Scotland, one of which resulted in a Destroyer attack and a possible kill.

Not long after our arrival at St Eval, the Station and No.217 Squadron Commander, Wing Commander A.P. Revington (a coincidence of names which meant that P/O Rivington escaped Orderly Officer's duties for his first month, the Orderly Room Sergeant thinking that his name a misprint for the CO's) received an invitation from the Mayor of Falmouth to send a party of officers to see a new film about the Air Force at War. It was called "The Lion has Wings". I volunteered to go. We were civic guests and were to attend a reception after the show. The film had been hurriedly thrown together after the outbreak of war and had a strong cast including Ralph Richardson, Laurence Olivier and I think Olivia De Haviland. I suppose there was some story line but the main theme was an enemy air raid on a British city. Clearly it had not been possible to produce flying sequences especially for this film, but the makers excelled themselves in this case. We watched in disbelief as the 'enemy' raiders changed from Battles to Hawker Harts to a whole Hendon display fly past (circa 1937) and finally and most incredibly, to a couple of ancient Curtiss Biplane bombers of the U.S.A.A.C.

No doubt we were restrained out of deference to our hosts from hooting too openly, but the British film industry could certainly turn out some rubbish around that time. 'The Aeroplane' magazine reviewed the film under the heading 'The Unicorn has Tail Planes' and, as I remember, did a fairly good debunking job.

Talking of 'The Aeroplane', its Editor at that time, the formidable C.G. Grey, had long been conducting a campaign against the purchase of American aircraft for the RAF. A particular target of his was the choice of the Harvard for training. According to Grey this was a dangerous aircraft, would flick into a spin without warning and had far too high a landing speed for a trainer. What was required was an aircraft which in his words would "land slowly and not burn up".

I wrote to 'The Aeroplane' suggesting that the Editor stopped 'knocking' a fine aircraft, and stating that I was a member of the first F.T.S. Course to be Harvard trained, that we had come through with only minor damage to two aircraft and without a scratch on any pilot. They printed my letter, but Grey himself was, I suspect, quite unimpressed. I think he had retired by then.

After about a month with no Orderly Officer duties, someone at last realised that Rivington was not a misprint for Revington. From then on I got clobbered along with all the other POs and FOs. There was not so much 'bull' involved as at Grantham, but the Orderly Officer had to sleep in the Ops Room. He was responsible for deciphering 'immediate' or 'most immediate' signals after the cipher staff had gone off duty. Sometimes one would be woken up at about 4 a.m. to decipher a long signal marked 'immediate' to find it was a spiel to do with airmen's boots or some other 'vital' subject.

There were few formal parades in wartime, but the Orderly Officer was expected to take the daily colour hoisting with 20 or

30 men on parade. The first time I did this I was desperately trying to remember how these things went at Grantham. After a round of:

"Parade atten-hup"

"Parade standat-ese"

"Atten-hup"

I went on with

"Parade form - fours."

This caused some consternation in the ranks, some men standing still and others stepping back onto the toes of the man behind to the accompaniment of barely suppressed giggles. The Station Warrant Officer restored order with a stentorian:

"As you were!"

He then came over to me, came to attention with a cracking salute:

"Sir, they can't form fours, they're in threes already" and his eyes added the unspoken word "clot!"

Of course I had forgotten that between the time of our last parades at Grantham and this one, the old drill book had been thrown out of the window and replaced with another, with the troops drawn up in threes not twos.

But not all the Orderly Officer's duties were so light hearted. On one occasion I was woken before dawn and told that I was wanted on the Aircraft Park where there had been an accident. I threw off the blankets, dragged on my flying boots and ran to my car, parked outside the Ops. Room. The shortest route to the aircraft led past the still uncompleted hangars. Unfortunately the contractors had left the flagstone covers off one of the channels running across the tarmac (designed to take pipes and wires). About two feet across, the trench was just wide enough for my front wheels to jump the gap, hitting the opposite edge with an almighty crash, and leaving the car stranded. I jumped out and ran the rest of the way towards the flickering torches that indicated where the trouble lay. A Corporal was lying under one of the engines of an Anson with his skull split from ear to ear and some of his brains lying on the grass. He had, it seemed, been turning the engine over with the starting handle, which was inserted into the engine nacelle just forward of the main plane. When the engine started he had walked forward into the propeller instead of moving outward. When there is an argument between a human skull and a moving aircraft propeller there can be only one result. Soon after my arrival the M.O. turned up with an ambulance and my part in the proceedings was over.

As to my car, some workmen lifted it over the open trench. The front axle was badly bent and the engine had moved an inch or two forward on its bearers. However it was just driveable and the Mawgan Porth Garage mended it in old fashioned style using a Blacksmith's forge and a welding torch.

When Christmas came in 1939 I was lucky enough to get leave. By now a flight of Whitley Mk.I's with Tiger IX engines were based at St Eval to give longer-range convoy cover than the Ansons were able to provide. One of these was being flown to Boscombe Down, the new home of the Aeroplane Development and Experimental Unit. I, heading for Devizes, was lucky enough to get a lift. I enjoyed the trip, sitting in the front gunner's turret, and when the familiar shapes of 'Oliver's Camp' and 'Picnic Wood' (features of the Down just north of Devizes) appeared dead ahead. I was able to crawl back and tell the pilot that if he wanted to get to Boscombe he'd better go right hand down!

On landing on the undulating grass airfield I was able to pick out a number of interesting new aircraft of which we had only heard rumours. These included a Beaufighter and that pretty little radial engined single seat fighter by Gloster, the F5/34, which was upstaged by the Hurricane and Spitfire and never went into production.

Had we known what 1940 was to bring I doubt if we would have entered the New Year with so much confidence. We were fed up with flying 'scarecrow patrols', and in early February 1940, to our great relief, the C.P.F. was disbanded and we were absorbed into No.217 (G.R.) Squadron.

5. *Over the Western Approaches*

We were, I think received on the Squadron with some reservations. None of us had completed the General Reconnaissance Course, a sine qua non for the Coastal Pilot and, more importantly perhaps, we had flown only single engined aircraft. However the Squadron possessed a dual control Anson and after a trip with the Flight Commander I was off solo in my first twin. The Anson had about as many vices as a Tiger Moth, and the most difficult thing to get used to was handling it on the ground. I don't remember practising single engine flight at this stage, but then the Cheetahs never seemed to stop unless asked to. This was just as well as the basic principles of an asymmetric flight although probably well understood at the rarefied level of the Central Flying School, did not seem to be well propagated at the lower levels.

With the introduction of high performance aircraft (as they then were) into the Service in the late 1930's, the old biplanes were replaced by Blenheims, Hampdens, Wellingtons and Whitleys. These brought with them new high-powered radial engines that suffered from teething problems, some caused by incorrect handling. So accidents happened when, after suffering engine failure on take off or landing, the aircraft out of control in a diving turn would hit the ground. I do not think the twin factors of critical speed and safety speed were well understood in the Service at that time.

A multi engined aircraft with engines in the wings, when flying with an engine or engines on one side inoperative, is an 'asymmetric power', and a turning movement is present. This can be balanced by applying rudder. Often the slipstream from the operative engine(s) will cause extra lift so a rolling movement is also present. This can be corrected by aileron, but the effectiveness of the rudder and ailerons is directly proportional to the airflow over them and the turning movement or asymmetric-power is proportional to the power. It therefore follows that under conditions of high asymmetric power and low airspeed, the effect of the controls may be insufficient to correct the turning, rolling forces and the aircraft will go out of control into a diving turn. This is exactly the position when an engine fails just after take off, so, as all modern pilots know, the principles are these:

At take off power there is a speed below which, in the event of engine failure, it will be impossible to control the aircraft. This is the critical speed. As speed builds, there comes a point when control can safely be maintained in the event of engine failure. This is safety speed. The aim on take off, therefore, is to reach this speed as quickly as possible, and speed offers much greater safety than height. These principles were not generally understood by a generation of pilots brought up on Tiger Moths, Hawker Harts, Sidestrands, and Heyfords, nor by myself when I first flew twins.

But to return to the delights of flying Ansons on convoy escort over the Western Approaches in the early months of 1940. If the radius of action of the Anson is marked on a chart of the North Atlantic, the impact we were able to make on the incipient Battle of the Atlantic will become clear. The Anson had a safe endurance of around 4 hours at 120 knots. Flying from St Eval this would allow a convoy to be met 100 miles west of Lands End and escorted for 2 hours, or if met 160 miles off Lands End, for 1 hour. Some aircraft had a 40 gallon tank in the fuselage which gave an extra hour's flying so the 100 mile convoy could be escorted for 3 hours and the 160 mile for 2 hours. The area beyond our domain was the Sunderland flying boats from Pembroke Dock or Mountbatten (Plymouth), and the Whitleys I have mentioned. Even they could cover only a fraction of the broad Atlantic. It was standard practice at the time in G.R. Squadrons to fly with two pilots who took it in turn to fly and to navigate. Ansons also carried a Radio Operator and an Air Gunner. Armament normally consisted of a fixed forward firing Browning gun for the pilot and a Vickers gas operated gun in the turret. Later in the year, after the fall of France and we started to encounter enemy aircraft, we fitted two extra Vickers gas operated guns firing through windows at the rear of the fuselage. Some of the older Ansons had a Vickers gun (belt fed) firing forward and a Lewis gun in the turret firing rearwards. This was exactly the armament carried by two-seater aircraft in the previous war, 22 years earlier! (No turrets then of course!).

The load was a mere 2 x 100lb anti-submarine bombs, carried internally with two more carried on external racks. So this was not an aircraft calculated to make Admiral Raeder and his U-Boat Commanders tremble in their shoes, especially in the light of what was later discovered concerning the ineffectiveness of the pre-war designed a/s bombs. The airborne anti-submarine forces did not become really effective until they started carrying depth charges.

This was a typical operational sortie by a No.217 Squadron crew on convoy patrol in the early months of 1940, when, as far as Coastal Command was concerned, there was nothing 'phoney' about the war. The crew would very likely consist of a Pilot Officer pilot, a Sergeant pilot, a Sergeant Wireless Operator and an L.A.C. air gunner. I don't remember anything formal being laid down as to which pilot would be captain of the aircraft. If the experience of the pilots was roughly equal, then the one whose turn it was to fly would be captain. If, however, one was vastly more experienced than the other, then he would make the decisions should anything untoward occur. This applied irrespective of rank, and as a green Pilot Officer I would defer to a vastly more experienced sergeant. Members of the other two services sometimes found this difficult to understand.

The crew would have seen from the flying programme that they were due for a 0545 hours call and, if they were wise would have got to bed the previous evening reasonably early, reasonably sober. It would seem that they had hardly shut their eyes before being shaken awake with a cup of tea (for the officers anyway). So that there could be no falling asleep again, an early call book would have to be initialled before the befuddled victims were left to dress and stagger to the dining room for the obligatory pre-flight breakfast.

After the short drive to the airfield the crew would assemble in the Operations Room for briefing at about 0630 hrs. They were to relieve the aircraft that had taken off an hour earlier to meet a convoy at first light some 150 miles west of Lands End. Take off was at 0730 hrs. to rendezvous with the convoy at 0900 hrs. The navigator would now be busy working on his charts, while the pilot consulted the Met Officer. The radio operator would be checking his frequencies, recognition letters and colours. These last were vital as the Navy had the reputation of shooting first and asking questions afterwards.

Half an hour before take off the crew would be driven out to their aircraft already checked by the ground crew. The Captain would sign the Form 700 and they would pile aboard with their bulky navigation bags and parachutes. (All crew members used Observer type parachutes with clip on packs, life jackets, and flying suits would be worn under the harnesses).

Ten minutes before take off time the engines would be started and checked, then the aircraft would be taxied to the take off point. Although it might by now be nearly full daylight, the flare-path would probably still be in position and its line would be used for take off. This was before the days of Air Traffic Control and runway control vans and in any case the aircraft had no R.T. (voice radio). Once airborne the aircraft might set course direct from the airfield or perhaps from some convenient land-mark, say St Agnes Head.

With the aircraft on course the navigator would be busy checking his forecast wind. Flying at 1,000 ft. there would be little difference between the wind at that height and on the surface. With experience the wind speed and direction could be estimated very accurately by the state of the sea. The number and size of the white caps would indicate the speed while the direction could be clearly seen from the 'wind lanes' or streaks that appear on the sea surface. Satisfied with the course the navigator would give the pilot the E.T.A. at the convoy. He might then move from his chart table behind the pilot's seat to the folding seat alongside him, or perhaps forward to the bomb aimer's position in the nose, to measure the drift and get yet another check on the wind. It may seem odd but the white caps on the sea do not move with the wind, and can be used for drift finding, as they are virtually stationary.

The Radio Operator at his set behind the navigator would, by now, have wound out his long trailing aerial and made contact with base, just a brief coded signal. His task from now on would be to maintain a listening watch. The Airgunner in his turret might now ask permission to test his gun and the pilot would probably fire a test burst from his also.

Now, for an hour or so, there would be nothing to do but watch the sea. The rocky Cornish coast would have fallen below the horizon on the port beam. The crew would be surrounded by a wide circle of restless grey, flecked with white, a sight to become so familiar to Coastal Command air crews (I don't believe we used that term in early 1940) in the long years to come.

Five minutes before E.T.A. at the convoy, in good visibility, smidges of smoke might appear on the horizon, to the great relief of all in the aircraft, but in poor visibility, the tension mounts. Will the convoy be found? If not, whose fault will it be? Of course if the visibility is less than about 5 miles, a convoy is a very small speck in a very large ocean. In cases where the convoy did not come up on E.T.A. the drill was to fly on for a further few minutes and then to turn out the reciprocal of the convoy's course. Experience had told that convoys were usually late rather than early and were often found back along their track. If the ships were still not sighted after about 10 minutes, then a square search was started and continued, if necessary, until it was time to return to base.

In our case, however, the convoy comes up on time and our aircraft must identify itself to the Officer Commanding the surface escorts and to the aircraft to be relieved. Identification would be achieved by flashing the letters of the day using an Aldis lamp. The letters being changed several times during the 24 hours. In an emergency, the colours of the day, also frequently changed. These could be fired from a Very pistol that used a two-star cartridge.

Once the take over has been completed and the aircraft relieved has set course for home, the new escort can settle down with its flock, counting them carefully and noting any stragglers. It spends most time ahead and to the flanks of the convoy, with occasional sweeps to the rear, just in case some cunning U-Boat Commander is following the convoy and waiting his chance to close for an attack.

By about 1100 hrs. it would be time to leave, and a relieving aircraft should have appeared. Once away from the convoy a routine leaving signal could be sent, together, perhaps, with a message or two from the Senior Naval Officer Commanding, to his base, these having been passed to the aircraft by lamp.

All signals were encoded by a simple machine called a Syko. I forget the exact details, but recall that the key was a card placed under a system of sliding letters and numbers. When the message was spelt out in clear, the coded signal was revealed on the card. As the cards were arranged completely at random and changed twice a day, no card being used twice, the code was completely secure unless the enemy could get hold of a future supply of cards.

By about 1215 hrs. our crew would have the Cornish coast in view once again and by 1230 hrs. the aircraft would be on the ground at St Eval. A visit to the Ops. Room followed, to hand over the navigator's log to the duty controller, report briefly on the sortie, and then back to the hotel for a beer lunch and a well earned snooze in the afternoon. With trips taking up to 5 hours, it was now commonplace, say, to take off before lunch and land late in the afternoon. This seems a simple thing, but when previously one's day had been organised into compartments around meal times, it seemed odd at first to have these broken down.

Social life in these early war days was most enjoyable. As we had no proper mess, we had to make our entertainment outside. The hotels in Newquay (with the exception of the 'Atlantic' which, I believe had been earmarked as a hospital) were still in their pre-war condition. I particularly remember the 'Bristol' on the seafront out towards Porth, which we used as an unofficial junior officers' mess, and the 'Headland', where excellent dances were laid on. The barman there boasted that he could provide any drink that anyone asked for. He had achieved this, he said, over the years, by always obtaining a bottle of anything he was asked for and could not provide. The point had arrived when he was virtually never caught out. It was still quite a novelty to have large numbers of young men in uniform about, and a good time was had by all.

There was, of course, a great deal of drinking. While I understand the accident rate in the blackout was horrifyingly high, proportional to the traffic density, the actual number of accidents was quite low. No doubt we all had narrow escapes but I don't remember anyone having a serious accident in spite of the fact that masks on headlights, reduced already poor headlights (no sealed beams in those days) to a mere glimmer, and all street lighting was off. I remember a young Pilot Officer with a sports car that seemed to spend more of its time on its side than right way up. It was said of its owner that he need have no fear if his engine ran out of fuel as the engine would run quite happily on his breath!

Sometime in March the Squadron was asked to provide a junior officer pilot to sit on a Court of Inquiry to be held at Hooton Park Aerodrome near Liverpool, to investigate an accident to an Anson of the squadron stationed there. My name came out of the hat, and I collected petrol coupons and set off in my little Morris 8 for the North.

The President of the Court was Wing Commander Kellet A.F.C., well known in the Service for his pre-war long distance flights. It seemed that the Anson, returning from patrol, was following the North Wales coast in poor visibility. Running into heavy snow the aircraft had crashed on the beach at Prestatyn. We went to take evidence from the pilot in hospital. I don't remember seeing any other crew members so perhaps he was the only survivor. I was shocked at his appearance. He had not suffered any serious injuries, but for a man of 28 or 30, he looked 50 years old.

I think our findings were that the aircraft had flown into the ground in poor visibility, probably because the pilot had tried to maintain visual contact when this was no longer possible. After two or three days at Hooton Park I drove back to St Eval again.

Spring was now well advanced in Cornwall, and we were looking forward to the better weather, but as our work covered all the hours of daylight, the longer days meant much longer hours of flying.

There was now talk of re-equipping the Squadron with Beaufort torpedo bombers, but before anything materialised, I was on the move again - to Wick of all places. Now there were few RAF Stations in the United Kingdom more widely separated than St Eval, 40 miles from Lands End, and Wick, 15 miles from John O'Groats. It appeared that operations were just commencing from that airfield in the far North of Scotland and they needed the loan of an 'experienced' Coastal Command pilot to act as Ops. Room navigator. Now it is well known that when a squadron gets a 'request' such as this, they send their most inexperienced 'sprog', in this case, me. So I once more pointed the nose of my little car northwards.

6. *Scotland*

The journey from St Eval took four days and I spent nights at Hooton Park (where I had to call to sign the findings of the Court of Enquiry), Ayr and Inverness. The halt at Inverness was enforced, as at that time Scotland, North of the city, was a restricted area, where all sorts of secret training was presumed to be taking place, and to get past Inverness was like trying to get through the Berlin Wall. However, I arrived eventually at Wick, my worst mishap being a broken spring on the shocking coast road up past Helmsdale and Lybster.

Arriving at Wick I looked, not unnaturally, for the RAF Station and found, to my consternation, a sea of mud even worse than that at St Eval the previous autumn. There were no buildings or hangars, Station Headquarters and the Ops. Room was in a nearby school and everyone was billeted out in town. I was found a bed for the night in a private house and soon after I had settled in, a charming maid came in and asked me "Have ye no had ye tea?" Now, as it happened, I had had a cup of tea some 30 miles back down the road while a local blacksmith welded my spring, so I told her I had had tea, and sat down to wait for supper. I was soon to find out that in Scotland, when you've had your tea, you've had it (to use a phrase popular at the time). However, again according to Scottish custom, I did get a cup of cocoa and a biscuit at around 10 p.m.

Wick at that time was becoming a busy Coastal Command base and housed, in addition, a squadron of Hurricanes charged with the defence of the Naval base at Scapa Flow. The Coastal Command task was to patrol the Northern channel between the

Orkneys, the Shetlands and the then neutral Norwegian coast, the route taken by U-Boats, and surface raiders slipping out into the Atlantic. The main burden of this task was carried by No.224 and No.233 Squadrons equipped with Lockheed Hudson aircraft. Their main base was at Leuchars near Dundee but they each kept a flight detailed at Wick. The Hudsons were backed up by the Ansons of No.269 Squadron, based at Wick, and used for the shorter range work.

The Hudson was a military version of the well known Lockheed 14 airliner, and had been, with the Harvard, the first American aircraft to be ordered by the RAF in the immediate pre-war years. It was a fine aircraft, if something of a stop-gap, and did yeoman service with Coastal Command in the first years of the war and later overseas in a number of roles. The United States Air Force used it as the A29. It had, however, one serious failing. Being a short wheel base tail wheel aircraft with a comparatively high ground angle, it had a tendency to swing both on take off and landing when the tail was down. The locking tail wheel helped to correct this and it probably was not a factor to worry about when the aircraft was being flown by experienced airline captains, but with young inexperienced RAF pilots, things were different. A bad swing usually resulted in the collapse of one or both undercarriage legs, which would often be forced up into the wing. As the fuel was carried in tanks integral with the wing structure and with no self sealing system, fire frequently resulted. Normally these were low speed accidents, and the crew was able to escape before the fire got a serious hold. For this reason it was said that the ability to do 100 yds in even time wearing full flying gear, was a useful qualification for a Hudson crew member.

The Fighter squadron at Wick was a fashionable Auxiliary Squadron (*No.43 Squadron*) which had arrived from Acklington in February 1940. At this stage in the war its peacetime membership was largely intact. I remember their uniforms with exotic scarlet silk linings. They flew Hurricanes and were frequently in action chasing daylight raiders away from Scapa Flow, or trying to interfere with the night bombing raids that were a frequent occurrence. I saw my first enemy aircraft when one of their Hurricanes forced a Heinkel 111 to make a belly landing on Wick airfield. The shambles that was the rear gunner's cockpit clearly showed the devastating effect of eight Browning guns at close range.[4]

The even tenor of life at Wick was rudely shattered early in April when the Germans invaded Denmark and Norway. The Hudsons were now expected to operate across the North Sea over the Norwegian coast. They carried out every task, even including 'Fighter' patrols over our troops when they landed. As the Germans quickly brought up Me.109's to the Norwegian airfields, this was hardly an enviable duty.

The Hudson was armed with two fixed Brownings firing forward, and two more in a turret towards the rear of the fuselage. The large twin tails interfered seriously with the field of fire of this turret, and when attacked from below the aircraft was quite defenceless. One of the Mess songs of the time, sung to a popular tune, went like this:

> *Hudson rolling down the Skagerrak*
> *with a 109 behind,*
> *Hudson rolling down the Skagerrak*
> *with a 109 behind,*
> *Now a Hudson is a Yankee kite*
> *A Messerschmit is a Hun*

---

[4] This incident occurred on 8th April 1940 when the squadron met two attacks in which three He 111s were shot down and two damaged. It was one of the latter that force-landed on the aerodrome with two of the crew dead.

And when the two of them get together
There's bound to be lots of fun!
Hudson rolling etc. etc…

Hun and fun yes, but mainly for the Hun.

The danger to the Hudson came not only from the enemy. One crew were briefed for a "battle flight" over the Norwegian coast and were instructed to 'show the flag' to the troops and R.N. ships at Andalgnes. To this end they carried an unofficial load of newspapers and magazines to be dropped over our positions. Unfortunately the British had not seen a friendly aircraft for days and were extremely trigger-happy. Their motto was, 'all aircraft are hostile' and those with double tails (like the Dornier) doubly so. The AA fire was accurate and one aircraft was shot down and another seriously damaged. This staggered up into the cloud and miraculously made the 300 miles back to Wick on one engine, the newspapers and magazines, of course, forgotten. Later a photo of the damaged aircraft appeared in the press, with the heads of the crew poking up through the hole in the wing, to show the world what punishment our aircraft could take and still get home; of course, no mention was made of the source of its punishment. At the time we thought an Army Bofors battery was the culprit, but Andrew Hendrie, in his book on the Hudson *Seek and Strike*, laid the blame on the AA cruiser HMS *Curacao*, which was lying in the fjord at the time. Incidentally, one of the pilots of the surviving Hudson was Tolly Rothwell, late of No.19 ERFTS and No.12 FTS Grantham.

At Wick I discovered an old school-friend, P/O Alfie Hayter, was flying with one of the Hudson squadrons. We had played cricket and rugby together; he was a useful left-hand bat and a good outside half, making the most of my shaky service from the base of the scrum. Sadly, his aircraft failed to return from a sortie just a few days later and he was subsequently reported killed.[5]

It was at Wick that I flew my first bi-plane, an Avro Tutor belonging to the station flight. It made no great impression on me except that I remember to start the engine one had to twiddle a little handle in the cockpit while the engine was being turned over by an outside crank. This was to operate the starter magneto and the Tutor was the only aircraft I ever flew with this device, common I believe in 20's and 30's aircraft.

Wick was, at this time, a 'dry' town. One could not get a drink unless one was a hotel resident, and then one had to retire to a back room. The story going around at the time was that the wives of Wick voted the town dry by referendum when all the fishing boats were out, and the men deprived of the votes that would almost certainly have kept the town 'wet'. Be that as it may, when I was there some of the hotels seemed to have at least ten guests for every room, especially on Saturday nights.

Just as the late northern spring was making itself felt, news broke of the German offensive in Northern Europe. Norway was at once relegated to the status of a sideshow and not long afterwards 217 Squadron indicated that they wanted their wandering boy back. So my Morris 8 headed south once more...

---

[5] P/O Alfred Henry Hayter was serving with No.269 Squadron when he was killed on Wednesday 1st May 1940. His name appears on the Runnymede Memorial and on Dauntsey's School War Memorial. Three Hudson I's took-off from Wick early in the morning to bomb Stavangar aerodrome. The three aircraft carried out the bombing run line astern. The first Hudson successfully dropped its load on the target at 0820 hours without experiencing any opposition. The second Hudson did the same but an enemy aircraft was seen to take-off between the two drops. The third Hudson N7278 with Sgt. Bell, P/O Hayter, Sgt. Kelly and LAC McKenzie was observed making its bombing run towards the target but was not seen again and failed to return to Wick. [Ed]

7. *Earmarked For Overseas*

At St Eval I found the Squadron somewhat extended. One flight was non-operational, converting to Beauforts, which left the remainder to cope with a much increased work load due to increasing evening action over the Channel, and the long summer days. The evacuation from Dunkirk kept many squadrons busy in the East and it was not long before enemy aircraft started to appear around convoys in the Western Approaches.

We armed our Ansons with two extra Vickers gas operated guns, mounted to fire out of the rear fuselage windows, but there was little we could do against our enemy, who often ducked out of the clouds, bombed and disappeared again in seconds. In any case, even a Ju.87 could out run our old aircraft.

No ship was hit when I was on convoy patrol, but on a number of occasions attacks were made by aircraft we hardly saw. Frantic lamp signals from the escorts that "he went that-a way" hardly helped. On one occasion a Heinkel 59 floatplane was reported to be down on the sea off the South Cornish coast. An Anson aircraft was sent to investigate. The enemy aircraft was sighted at a range of about 10 miles and soon afterwards began to take off. A chase ensued with the Anson steadily gaining. Our pilot eventually got in a few bursts at extreme range. The Heinkel then started to lose height, probably due to the engine trouble that had forced it down in the first place. This time, however, it crashed and turned over on alighting on the water. The Anson's Air Gunner, a somewhat belligerent character started hammering away at the crew struggling in the water, and had to be forcibly restrained. I imagine the Germans were eventually picked up and taken into captivity as they were not far from the Cornish coast.

I remember clearly the occasion when the news of the French capitulation broke. It was not a total surprise after Churchill's offer of joint citizenship had been turned down. Nevertheless, it was a shock to realise our principal ally was knocked out, and we were left alone to continue the war. In the group clustered round the radio, one spoke: "Well, we can't win now." At once he was shouted down with cries of "Rubbish!" "Nonsense", "Clot, of course we can", and so on. I can honestly say that from that moment, I never heard any serviceman express any doubt as to the eventual outcome of the war.

At about this time a number of very odd looking aircraft started arriving at St Eval, wearing their roundels back to front (red on the outside); some appeared like the camel to have been designed by a somewhat eccentric committee. They belonged to the French Armee d L'Air or, in one case, I believe, Aeromarine, and were overloaded with French men and women (some men had brought their wives) who had decided to join de Gaul in this country rather than suffer life with 'les Boches'. In fairness to their aircraft, I suppose they had picked up anything they could find that was fit to fly, but they were a very odd assortment. We offered them what hospitality we could, but they were anxious to get on up to London and were in the mood to celebrate.

We received more tangible evidence of the German presence in Western France when a number of hit-and-run raids were made on the aerodrome. By now we had a Spitfire squadron with us, and their presence, no doubt, made the evening visits fleeting and circumspect.[6]

---

[6] This was No.234 Sq. that arrived from Church Fenton with Spitfire I's in June 1940. [Ed]

As the summer drew on there seemed to be a lull in the war. It was, as we now know, the lull before the storm.

Our escort duties became less as more and more convoys were routed to the North of Ireland, to take them away from the enemy bases being set up on the west coast of France. Clearly, the Anson was no longer up to the tasks being required of it, which included operating off an enemy held coast in daylight, but soon the Squadron would be operational on Beauforts. Before I could become involved in the change, the fates intervened once more. A Unit was to be formed at St Athan in preparation for overseas service. Three crews from No. 217 Squadron were required. So, in early August, a small group from St Eval, myself included, found themselves members of No. 417 (G.R.) Flight, St Athan. Our new CO was to be Squadron Leader L. Rankin. (I believe that his true initials were W.E., but for some reason that now escapes me, he always styled himself 'L'.) On the day after our arrival in South Wales he told us what he could of our new unit. We were to be equipped with Ansons (Oh no, not again!) which were at present on a quayside waiting for the word that would send us across the high seas to ... where? Well, that was the snag. The operation was so highly secret and sensitive that he couldn't tell us where we were going, only that we were to be issued with tropical kit and to have every inoculation under the sun, including yellow fever. He could tell us, however, that our mission would be a vital one, most important to the war effort and one that we would be proud to be involved in.

So we were condemned to a period of what a friend called 'Also serving' ('They also serve who only… etc, etc.'). This was made even more frustrating by the fact that the war was moving into the phase later to be known as the 'Battle of Britain'. At the time the issues were not seen in quite such a clear-cut way, although Winston Churchill had coined the phrase in a speech some time previously ("The Battle of France is over, the Battle of Britain is about to begin!") What seemed to be clear, however, was that the all-out German onslaught on these islands could not be long delayed and almost everyone thought an invasion attempt was a near certainty. It was therefore doubly hard on a frustrated incipient fighter pilot (I still thought of myself as such) to be inactive at this time. We managed to borrow a couple of Ansons to keep ourselves in flying practice, but still had far too much time to spare, playing snooker in the mess or going in to Cardiff to the 'Queens' or to see 'Gone with the Wind' at the cinema. One morning after breakfast, when we were finishing our coffee in the ante-room, the Station Adjutant put his head round the door:

"Anyone here flown a Maggie?"

Naturally, my ears pricked up.

"Yes me," I called, ungrammatically.

It turned out that a Medical Officer had to go to Yatesbury and the Senior Admin Officer had agreed to get him a lift in the Station Flight's Magister; all they needed was a pilot, and now they had found one. I was particularly pleased because, not only would it be good to fly a Magister again, but also Yatesbury was near my home town of Devizes and it is always interesting to view familiar places from the air. Accordingly, after I had dropped my passenger, who was not coming back with me, I planned to make a little sight-seeing tour.

All went according to plan… at first. I put the MO in the front cockpit, as I would have to return solo, and climbed into the familiar rear seat. Everything came readily to hand, although those days at Gatwick seemed now to belong to another world (which in a sense, I suppose they did.) I took a route to the South of Bristol to avoid the barrage balloons, via Weston-Super-Mare and Bath and then along the A4 past Chippenham to

Yatesbury. My passenger disposed of, I headed south past the Monument and the White Horse on Cherhill Down, over Morgan's Hill and 'Picnic Wood' of childhood memories, and so to Devizes. I spent a few minutes picking out well-remembered places and then on south towards the village of Worton, where my sister still lived. She may have waved from the garden, but she had no way of knowing that the little yellow monoplane she was waving at contained her brother. Then on to Dauntsey's and a few more minutes of pleasurable nostalgia.

By this time I was getting somewhat chilly. I had probably forgotten that an open cockpit, even in summer, is not the warmest of places. I suppose I was wearing the civilian-type cotton flying-suit that many of us used at the time – the regulation 'Sidcot' suit being too bulky – and there was no equivalent to the modern aircrew overalls. An Irvin flying jacket would have been ideal, but not all of us were lucky enough to possess one.

As it was, by the time I was crossing the Bristol Channel on my way home I was thoroughly chilled. To make matters worse, I was only making slow progress against a stiff westerly wind, so when I saw the aerodrome ahead and no other aircraft in the circuit I decided to make a straight-in approach to land. I lined up between two hangars, cut the speed to 70 mph, lowered the flaps and prepared to touch down as early as possible, to avoid taxiing. This I did, on the first piece of grass after the tarmac. The aircraft ran about ten yards and was then brought to a standstill with a violence that threw me forward against my straps.

The propeller was stationary and when I gathered my senses I could see that the aircraft had been arrested by a dense coil of barbed wire after the manner of an aircraft carrier barrier landing. One or two small holes had been knocked in the wings by the iron stanchions supporting the wire, which was coiled round the propeller and over the cowling. With a little less luck I suppose a strand could have swept across the cockpit, removing my head! The whole performance was watched by an impassive Dutch soldier with rifle and fixed bayonet who was standing on the pill box that the wire was sited to protect. I had, of course, fallen foul of the sort of defence works that were appearing on airfields all over the country.

There was no excuse for my carelessness. Straight in approaches are permissible and no one will complain, provided all goes well. If not, the pilot tends to be in trouble. In my defence I could say that the wire encroaching on the landing area should have been very clearly marked, but it was not. I suppose I had to render the usual accident report (form 765 C) but I heard no more of the incident. The Group Captain (Admin) – this big station was commanded by an Air Commodore – was said to have made half-hearted efforts to find out who the clot was who had 'pranged' his Maggie, but being a busy man he did not pursue the matter.

So now, during those now-famous weeks in the late summer of 1940, we were left kicking our heels at St Athan, waiting for some crucial happening that would send us sailing off to tropical climes. In the event this never occurred and as summer turned to autumn I think we all sensed that our unit was not going to be needed. What had it been formed for? I still don't know for certain, but I think the reasoning may have gone something like this:

The Germans, having swept France aside, would probably not stop at the Pyrenees. Franco was their friend; if he accepted German 'protection', Portugal would almost certainly fall. In this event it would be vital to have a force standing by to occupy the Portuguese Atlantic Islands, especially the Azores, lying as they did across our vital convoy routes. Of course much later on, when the threat to the Iberian Peninsula had subsided, Portugal did allow the Azores to become a vital allied base in the Battle of the Atlantic.

If that was it, the threat was not going to disappear overnight, and we were clearly in for a long wait. However, early in October word must have been given that our warning time had been extended from days to weeks, and while No. 417 Flight was not to be disbanded, we were available for other duties. Sergeant Pilot Mott, an old hand from No. 217 Squadron, and I were sent to RAF Bircham Newton, near Kings Lynn, for, of all things, flare-path duties.

The position was this. The Luftwaffe was starting to interfere with our night operations by attacking airfields where night flying was in progress. We also had started these 'night intruder' operations over their bases in Northern France. As it is impossible to fly at night without showing some light from the ground, it is common sense to conduct night flying from 'satellite' landing grounds, with a minimum of permanent buildings, well away from the main base. There were no full time air traffic controllers in those days, so 'gash pilots' were needed as flare-path officers at these satellites. At the time, Mott and I came under the heading of 'gash pilots'. In fact these potentially dangerous evening tactics were not persevered with after the winter of 1940/41, and I understand that this decision came from the highest Nazi levels. This was lucky for us. Imagine the havoc that a small group of determined squadrons could have caused amongst the massed allied bombers later in the war.

8. 'Paraffin Pete'

On arrival at Bircham Newton we found that the satellite was at nearby Docking, but soon afterwards a bigger field became available at Langham, some 15 miles east, along the coast. It was here that we settled. We lived in 'The Hall' (taken over by the RAF) in the centre of the village. The airfield was about a mile down the road, just a number of flat fields with the hedges bulldozed away and no building of any kind.

With winter approaching the aerodrome had to be ready for night flying by about 4 o'clock in the afternoon. The duty flare-path officer would go out with the flare-path party at about 3pm, assess the wind direction and lay out the flare-path accordingly. This consisted of 800yds of electric cable with a white lamp plugged in every hundred yards. With the cable connected to the mobile generator on the 'chance' light (a floodlight used to help the aircraft land), which was stationed at the down-wind end of the flare-path, the lights could be switched on and off as required. White 'glim' lamps were used to make a 'T' at the up-wind end of the flare-path and red 'glim' lamps at either end to mark the airfield boundaries. These 'glim' lamps were battery operated and so constructed that they could be seen from the ground or when approached from the air at low level, but were invisible when viewed from above. This laying out duty sounds quite straightforward, and so it was when the wind was fresh and steady, but under light and variable conditions and in the knowledge that aircraft, heavily laden with bombs and fuel, were to operate, the responsibilities of a flare-path officer were considerable. Some of the aircraft involved, the fully laden Wellington 1c, for instance, had a highly marginal performance when taking off on wet grass and with little or no wind. On one occasion two of these aircraft, belonging to a Czech squadron, failed to get off the ground and crashed before we stopped the operation. In our isolated situation there was no senior officer to refer to – quite a responsibility for a newly-promoted Flying Officer, as I was at the time. I'm happy to say that in both cases the crews walked away from their aircraft, which had simply stayed firmly on the ground and bulldozed a couple of hedges. One gave us some anxiety however, as we arrived with our fire tender to find incendiary bombs scattered about, one or two of them burning. As there was fuel leaking from several tanks and we had no means of knowing if anyone was trapped in the wreckage, things were somewhat fraught for a time. However, we soon found that the entire Czech crew had wisely removed themselves from the scene of the crash – the aircraft, in addition to its load of incendiaries, was carrying a number of 500lb bombs!

The flare-path officer would have a copy of the night flying programme and aircraft that were due to operate later in the night would probably have landed just before dusk to await their time of take off, their crews being taken to the comparative comfort of the Hall.

During the night there might be aircraft going off on anti E-Boat patrols, mine-laying, bombing barges in various continental harbours (invasion was still thought to be very much on the cards) and perhaps a couple of crews doing night familiarisation 'circuits and bumps'. If there was a lull in the flying, the flare-path crew could retire to the 'comfort' of a caravan at the edge of the field. There were bunks of a sort, but it was normally too cold to sleep.

A mile or so from the field a red beacon flashed the code letters for Langham. The beacon was moved every few nights with its new position known to the aircrews. Thus the flare-path could be kept off until the landing aircraft had identified itself and was on its down-wind leg. The 'chance' light would be switched on when the aircraft was on short finals and switched off when it was safely down. Then a van, with an airman holding a torch at the back, would go out and guide the aircraft to its dispersal point.

This system gave rise to some 'amusing' incidents. Anyone who has driven a car and taxied an aircraft over a grass airfield knows that while the oleo leg suspension of an aircraft gives a comfortable ride up to almost any speed, an old Commer or Standard van of 1939 vintage, will rattle your false teeth at anything over 10 mph. Add this to the fact that when taxiing an aircraft in the pitch dark it is very easy to underestimate your speed, it will be seen that manning the guiding vehicle could be a somewhat hairy job! It was not, as can be imagined, very pleasant being chased by a roaring, flame-spitting monster with two whirling, 12-foot metal propellers capable of making scrap iron of the van and mincemeat of its occupants in the time it takes to blink an eye. Thus there was a tendency for the van driver to go faster and faster to maintain a safe distance from the aircraft – a race, as was frequently pointed out, that was not a fair one.

On one occasion the van was manned, in addition to the usual crew, by the Corporal I/C the parking crew. The speed was increasing and the bumps getting worse, when the van hit an especially vicious ridge.

Torch holder: "Hey, hold it! The Corporal's fallen off!"

Driver: "F--- the Corporal, I'm getting out of here!"

Luckily the Corporal had the sense to lie 'doggo' – like a Grand National jockey parted from his mount – until the propellers and main wheels had passed him and he could roll clear of the tail-wheel.

On another occasion when the race was on and the airfield boundary reached, the driver drove in panic through a gateway for safety. Unfortunately the airman omitted to switch off the torch and the aircraft followed, straight through the hedge, so both aircraft and van ended up neatly parked in somebody's ploughed field!

The aircraft we had to deal with were mainly from the Squadrons at Bircham: No. 206, equipped with Hudsons, No. 500, equipped with Ansons and No. 235 equipped with 'fighter' Blenheims. These aircraft acted as a stopgap in Coastal Command until the Beaufighters arrived. They were fitted with a pack of four .303 Browning machine guns under the nose, giving five forward firing guns, plus one or two in the turret, but they didn't have the performance satisfactory to fulfil a fighter role. We saw little of them, as they operated mainly by day.

No 500 Squadron was a pre-war Auxiliary (County of Kent) Squadron, and though based at Detling, near Maidstone, kept a flight detached at Bircham. Their home station had suffered badly during the Battle of Britain period, when it attracted more than its fair share of bombs, offering a tempting target for enemy aircraft flying up the Thames estuary towards London. Perhaps the Germans thought it was a Fighter Command airfield, anyway, it was here that the Ops Room suffered a direct hit and casualties were high, including a number of WAAFs. However, they did not suffer totally in vain, for as far as the 'Battle' was concerned, every bomb on Detling was a bomb wasted.

In addition to our 'home' squadron we had to deal with a number of visitors, in the shape of Bomber Command Wellingtons, Hampdens, Whitleys and Blenheims which either came to us as a planned operation, sometimes landing in the afternoon for Operations that night, or dropped in unannounced on their way home; short of fuel, damaged or due to bad weather at their home base. All were made equally welcome.

Not all our visitors, however, were as welcome. As I have indicated, the German Air Force began to realise that an economical way to deal with the night raids their country was beginning to suffer would be to harry the bombers at their home bases. Good results could be achieved from a comparatively small effort and there is nothing more morale-sapping for bomber crews than to know that there is no safety, even in the circuit of their own home base. Despite the fact that we kept the flare-path switched on for only the shortest possible time, every now and then, as an aircraft was landing, a dark shape would sweep across the airfield a few hundred feet up. Possibly it would be preceded by the crackle and flash of tracer bullets and followed by the louder crack of light bombs. Occasionally we were lucky and only a few craters in the aerodrome resulted, but sometimes an aircraft would be hit. One Wellington was shot up just after touchdown, starting a fire in one wing. Our fire crew had the unenviable job of taking their tender out to deal with the fire, knowing that the enemy might well repeat the attack on the now clearly visible target. Fortunately, the German pilot, having overestimated the strength of our defences, must have decided that it would be tempting fate to make another attack.

The truth of the matter was that, to start with, we had no defences at all. Later we obtained a Lewis gun (Army type, on an AA mounting) and stationed it by the 'Chance' light. The trouble was that the engine that provided the power to light both the 'Chance' light and the flare-path made enough noise to mask other sounds until an aircraft was within 100 yards or so. After that, even if the target could be distinguished, everything was over so quickly that there was no time for defensive fire.

On one occasion the first indication I had that we were being attacked was the appearance of a flower like 'firework' some two or three hundred feet up and down-wind of the flare-path. This was immediately followed by the 'woosh' of a low flying aircraft and the crash of exploding bombs. I realised afterwards that when I thought I was seeing a firework in the sky, I was probably looking straight down the barrel of a MG-15 machine gun spraying tracer from the nose of the enemy aircraft!

We alas had problems communicating with our own aircraft, both on the ground and in the air. An Aldis lamp flashing Morse-code was our main method of communication, though we did have a primitive TR9 R/T set on the flare-path. I don't remember ever getting this to work, so if we wanted to send a message to an aircraft waiting to take off, the easiest way was to hold it stationary with a red light and then send a man over with a message for the pilot. On one occasion I was using this method with a Hudson waiting to take off. I sent a man over to open the door at the rear of the fuselage and pass the message. After a minute or two the aircraft signalled with its downward identity light that it was ready to go. It was given a 'green' and moved off into the darkness. No one noticed that the messenger had not returned. A few minutes later one of the flare-path crew felt someone pulling at his legs and looking down saw the missing man, on hands and knees, his face covered with blood from a nasty head wound. He was taken at once to the Hall and the local GP who did duty as our MO was summoned. Luckily the wound, although quite horrific to look at, proved superficial. The man was new to the job. Previously he had been used to Wellington aircraft. To enter a Wellington one used a trap door under the fuselage between the undercarriage legs. This door was well clear of the propellers and could be safely used with the engines running. The Hudson, on the other hand, being designed as an airliner, had a side entrance door; the position under the fuselage corresponding to the 'Wimpy' door was very close to the propellers. This man, thinking of the 'Wimpy', had walked under the Hudson and started to knock on the underside of the fuselage, looking for the trap door. One of the propellers caught him a glancing blow on the head. When the aircraft pulled away he was lucky not to be run over, and was able to crawl back to the 'Chance' light. He was a very fortunate young man; few people survive being hit on the head by an aircraft propeller!

Christmas came and went at Langham with no noticeable pause in operations and by this time we had built up a very happy relationship with the two elderly ladies who kept the 'Blue Bell', just across the road from the Hall. On New Year's Eve I was lucky enough to be off duty, and saw 1941 in, in grand style. I'm afraid that I had to be helped back across the road to my bed at some very unearthly hour.

New Year's Day 1941 I shall never forget, partly because I had the father and mother of all hangovers, but mostly because of the way it was cured. I should have mentioned that, for one reason or another, telephone communication between Langham and Bircham was erratic. Pilots from Bircham often announced their arrival at Langham by 'shooting up' the Hall so that we could get the fire tender and crew transport out to the aerodrome for their landing. Experienced pilots will now guess what is to follow.

On this New Year's Day, at about 1330 hrs, I was sitting unhappily in front of the fire in the room we used as our Mess, having been quite unable to face any lunch. In the distance I heard the unmistakable rumble of a Hudson's Wright Cyclones. The sound grew louder and louder and the aircraft swept over the building, seemingly much lower than usual. There was a crash, the rattle of falling masonry accompanied by a few muffled explosions ... then silence. We rushed outside to see the roof of the barn behind the Hall in ruins. Fearfully, we ran to the field beyond. The wreckage of the aircraft was spread over about 100 yards. Destruction had been too complete for there to be much in a way of fire. A blackened patch here and there showed where the fuel had exploded. Eight bodies were dotted about amongst the debris. The first I came to was that of the pilot. I recognised him at once; I had spent part of the previous day at Bircham and he and I had played snooker after lunch. But this was not the friend I had known; violent death is kind in this way, clothing its victims in an impersonal cloak. Of the others, only one showed any sign of life. We got him into our ambulance, but I don't think he lived more than a few minutes. By the time the doctor arrived from Blakeney (we had an arrangement with a local GP, who we could call on in emergency) there was little he could do. A phone call to Bircham brought ambulances and a horrified Squadron CO. It was getting dusk on that winter's evening before we had finished our sad task.

About 45 minutes after the crash a lorry arrived from Bircham bringing rations and so on. From this jumped a white-faced boy, our Mess Orderly. He had been at Bircham and was due to return to Langham by road. Someone had told him that an aircraft was going over, so as an airlift would save him time and a bumpy lorry ride. He had run to the airfield when the aircraft was just about to taxi out. Opening the door he had asked one of the passengers to find out if the pilot had room for one more. After some hesitation the answer came back, "Sorry chum, we're full". Cursing his luck, he had returned to base by road.

On such fine threads hang life and death.

The tragedy of the disaster was multiplied because, in addition to the normal Hudson crew of four, there were on board four pilots new to the Squadron, who were being shown round the area – that being the purpose of the flight.

As for my hangover, when at last we got back to our Mess room for a much needed cup of tea, it was completely gone. The cure, however, was rather too drastic to be recommended for normal use.

During the subsequent enquiry into the accident, the fact emerged that pilots had for some time been flying low over the Hall, for the purpose already stated, and we came in for a certain amount of criticism for not reporting this and having it stopped.

It is easy to be wise after the event.

Early in 1941 I started to make efforts to get back on flying duties. Charles Green, our senior pupil at Gatwick and Grantham, was with No 235 Squadron (Fighter Blenheims) at Bircham and put in a word for me, but with no result. However, Mott and I had better luck with No 500 Squadron. We offered ourselves as a two pilot team (this was still the pattern in Coastal Command) and as replacements were available at Langham, we were accepted, whether on an official or unofficial basis I'm not quite sure. Anyway, we teamed up with a Radio Op and an Air Gunner and were 'back in business', flying Ansons.

The work consisted mainly of protecting the East Coast Convoy lane between the Thames Estuary and Flamborough Head. There was a swept channel marked by buoys and this had to be patrolled. Submarines were not the main problem here. The convoys were liable to attack by enemy aircraft by day and by E-Boats (fast MTBs) by night. These had a habit of tying up to one of the marker buoys and waiting for a convoy to turn up. There was quite a lot of night flying to counter this threat, though the chances of making a successful night attack on such a small target must have been slim.

Then someone had a bright idea. A 20mm cannon was fitted to an Anson, fixed to fire forwards and downwards through the cabin floor at an angle of about 45 degrees. The theory was that when an E-Boat was spotted, probably only its wake would show up at night. The aircraft would fly over the target, firing the cannon at the appropriate time. In view of the fact that the aircraft would have to fly straight and level at about 1000ft, directly over an E-Boat which was probably armed with at least four 20mm cannon on proper anti-aircraft mountings, it was just as well we never encountered one on any of our sorties with the cannon-equipped Anson. I hardly think it would have been a fair contest. As far as I know, the gun was never fired in anger.

Life at Bircham was pleasant and busy. Coastal Command at this early stage retained much of its pre-war character, still being small enough to give the feeling that we all knew each other. There were casualties of course, but they were not heavy, and much of the work was still of a routine defensive nature.

One of the saddest days I remember was when two crews, one from No 206 Sqn and one from No 500 Sqn were lost in one night. The missing pilots lived out with their wives in two caravans parked in the same field. It remained a moot point whether operational aircrew should have their families with them. There were arguments for and against, but in this case it made the tragedy doubly poignant. No doubt later in the war, with the mass bombing raids, such incidents became commonplace, but in 1941 we weren't hardened to that sort of thing.

Spring came and turned into summer. The routine E-Boat and anti-submarine patrols continued. It was from the radio set in the Mess that we learned of the breakout of the *Bismark* and the *Prince Eugene* and of the tragedy of HMS *Hood*. I well remember the deathly silence that greeted that news and the announcement that *Bismark* had evaded her shadowers. Later I remember the cheers when she was found again and the even greater celebration when she was sunk. A minor consequence of this episode was the re-writing of a popular RAF chorus. It used to go…

"So roll on the Nelson, the Rodney, the Hood,
for this 'effing' Air Force is no ruddy good!"

The modified version ran thus:

"So roll on the Nelson, the Rodney, Renown.
We can't sing 'The Hood', 'cos' the bugger's gone down."

As I have said, I'm not sure whether Mott and I were officially on the strength of No 500 Squadron or whether we were still members of the moribund No 417 Flight. In any event, early in June we were ordered to proceed on embarkation leave, prior to reporting to RAF Winslow for overseas posting. We had, of course, already had all the inoculations, so on 26th June 1941 we embarked in H.M. Transport *Anselm* at Liverpool docks, bound for who knew where?

9. *Things That Go Bump in the Night*

In the summer of 1940, the defeat of France and Italy's declaration of war closed the Mediterranean to Allied shipping, leaving Air Chief Marshall Sir Arthur Longmore's ME Air forces dependent for re-enforcement on shipping making the long haul round the Cape of Good Hope. But there was an alternative, for in 1936 a chain of airfields had been built, linking the west coast of Africa with Sudan and a weekly Imperial Airways passenger and mail service established, using DH Rapides. In July 1940 Group Captain, soon to be Air Commodore, H.K. Theobald, arrived at Takoradi on the Gold Coast with a small RAF advance party. In September the first convoy of re-enforcement aircraft (1 Blenheim and 6 Hurricanes, only five of which arrived) set off on their 3,000-mile, six-day journey to Egypt. This trickle turned into a flood that was to deliver 5,000 aircraft in the next three years. It has been said that victory in Egypt came via the Takoradi route.

Anselm was an unimposing 7,000-ton single-funnel Booth Line cargo liner. Her peacetime task had been to ply between Liverpool and South America and thence up the Amazon for an amazing 1,000 miles to the port of Manaus. For this she had been designed with a very low draught – a flat-bottomed tub that would roll devilishly in anything like a sea. In peacetime conditions she would take up to 40 passengers in 20 cabins, placed amidships in her central superstructure. Cargo was carried in two holds, reached by means of hatches in her forward and after well decks. As a trooper she had accommodation for some 80 officers in her passenger cabins and 1,500 other ranks in her holds, converted to Mess decks with wooden staging. No doubt these quarters were palatial compared with those provided in 18th century slave ships, but after seeing them I was very grateful for my cabin for two, shared with three other junior officers.

One thing we were to discover about our floating home was that the food on board for the officers was magnificent; doubly so, after suffering nearly two years of wartime rations. She had last taken on supplies in South Africa, which accounted for the excellence of the fare. She was an RAF ship with a permanent staff, including a Squadron Leader OC Troops, but had retained her pre-war crew, including chefs and stewards. There was a very pleasant well-stocked bar with a veranda overlooking the after well deck. (This was some time before American influence had made all troop ships 'dry'.)

Her main drawback, as we were soon to discover, was lack of speed. We sailed from the River Mersey in a most imposing convoy, including the old *Mauritania*, the *Empress of Britain* and *Otranto*. It was soon clear that we could not keep up with these ocean greyhounds. Sailing north from St Georges Channel we fell further and further behind and drew the disapproving attention of a number of escorting destroyers, which steamed alongside, urging us to get a move on. When it became clear that we were quite out of place in a fast troopship convoy we were curtly dismissed to head for the Clyde and await further orders. We lay for 24 hours in Greenock roads, surrounded by the green hills of Scotland, the last view of home that many of our number were to have, and then sailed once more in company with three corvettes and an R.N. survey ship, HMS *Challenger*.

For several days we sailed uneventfully through the benign Atlantic, on its best behaviour in mid-summer. Even so, quite a few places were empty at meal-times, mostly those of non-flyers, for a stomach used to aircraft movement should be immune to sea sickness in anything but quite rough weather. We spent the days lounging in the sun and the evenings sitting outside the bar, watching the troops in the after well deck playing 'housey' or 'bingo', as it is now called.

Our orders were to keep lifejackets with us at all times, and to go to bed fully clothed, but after about a week the order came round, "From tonight officers may undress to turn in". We should have been warned! Next morning, at first light, it happened. When one is awakened from a deep sleep, it is often difficult to know the cause. There seemed to have been a very loud noise, like someone banging a great gong just outside the cabin door. The ship gave a great lurch that shot me off my top bunk and onto the floor. Then the unmistakable smell of burnt explosive told us the truth. It was clear that we had been torpedoed and by now alarm bells were ringing all over the ship and the siren was giving a series of short blasts. I groped round for something to put on over my pyjamas and found a raincoat. I felt on the floor, found two shoes, grabbed my lifejacket and made for the aft well deck and my lifeboat station.

Dawn was breaking and in the grey light the sea rose and fell, unruffled in the long Atlantic swell. The ship was stopped on an even keel but distinctly down by the bows. *Challenger* was circling at a distance of about half a mile and the three corvettes, one on each flank and one ahead, lay, seemingly, motionless against the grey background of sea and sky. It seemed wrong that they should be so still. Why weren't they dashing about with white foam creaming from their bows, dropping depth charges on the submarine that must be lurking close by? No doubt we had been fed on too much romantic fiction. The truth was, as we heard later, that two of the corvettes had suffered Asdic failure, the remaining one was obviously unable to provide adequate cover, and the submarine was making good its escape, no doubt wondering at its immunity from attack.

On board, preparations were being made for lowering the lifeboats. These, however, seemed to be badly rusted in their davits, and to make matters worse, there was no sign of the crew members who were supposed to supervise the lowering. There were four lifeboats in the after well deck, two on each side, rigged one above the other. The lower boat had to be swung out and lowered before the upper could be moved. I was allocated to the upper boat, starboard side.

At my station there were problems in getting the first boat away. Not only were there no seamen there to take charge, but the condition of the tackle seemed to indicate that the boat had not been moved for many months, but, by trial and error, the boat was eventually swung out, lowered and pulled away with its full complement on board. Now it was the turn of the upper boat. No amount of coaxing would shift it. Higher up and more exposed to the weather, the davits were well and truly rusted up. It seemed criminal to us then, and still does to me now, that no attempt was made to hold a boat drill during the long hours we were lying in the Clyde. Eventually, someone climbed up into the boat and found an axe. In desperation he started to chop at the ropes holding the boat. For a while nothing happened, then he must have cut a vital support. The boat crashed to the deck, slithered over the side and landed in the water with a great hole torn in its bottom. But worse than that had happened. Just before the final rope was cut, a man had gone to the side to look over and check that the first boat was clear. In its fall, our boat hit him and left him lying seriously injured on the deck. He was carried as gently as possible and put into one of the port boats that was about to be properly lowered.

After this, there wasn't much point in waiting at the boat sta-tion. I climbed onto the flat roof of a temporary bake-house erected on the port side of the well deck. Seeing the trouble being experienced with the boats, *Challenger* was approaching us and placing her bows as close as possible to our stern, her crew were encouraging men to jump across the gap onto the smaller ship. The movement of the two ships made this a hazardous business, but a number had successfully made the leap and many more were collecting to take their turn. There didn't seem to be much point in joining them as it was obviously going to take a long time to get everybody over.

The attitude of the ship had not changed much during the 30 minutes or so since the torpedo struck. She was still on an even keel but down by the bows. We understood later that plans were being made to take her in tow. Then there was a muffled report from somewhere down in the ship and things happened very quickly. The bows started to go down and the stern to rise. As it was quite clear that she was going down fast, I came down from the bake-house roof, ran to the side and jumped into the water. My kapok lifejacket came up over my face as I went under and as I came up I felt my leg entwined in a trailing davit rope. Three or four desperate kicks released it, and I struck out as best I could, away from the ship.

As I turned, a terrible sight met my eyes. *Challenger* had rap-idly backed away and the bows of *Anselm* were slipping under the water, her stern rising. Those who had jumped when I did were now just clear of the ship, which moved forward in her final dive. Others who had hung on were 50 feet or more above the water. Some continued to hang on; some fell, to crash into the water among their comrades. The ship was now rapidly approaching the vertical and from her came the most fantastic noise. Ships, I suppose, are designed to tolerate a certain degree of pitch. Marine engineers would know how much, beyond that point all loose, and much of the fixed, equipment will start to move, in this case towards the bows. Bulkheads would probably not be strong enough to restrain much of this movement. Anyhow, as *Anselm* reached an attitude when she was literally standing on her bows with half her length out of the water, the noise from within her was as if all the beasts in Hell were roaring and screaming. Then she slipped quickly down, for all the world like a perfect diver, and in a few seconds was gone, leaving only wreckage and swirling water to mark her grave.

But *Anselm*, in her last act, had done us proud, for there must have been hundreds of men in the water only yards from her when she went down. Had she rolled over she would have carried many down with her. As it was, I imagine that most of those clinging to her stern were simply washed off into the water.

One minute the ship was there, representing all that was solid and safe, the next she was gone, leaving only a mass of floating debris. The feeling of desolation and of sheer disbelief was absolute. It must be like this to see one's home destroyed by a bomb, except in that case one is at least on *terra firma* with wreckage to sift through and something to be salvaged. In this case there was nothing.

The sea was a mass of bobbing heads. Most survivors were quite calm, shouting encouragement and advice to one another, for there was no immediate cause for worry, the sea being calm and reasonably warm. *Challenger*, with one of the corvettes, was edging in, preparing to pick us up. I saw a lifeboat with only a few men in it not far away and struck out towards it. When I reached it and climbed aboard, I found it was full of water. Taking off a shoe I started to bale it out, but realised almost at once that this was a waste of time, for it was 'my' boat, the one damaged in the lowering attempt. There didn't seem to be much point in staying with that, so I set off again, swimming this time towards *Challenger*, which was by now hove-to and lowering ropes over her side.

I remember passing a sergeant who had his forage cap on at an immaculate angle and was lying on his back 'reading' a book! Unfortunately there were also quite a few bodies floating around, either killed by the torpedo or drowned in the panic when the ship went down. Tragic, as the Kapok life jacket kept one very comfortably afloat and rescue was at hand.

By now I had reached *Challenger* and it was just a case of waiting one's turn to be hauled aboard. On the deck the scene was one of organised chaos. Quite a number of injured men, some in a serious condition, were being attended to while the uninjured were being guided down below. I was directed to the wardroom, designed for perhaps half a dozen officers. It now held fifty or more. For the first time it was possible to talk over what had happened, especially in the forward part of the *Anselm*.

The torpedo, it seemed, had struck in the region of the forward hold. The explosion had no-doubt killed many men and wrecked much of the wooden staging and companionways that had made up the mess decks. The hold had rapidly flooded, drowning most of those who had survived the explosion. I could imagine the scene, as during my tours of duty as ship's Orderly Officer, one of my duties was to inspect the mess decks. I have to confess that the combined stench of sweat, stale food and vomit made me limit my inspections to as brief a time as possible.

After the torpedoing, the forward hatch covers had been pulled away, revealing a horrific scene. Men were struggling in the water among bodies and wreckage. The companionways to the deck were completely gone and there was no way of escape. I do not know if any men were rescued from that hell, but I do know that one of the RAF Padres on board, Rev Pugh from

Essex, insisted on being lowered down into the hold. An act of almost insane bravery, one would think, as apart from other dangers, no one could tell how long the ship would stay afloat. At all events, he said he could not stand by and see fellow men going to almost certain death. Shortly afterwards the bulkhead, or whatever, gave way and the ship started its final dive. Padre Pugh was last seen in an attitude of prayer as the water closed over him. He was later awarded a posthumous George Cross.

On board *Challenger* we were a very bedraggled crew. I found that in the confusion following the torpedoing, the raincoat I had grabbed was someone else's and the two shoes were both the same foot and neither of them mine. *Challenger* officers provided what creature comforts they could in blankets, sweaters, soup and cocoa, but not much moral support. They seemed to be amused to have this large group of nervous 'crabs' in their ship. ('Crabfat' is the RN name for RAF, don't ask me why). The Corvettes were still dropping the occasional depth charge, on a 'bird scaring' principle I imagine, and each sounded as if the side of the ship was being hit with a sledgehammer.

"No U-Boat Captain would waste a torpedo on us now, would he?" asked someone hopefully.

"Wouldn't he just..." came the reply. "We're towing a string of your boats, so he'd know we've got survivors on board and would make a special effort to get us."

"But surely, a torpedo would pass right under this little ship?"

"Not on your life; he'd use a shallow running one. See that bulkhead? The magazine's through there, we'd never know what'd hit us!"

Charming! No doubt the Navy's idea of a joke, but we were in no mood to appreciate their sense of humour.

We were on board *Challenger* for just over two hours and in spite of the dreadful inconvenience we must have caused in their little ship, the crew never treated us other than as guests they were pleased to help.

Several of the injured died during this time, including the man who had been crushed by the lifeboat. We heard later that the total *Anselm* casualty list came to around 600 out of 1,500 men on board. The *Challenger* officers told us that the torpedoing had taken place 600 miles north of the Azores and we were now steaming south to rendezvous with a large naval ship that would take all survivors on board.

Sure enough, some time after dawn on the day following the sinking, we were invited up on deck to see the looming bulk of a large ocean liner which was waiting to receive us. She was an ex-P&O vessel, now an Armed Merchant Cruiser manned by the Navy. Scrambling nets were lowered and the two ships edged together. After returning sundry pieces of loaned clothing and making our grateful farewells, we climbed up to the broad decks of HMAMC *Cathay*. We looked a motley crew, wearing whatever we had managed to grab on scrambling out of our bunks in the *Anselm*. When we entered the wardroom to join the ship's officers in their immaculate white tropical rig, it looked as if half the down-and-outs of London had wandered into the Savoy Hotel.

Anyway, 'slops' (stores to us RAF types) soon provided us with a minimum of clothing and we were all allocated sleeping space. I and six companions came off well, we were given what we were assured had been the bridal suite, high up on the boat deck, with mattresses spread on what we insisted on calling 'the floor'. Where first-class passengers had formerly sipped their cocktails, the wardroom bar now served gin at tuppence a tot. Life could have been a great deal worse.

So we continued our interrupted voyage south, bound, we now discovered, for West Africa; but what we were to do when we got there was none too clear. After about five days we noticed that we were now steering due east and paravanes were deployed, streaming back from the bows. It was clear that we were now in shallower water, with the risk of submarine-laid mines, and all eyes were strained ahead for the first sight of land. Soon rows of palm trees appeared on the horizon and then the cloud- covered mountains behind them came into view.

We dropped anchor off Freetown, Sierra Leone and were allowed a few hours ashore, but our final destination was to be Takoradi, further down the coast. A first experience of Africa is always memorable, even if it's at Freetown, at that time not the most impressive of places, with a preponderance of corrugated iron. It was just over a day's steaming to Takoradi and we arrived there on the 22nd July.

10. 'The Taki Route'

There are few natural harbours on the West African coast, so at Takoradi an artificial one had been built. This enabled quite large ships to berth alongside, cutting out the difficult business of bringing everything ashore through the surf in small boats, as was the rule further along the coast at Accra. *Cathay* was, therefore, able to tie up at the jetty and we could walk ashore down a gangway.

The Mess at Takoradi was a low group of huts for the more junior officers and a rather more imposing two-storey building for those of Wing Commander and above. These had been built by the gold mining company based at Takoradi about 100 miles up country. In peacetime they were used as rest houses for their employees, built on rising ground overlooking a small lagoon and the nine-hole golf course. They could hardly have been better situated. In fact, with the pounding Atlantic surf and the palm-fringed reef, the scene was almost too good to be true.

A small settlement had been built up around the harbour in pre-war days, and now this community had a large RAF Station imposed upon it because of the harbour and the nearby aerodrome. This last had one usable north/south runway some 900 yards in length. The second, much shorter runway was not suitable for 'modern' aircraft and was used as a parking area. Landings and take offs were always made heading south, which enabled aircraft to take off over the sea, although the final approach had to be made over low bush covered hillocks.

The purpose of the RAF Station was to assemble aircraft brought in by sea in crates, test fly them and send them off in convoys across Africa to Egypt as reinforcements for the hard pressed Desert Air Forces which, in 1941 were not having things entirely their own way. The saving of time and shipping compared with the route round the Cape made worthwhile the wear and tear and inevitable aircraft losses involved. This much we learned on our first night in Africa, and the sight of a large black scorpion crawling out of my room made me take seriously the advice to examine shoes carefully and in fact, all clothing before use.

That first night at Takoradi, under an unaccustomed mosquito net, I was woken up some time after midnight by a Squadron Leader Engineer Officer, one of the *Anselm* survivors, an ex-Warrant Officer I think, and a kindly man. "Have you a brother in the Service?" he asked, and handed me an Air Ministry signal.

To: F/O P.S. Rivington
From: Air Ministry, Personnel Branch

Deeply regret to inform you – your brother – Aircraftman 2nd class, Paul S. Rivington – killed in a flying accident 10th July 1941.

It took some time for the meaning of this to sink in. Paul had been my twin brother. We were not identical twins and were quite different in looks and character, but we had been continually together for 18 of our 21 years and were part of one another. His talents were quite different from mine, lying in the direction of artistic things, in writing and acting. Although not good at ball games, he was a keen spectator and we used to bicycle many miles in the summer holidays to watch county cricket. He took a leading part in school plays and operettas, and on leaving obtained a place at the Royal Academy of Dramatic Art. He had just finished his first year when war broke out. Without hesitation he volunteered as an RAF pilot, and was called up soon after

Christmas 1939. Predictably, he failed his Pilot's Course at White Waltham. I say 'predictably' because eye and muscle co-ordination had never been his strong point – he took a long time to learn to ride a bicycle and to drive a car. Nothing daunted, he re-mustered as a Radio Operator and it was during his training that he was killed at Cranwell.

Paul and Peter Rivington together on leave in 1940. *Photo: Kate Anstie*

I learned the details some years later. He was flying in a Proctor with a Polish pilot when, quite unexpectedly, low cloud rolled in over the airfield. His pilot did what all of us had been tempted to do and went down to see if he could get underneath it. I don't suppose they saw the trees they hit. Both were killed instantly. Perhaps I was lucky being thousands of miles away from his military funeral, which was over before I heard of his death. It's odd to think that if I had had a little less luck and he a little more, our positions could have been reversed. It is said that things that happen in one's early years leave an indelible mark. It is certainly true that after more than 40 years, Paul is the person who figures most often in my dreams, and he is still only 21.

"They shall grow not old as we that are left grow old…"

Paul Rivington

Our first task in the morning was to get some clothes made. The camp tailor, African of course, measured us up for shorts, bush shirts and slacks. We were able to draw certain items from stores – shoes, socks, braid for badges of rank, and the RAF flash for the 'Bombay bowlers' obtained from a local shop in Secondi. When it comes to clothing, the RAF, in common I suppose with the other Services, always seems to be equipping one for the war before last. The knee-length shorts, narrow slacks and huge 'solar topees' on offer were of the 'Gunner Sugden' variety. Those readers who remember the TV series *It A'int 'alf Hot Mum* will know what I'm talking about!

The aircraft at Takoradi in late 1941 were mainly British-built Hawker Hurricane Mk Is and IIs and Bristol Blenheim Mk IVs, with a sprinkling of American-built Martin Marylands and Curtis Tomahawks (the original P-40s with the Allison engine). These were assembled, tested and passed on to the Despatch Flight, who organised their onward transmission to Egypt.

On our arrival it was decided to organise a Defence Flight with Hurricanes and Blenheims. Takoradi had suffered a couple of hit-and-run bombing attacks by Vichy French Marylands from Dahomey and the Hurricanes were to discourage these. Enemy submarines were known to lurk in the shipping lanes round West Africa and the Blenheims were to deal with these. Because of, I suppose, my Coastal Command experience, I was attached to the Defence Flight as the Blenheim pilot and there were three Hurricane pilots: Flt/Lt Ken Dewhurst (Flight Commander) and F/Os Bob Rutter and Dave Thatcher. All of us were *Anselm* survivors and had operational experience in the UK. Ken, in fact, was one of those who had fallen from a great height from the stern of the ship as the *Anselm* went down. He hit the water flat on his back and attributed his escape uninjured to the wearing of his heavy RAF greatcoat.

The Blenheim was by far the most powerful aircraft I had encountered, and it had not entirely lived down its reputation as a 'killer' – gained, I imagine, in the immediate pre-war years when pilots, used to mild-mannered biplanes, had found it something of a handful. It was not long before I found myself face-to-face with a long-nosed Mark IV, equipped, I was relieved to find, with dual controls, which were to be handled by a fellow officer with the re-assuring name of Paynter (older cricketers amongst my readers will understand the reference).

One mounted a Blenheim via hand and foot holds to a walkway on the port wing root, leading to a sliding hatch in the cockpit roof. Whilst wearing a seat-type parachute, this was quite an effort and probably accentuated the feeling of claustrophobia brought on by the poor sideways view from the cockpit, restricted as it was by large engine nacelles obscuring both wings. Once installed, the atmosphere in the cockpit was typically British, that is to say, that apart from the excellent standard blind flying panel it seemed that the other instruments and controls had been attached to the cockpit sides and bulkheads to suit the manufacturer rather than the pilot.

After one trip in a dual-control Blenheim IV L8862, I did my first solo. From now on I have a detailed record of my flying (my first log book, of course, went down with the Anselm). The Bristol Blenheim was the first high-speed twin-engined monoplane medium bomber to be ordered by the RAF. Derived from a private venture design – 'Britain First', built for Lord Rothermere, it equipped several groups of Bomber Command until replaced by the Boston in late 1941/42. It continued to be used in the Mediterranean theatre until much later and in the Far East until the end of the war. The power-plants were 850hp Bristol Mercury IV radial engines. It was very pleasant to handle, although its single engine performance with anything like a load was marginal. This was not helped by its De Havilland two position non-feathering airscrews, so that all the pilot could do to reduce drag if an engine failed was to put its propeller into coarse pitch.

The pitch controls were placed on the bulkhead behind the pilot's right hand, two knobs pushed in for fine and pulled out for coarse. Next to these were two exactly similar knobs, the engine cut out controls. Although these had a guard over them, I believe that accidents did occur when they were operated by mistake instead of the pitch controls. This rather illustrates the way in which most British cockpits of that era were laid out. Then the Blenheim undercarriage and flap controls, although placed quite conveniently under the pilot's right hand, were dangerously alike and surrounded by sharp cutting edges. Admittedly, the former control was guarded against inadvertent operation by a hinged flap, but this made the retraction operation rather like feeling through a covered letter box slit from the inside. In a climate where gloves were seldom worn, one could easily pick out Blenheim pilots by the absence of skin on their knuckles.

The design chaos in the cockpits of British aircraft was in marked contrast to the neat layouts of the American-made machines, which tended to follow their automobile practice, giving the impression that, if not exactly styled, the cockpits were at least designed by a pilot with a eye to visual effect. Only in one important respect was the British cockpit superior, and that was in the layout of the blind-flying instruments. All British aircraft were fitted with a standard blind-flying panel, separate from engine and other instruments, whereas American aircraft had vital flying instruments mixed up with all the rest.

It was discovered very soon after the outbreak of war that aircraft such as Blenheims were unable to operate in the face of fighter opposition, even in formations that were supposed to give sufficient firepower for defence. In order to provide a little more protection, the aircraft was loaded down with armour plate and extra machine guns, two in the turret and two in a 'chin' mounting under the nose, and firing backwards, in an effort to provide protection from attacks from astern and below. The guns were operated by the Observer, lying in the nose and peering into a system of mirrors. The 'chin' guns had a very restricted field of fire and provided only a scare value. Nevertheless, they all added weight and reduced performance, so we got the well known progression; an aircraft lively and a delight to fly is found to be easy meat for enemy fighters … so it is given more guns and armour and becomes heavy, slow and sluggish and is even easier meat for enemy fighters. This was the fate of the Blenheim. I had two flights in the short nosed Mk.I version and it was a revelation to fly. Wonderfully manoeuvrable and fast, even with the lower powered Mercury VIII engine. The Blenheim IV was that much worse, even with the greater power of Mercury XVs, and later when flying Blenheim Vs with constant-speed propellers, and Mercury XXVs, one got the impression that the things could hardly drag themselves off the ground.

The first task at the Defence Flight was to get the Blenheims operationally serviceable and I see from my log book that a lot of time was spent on radio (WT only) and gun tests. We began anti-submarine patrols as soon as the aircraft were ready. These usually lasted between 3 and 4 hours and sometimes involved escorting ships into Takoradi or Lagos. In between whiles the Defence Flight Blenheims were made into maids of all work, carrying out communications duties between Takoradi, Accra and Lagos, and providing practice targets for the local army's AA batteries. Sometimes we would get a request to 'show the flag' over some town or other. We demonstrated over Takoradi, a gold-mining centre about 100 miles in land, and Lagos, and took part in a display over Kano in Nigeria. Accra was about 40 minutes flying time from Takoradi in a Blenheim. Lagos was about 2hrs 15 min and Kano about 3 hours from Lagos.

The visit to Kano was quite a relief. Some 500 miles northeast of Lagos and 1,500 feet above sea level, it lies on the edge of the Sahara Desert. The climate is hot and dry and it is quite possible to be comfortable at a temperature of 100 degrees F, whereas on the coast, where rainfall and humidity are high, it can be unbearable at 80 degrees. Flying from Kano to Lagos, as one descends below the clouds to land, it is like going through the door of a heated swimming bath.

The Gold Coast was sandwiched between two Vichy French areas, Ivory Coast on the West and Togo and Dahomey on the East. Neither was very friendly and one of our jobs was to keep an eye on them to check that they were not giving sanctuary to U-Boats or building airfields that enemy aircraft might use to attack our bases or our sea and air convoys. Occasionally we saw Vichy French naval ships at sea and would stand off and photograph them for the record. As long as they made no aggressive moves our orders were to leave them alone. Sometimes, when the Test Flight was busy and we were not, we would go over and help them. On one occasion, after I had done initial tests on a couple of Blenheims, I was met by the deputy Flight Commander, a Warrant Officer and clearly a brave man who said, "There's a Hurricane that wants an initial test, if you like…" I told him I had not flown a Hurricane, but his answer was that there's 'always a first time' and advised me to have a go. So I strapped myself into Hurricane Mk I Z4767 on 30th August 1941 for what was to be its first flight since emerging from its packing case and my first ever flight in a single-seat fighter. What would the modern pilot think about that? After a brief five minute chat, I was pressing the starter and booster coil buttons and watching the propeller jerk round and become a blur as the engine caught with that familiar cloud of blue exhaust smoke. Even at warming up revs it is quite an experience to sit behind a Merlin for the first time and running up the engine to test the mags and CSU gives one a taste of things to come. Taxiing out, I was very conscious of the long nose ahead and the poor forward visibility (Spitfires were even worse, as I was later to find out). A brief cockpit check, Trim, Mixture, Pitch, Fuel, Flaps, Gills (radiator flap on the Hurricane) and we were lined up ready to go. (No R.T. or Air Traffic Control at Takoradi at the time, just the pilot's eyeballs!).

Perhaps I opened the throttle too quickly, eager to raise the tail and achieve some forward view, anyway, I was quite taken by surprise by the violent swing to port which a boot full of right rudder failed to hold. It was a question of either mowing down some hangars that were very close to the runway, or reducing power to tame the swing. I somewhat naturally chose the latter course, re-applied the power when straight and the Hurricane shot off into the air after an untidy Kangaroo leap, leaving behind, I suppose, a number of somewhat shaken spectators and certainly taking with it a very shaken pilot.

Once safely airborne there was time to savour the experience of a first flight in a powerful fighter. This was supposed to be a test flight, but I was in no position to be too fussy about details. My impression was that, whereas the loudest noise in a Rolls Royce motor car at 70-plus mph may well be the ticking of the clock, when sitting a few feet behind 1,000+ hp of Rolls Royce Merlin, the impression is of thunderous thumping power, only slightly modified with the revs pulled back to 2,400 and the boost reduced to zero for cruising. The controls were a delight, light and responsive, and the whole impression was of a taut thoroughbred straining at the leash. A climb up to 10,000 feet, a few aerobatics (what a lot of sky a loop seemed to use and how easily she rolled) and it was time to land. No trouble here, down wind, check brakes, undercarriage down, mixture rich, pitch fully fine, flaps down while turning on to finals. Trim back as the flaps come down and cross the threshold at about 90 mph. The aircraft seemed to land itself, then one just had to concentrate on keeping straight and apply just a touch of brake at the runway's end.

"Was she alright Sir?" asked the Flight Sergeant.

"Oh fine, no snags," was my nonchalant reply.

That, of course, was not how I felt!

Our main work now still consisted of anti-submarine patrols interspersed with communication flights along the coast. One day we received a message from the Coast Guards at Cape Three Points. "There is a submarine that keeps taking off and landing on the water!" We got ourselves airborne in a Blenheim to investigate. As we approached the position the Coast Guard had indicated, a huge bulk seemed to heave itself out of the water and crash back in again. It was clearly a very large whale!

I was now able to take the occasional trip in a Hurricane, hoping against hope that the Vichy French would decide to make another attack on the aerodrome while I was airborne, but of course it never happened. Looking back, we did some very foolish things. It was the custom at Takoradi, when off duty, to take a few beers at the Golf Club of a Sunday lunchtime and then go back to the Mess for curry (very good, with all the trimmings). Most sensible people would then go to bed for an hour or so to sleep it off, but sometimes we would go down to the aerodrome, not completely sober, and get a Blenhheim and a couple of Hurricanes airborne and have a session of dummy attacks. On the odd occasion friends would be picnicking somewhere down the coast, perhaps with some nurses from the hospital, and we would go and 'give them a beat up'. All highly reprehensible.

Another thing that makes my hair stand on end was our flying Blenheims without using the Sutton harness safety straps. As we normally flew with the hatch wide open because of the heat, and the air was never smooth, the risk of being catapulted out through the roof must have been great, never mind the hazards of take off and landing. But again, we survived, but now that we don a safety harness before driving down the road, I can only think that a benign spirit was guarding us (and I am not referring to Messrs Walker and Gordon!). We also almost always flew without helmets in Blenheims, although we sometimes used cotton wool in the ears, this practice probably accounts for a great deal of the high tone deafness suffered in later life by old pilots.

Sunday 7th December 1941 started like any other day until the news broke of the attack on Pearl Harbour. I think we realised even then that this was the turning point of the war. Before this, we had been sure we were not going to lose, but could not quite see how we were going to win. We were soon to realise, however, that things would get worse before they got better. The following Wednesday we completed an A/S sweep to the east and landed at Lagos for fuel and lunch. While in the Mess the news came through that HMS *Prince of Wales* and HMS *Repulse* had been sunk off Singapore. We found it difficult to believe that these proud ships were gone. December 10th 1941 was a black day for the Royal Navy and for us all.

Even before Pearl Harbour we had been receiving direct help from the USA. As I have told, the function of Takaradi was to fly reinforcement aircraft overland to the Middle East. Once the aircraft had been delivered the pilots had to be returned to Takoradi for their next trip. This was done mainly by BOAC Empire Flying Boats routing via Khartoum, the Southern Sudan and the Belgian Congo. Soon after our arrival at 'Taki', some Pan

American DC3s turned up. These were to be used to ferry pilots back to the West Coast via the reinforcement route in reverse. Here were 'real' airliners, the first many of us had seen, flown by gum chewing Texans. Whether the aircraft were a result of 'Lease-Lend' I don't know, but we could not have managed without them.

Many of the Ferry Pilots at Takoradi were Polish. They were, in the main, fine flyers and when on the route had a sharp eye for a little profitable trading. Nigerian snake-skins for instance, fetched a good price in Cairo. On one occasion I was asked to sit in the right hand seat of a dual control Blenheim while a Polish Flying Officer, with an unpronounceable name, familiarised himself with the aircraft. My seat was very low and I could hardly see out. It will be remembered that the Blenheim IV had an 'asymmetric' nose to enable the Navigator to get to his chart table, and I could barely reach the rudder pedals. The Pole might well have been 'solo' for all I could do and I soon wished he had been. One general failing of his ilk was a lack of sympathy with things mechanical. Thus this chap's method of opening his throttles for take off was to move both from the fully closed to the fully open positions in one swift movement, taking perhaps half a second. The Mercurys, quite unused to this sort of treatment, seemed to give a gasp of surprise before bellowing out their full power. The aircraft then scuttled down he runway, being held straight (just) with plenty of rudder and differential brake. It was a most unpleasant business which we nevertheless survived without mishap.

With the opening up of the war in the Far East, the pressure on the 'Taki Route' increased and my days as a permanent resident were coming to an end as more route pilots were needed, especially convoy leaders. (I was by this time a Flight Lieutenant). Life at Takoradi had been very pleasant with the nearby nine-hole golf course, with its 'greens' of sand, a club house where drink was plentiful and the beer, though locally brewed, was quite acceptable. The monotony was relieved by frequent private parties in the Mess – for birthdays, promotions, in fact any excuse, and the prices were such that one could entertain ten or fifteen of one's friends, sending them to bed considerably the worse for wear, for a very few pounds.

I had one very interesting experience. The Wing Commander Flying had organised a trip up a nearby river in a nature canoe for himself and a friend. I'm not sure what happened, perhaps his friend let him down at the last minute, anyway he asked me to go with him. We drove about five miles through the forest on the usual dirt road. Every so often a black line appeared across the road. These lines were swarms of huge black ants on the move. We stopped once to have a look, clearly nothing was going to hold up their progress and so much the worse for any unfortunate animal that got in their way. When we got to the river the canoe was waiting for us. We sat in the stern and six Africans sat in front of us with paddles. Off we went, for all the world it was like a scene from 'Saunders of the River', we only lacked a Paul Robeson to sing.

The river was about 50 yards wide and we could clearly see and hear monkeys swinging from the trees in the thick jungle that came right down to the water's edge. Overhead, brightly coloured birds, mainly parrots I think, flew to and fro. It had been arranged that we should land a few miles up stream and see a native village. We drew into a small clearing and stepped ashore. The variety of insect life was amazing. In addition to the ants there were centipedes, millipedes, brightly coloured crickets and grasshoppers, and many kinds of brilliant butterflies. When we came to the village we were introduced to the Head man and the inhabitants followed us around on our tour of inspection,

showing the sort of friendly curiosity that is found among simple
rural people. I suppose we were offered refreshment, but I don't
remember that we took any, fearing, I suppose, that our weak
European stomachs would not stand the strain. We were told
that these people were absolutely honest; no crime, no stealing,
no need ever to trouble the policeman who called, maybe once a
month, riding his bicycle. This was in contrast to the situation
on the coast, where pilfering in the docks and in the Mess by
Africans was quite the norm. I'm afraid that we Europeans were
the corrupting influence, infecting the natives with our lower
standards.

On our way to the village we passed one or two palm trees
that had been cut, allowing the sap to run out into cups tied to
the tree trunks. This sap, when naturally fermented, made the
palm wine that was the native drink. Each tree had an owner and
to each one was fixed a second cup with a few pennies in it.
These, we were told, had been left by passers-by who had taken a
drink. We were assured that no one using this natural 'help
yourself' pub would fail to pay, and the suggestion that anyone
might steal money from the cup was quite absurd.

Now things at Takoradi were hotting up. Every morning convoys of aircraft were leaving on their long journey and I was
required to join in. Although I was to be a convoy leader, I had
to do one trip being led, to gain route experience. My convoy
was made up of the usual Blenheim IV, followed by a gaggle of
Hurricanes and one Mk I short-nosed Blenheim, which was my
aircraft. I was lucky in this as I don't remember seeing another
Mk I at Takoradi and, as I have said, it was a beautiful aircraft to
fly. The only snag was that it did not have the range of the Mark
IV, there being only one tank in each wing instead of two. We
also had some short range Hurricanes with us, without the two
40 gallon drop tanks normally fitted. I think they must have had

smaller tanks, as we managed legs of three hours, which was too much for a Hurricane with internal fuel only. This meant that we would have to make some extra stops and could not, for instance, make the Lagos-Kano leg without an intermediate stop at Oshogbo. I enjoyed a proving flight in the Mk I Blenheim and on the following morning of 17th January 1942, soon after dawn, set off on our long trek to Egypt.

The flight from Takoradi to Lagos normally took 2 hours 15 minutes and followed the coastline past Accra and then, as the land fell away to the north after passing the Volta river estuary, some miles out to sea on the direct track to Lagos. The Gold Coast shoreline had probably changed little since the times of the first white explorers and traders hundreds of years earlier. Their white forts, usually right on the beach, the small native villages with their surf boats and palm-fringed beaches, all made up a picture which exactly fitted one's pre-conceived ideas of Africa.

After something over an hour we were well out to sea from Dahomy (not only was this the direct route to Lagos, but it was not a good idea to give the Vichy French the opportunity of counting the aircraft that went by, and for all we knew, passing the information on to the Germans) when my port engine started to vibrate so badly it had to be shut down before it wrenched itself free of its mountings. The convoy, by this time, was disappearing in the distance and I judged it wise to turn northwards towards the coast, which could be faintly discerned some 15 miles away. Normally we kept clear of the Vichy enclaves of Cotonou and Dahomey, but in my position even Petain's men seemed preferable to the sharks that were undoubtedly lurking below. However the Mk I Blenheim was no problem on one engine and I was able to follow the coast past Porto-Novo, maintaining height comfortably. By the time I arrived at Lagos the rest of the convoy were parked by the hangars, with the crews standing in groups, speculating no doubt, on my fate. The convoy leader, a South African Air Force Lieutenant by the name of 'Shorty' Whitford, said that they had been sure I was either shark food or interned by the French. When the engine was examined it was found that two of the studs securing a cylinder to the crank case had sheared, allowing the cylinder to lift from its seating. It could have been only a matter of time before it came completely adrift and made an exit through the cowling. This fault, I was told, was not uncommon on the Mk VIII Mercury.

It so happened that there was a Mk IV Blenheim Z7757 at Lagos (previously left there unserviceable) that I could take on. It was, however, only to go as far as Khartoum. We were soon airborne again, heading north for Oshogbo over the dense green carpet of the tropical rain forest. We had been told that if forced down, the best thing was to attempt to land on the tops of the trees as if they were solid land. I never knew of anyone who had tried this, but I would not fancy his chances. This worry seemed to come mostly to single engine aircraft. With two engines we could hope to get to a reasonably open space if in serious trouble.

Oshogbo is several hundred feet above sea level and not quite so deep in the rain forest as the settlements near the coast. The climate is a little less humid and trying. My Log Book tells me that we night stopped there, but I must confess that I can re-member little of the place – one Mess hut in the African bush is very like another. The following day we got only as far as Kano, a flight of 22 hrs 30 mins. I'm not sure what kept us there but nobody minded. The chance to get clothes really dry (on the coast everything feels damp, and unused shoes and leather goods collect generous amounts of mould) and to get rid of 'prickly heat', that distressing skin complaint, suffered to a greater or lesser degree by almost everybody on the coast.

Kano, as I knew from my previous visit, is more of an Arab than a West African town. Terminus of the Trans-Sahara highway, it is in the savannah land that borders the great desert and at nearly 1,500 feet above sea level has a most pleasant climate – for that part of the world, anyway.

In the absence of any organised air traffic control an old man with a fantastically long trumpet was stationed at the end of the runway to warn all and sundry (especially herdsmen with animals) that an aircraft was about to land. In the city there was no shortage of characters wanting to sell us local goods: pottery, leather and Arab type daggers, mostly beaten out of old four gallon petrol tins and quite useless. For some things however, mainly snake-skins and leather goods, there was a profitable market in Cairo, a fact not lost on our Polish friends, as I have remarked.

The following morning we were on our way again at first light. The route now took us almost due east across the heart of Africa, over an area of savannah grasslands which wound only a hundred or so miles to the north, giving way to the sands of the Sahara. The first stop was at Maiduguri and then, on this trip, on to Fort Lamy. Normally this small airfield in French Equatorial Africa was overflown and used for emergencies only, but with our shorter range Hurricanes we could not quite manage the 3 to 4 hours flight from Maiduguri to El Geneina in Sudan. Luckily this French colony had declared for De Gaul – I suppose it had little choice, sandwiched as it was between the giant territories of Nigeria and Sudan. Had it chosen the path followed by the French Colonials on the coast, presumably we would have had to take it over by force. However, the Frenchmen were most co-operative and a short stop with them underlined the difference between the British and French colonial systems. While the British kept their roots very much at home, the French seemed to integrate with the local population, often taking wives (or at any rate, mistresses) from among them.

The Fort Lamy runway was only just long enough to get a Blenheim off. It was a question of opening up on the brakes, getting the tail up as soon as possible and holding on until the last few yards of runway were about to disappear under the nose. This runway consisted of red bricks forming a flat cobblestone surface, and although I only visited it once, I still have the picture in my mind's eye of the end of that red brick runway rushing all-too-quickly towards me.

Airborne from Fort Lamy we had a three-hour flight to El Geneina, which I understand translated, means 'the garden'. This underlined the difficulty of navigating across this part of Africa. There are no towns (the place names on the atlas denote settlements little larger than a fair sized English village) and of course no railways. The roads are mere dirt tracks, hardly distinguishable from the air and any rivers marked on the map will only have water in them for a few days in the year. For most of the time there is not a patch of green to be seen – only the uniform light brown of the dry grasslands. When the one month of rain comes, not only do the rivers spring to life but also the parched countryside turns green as if by magic. Thus, to a pilot or navigator who has experience of the route in the dry weather, this new landscape presents an entirely novel picture. With modern radio aids to navigators, it would be unimportant, but we were almost entirely dependent on map-reading with only a very unreliable and simple system of loop bearings as a backup.

On the leg from Fort Lamy to El Geneina we lost a Hurricane. A young sergeant pilot had arrived at Takoradi a few days before our convoy left. He was due for the Middle East and would do one trip along the route in a Hurricane on his way. He had not created a very favourable impression at Takoradi. During his practice flying he indulged in some quite unnecessary 'split-arse turns' (to use the somewhat vulgar term in vogue at the time) onto the runway before landing and in addition sported six-inch long red, white and blue streamers attached to the crown of his flying helmet, like some latter-day Biggles. Clearly, in his view at least, he was God's gift to aviation. During the early leg of our delivery flight he had been a constant worry to 'Shorty' Whitford because he insisted on flying two or three thousand feet above everyone else. It was the convoy leader's responsibility to keep track of his flock, counting them every few minutes (we had no radio contact) and this chap's insistence on doing his own thing brought him a dressing down at every landing point. Well, there we were, at about 10,000 ft above Central Africa and this chap was once more drifting about at 12,000 ft. One minute he was there and the next he was not. Of course there was nothing the convoy leader could do about that. The leg was a three hour one anyway, near the maximum that our Hurricanes could manage, so we carried on and landed at El Geneina hoping that our wandering boy would turn up. He did not, and we left the next morning still unaware of his fate. He did arrive at Geneina a day or so later on the back of a camel. His explanation? "Well, I just looked down to peel an orange and there they were, gone". Of course he had his maps of the route, and attempted, without success, to carry on and find the next landing point. When his fuel was about to run out he had no choice but to make a belly landing on the smoothest piece of ground he could find.

It was quite extraordinary but when an aircraft was forced down in this trackless and seeming uninhabited region, after half an hour or so, some bloke would turn up on the back of a donkey or a camel. It was then just a question of getting to the local village and eventually to the nearest staging post. The only snag was that an hour's flight in a Blenheim or a Hurricane, became a week's journey on a camel! I hope that this lad's somewhat humiliating experience cured him of some of his over confidence. If not, I fear that his flying career might well have been a short one.

Our first leg the following day was a short one of only just over an hour across the Marra Mountains to El Fasher. If the terrain at the lower levels in this part of Africa looks uninviting, what can one say about the mountainous regions? The peaks rise to around 10,000 ft. and appear desolate beyond belief. It is not for nothing that an African range is called The Mountains of the Moon. But it was pleasant climbing into the cool morning air, clear at this time and free from the rising dust that cuts visibility later in the day. We needed to climb to 11,000 ft. to clear the peaks and as we did so a plume of dust could be seen 50 miles to the East, where an aircraft engine was being tested at El Fasher. El Fasher was much more of a desert aerodrome than Geneina, and from here on the route to Cairo was over the desert, relieved only by the verdancy bordering the Nile. El Fasher had a surprise for the first time visitors. There were no buildings to speak of at the airfield, just a few grass huts for storing tools and equipment, so the transit crews would often rest in the shade of a mainplane while their aircraft were being refuelled from the ubiquitous four gallon cans. To the huge delight of the old hands, the unwary first time visitor would find himself enwrappped from behind in a huge furry embrace, with two paws the size of saucers clasped across his chest. This was the El Fasher tame lion cub, who was treated like a dog by the resident staff, sleeping in one of the airfield grass huts and helping, I suspect, to keep the hands of light fingered local gentry off the equipment. Unfortunately, as he matured, his play became just a little too boisterous, and I understand he was eventually found a berth in the Khartoum zoo.

As I have said, the route from now on was across the desert, some of the nastiest in the world. So much so that the direct track from El Fasher to Khartoum was not followed, and all aircraft were routed via El Obeid where there was an emergency landing ground, avoiding a three hour flight over the unfriendly Nubian Desert. Khartoum was a pleasant sight after the desert with the well laid out modern city to the east and the old native capital of Omdurman to the west. It was fascinating to look down on these cities, so steeped in recent British history, linked with the names of Gordon, Roberts, the Mahidi and the youthful Winston Churchill. Ones first sight of the great river Nile was an experience not to be forgotten.

Our transit base was not at the main Khartoum airfield but at Wadi Sidina, a few miles down river. Here there was a large newly built college or university whose buildings had been taken over by the RAF, and adjoining these was a flat area of sand suitable for an airfield. My Blenheim was to remain at Wadi Sidina. The following day, when the convoy set off on the last lap to Cairo, I was passenger in another aircraft flown by, you've guessed it, the Polish Flying Officer with the unpronounceable name who had given me such an unpleasant ride at Takoradi. The route took us up the Nile past Atbarah as far as Abu Hamad. Here the river takes a huge loop to the west, but the railway line from Khartoum to Cairo carries on in a North Westerly direction across the Nubian Desert, rejoining the river at Wadi Halfa. The drill was to follow this railway, thus keeping in touch with civilisation in case there was any trouble.

My Polish friend landed at Wadi Halfa without mishap and, after refuelling, we were heading north once more for Cairo. After a further four hours the urban sprawl of Cairo appeared on the hazy horizon. We were bound for Landing Ground 222, known as Fayoum Road, not far from the Pyramids. As with most desert landing grounds this merely consisted of a level area of firm sand, from which the larger stones and boulders had been removed. A large number of aircraft were parked all around the perimeter of the landing area, and these, and a windsock or two, were the only things that distinguished the 'airfield' from the surrounding desert. My pilot lined up into wind, lowered the flaps and made a reasonable approach. Passing over a group of parked aircraft with rather too much speed, he proceeded to concentrate on his landing. Unfortunately, during the rather long float, he allowed the nose of the aircraft to swing to port, so that instead of touching down with several hundred yards of clear sand ahead, we were almost immediately in amongst the parked aircraft. At some 70 mph he had little chance of taking avoiding action and cut through the parked aircraft like a centre three quarter through a scattered group of opposing forwards; by some miracle he avoided hitting anything. Parked in our allotted dispersal area, I have never been so glad to climb out of a cockpit and jump down on to terra firma.

When in Cairo the ferry crews lived on two houseboats with moorings at Gizera Island. The 'Egypt' for the officers and the 'Nile' for the NCOs. The flight across Africa had taken something over 20 hours flying time in five days, so a short rest was in order. It was not until a week later on 29th January 1942, that I boarded a Pan-Am DC.3 to fly back along the route to Takoradi. The Pan American pilot had arrived in West Africa a couple of months before Pearl Harbour, to help with the movement of crews. They were civilians flying civilian aircraft, and I imagine they were seconded under the Lend/Lease Agreement.

The week in Cairo made a most welcome change after the 'comforts' of the route and the isolation of Takoradi. A large city with no food rationing and a minimal blackout was something I had not experienced for some time, and wartime Cairo was fun.

One could swim, eat and drink at the Gizera Sporting Club, there were real live girls to ogle and friends to meet at Shepherd's or the Continental. In the evenings there were cinemas showing reasonably modern films and restaurants and nightclubs. A week went all too quickly. The flight back to Takoradi was tedious. A DC3 at 10,000 feet over Africa is not too comfortable and many pilots were bad passengers. We night-stopped at Wadi Sidina, El Geneina and Maiduguri, completing the last leg from Accra to Takoradi in a USAAF Lodestar.

Back at Takoradi I had the chance of a first flight in a Tiger Moth. This particular aircraft was fitted for spraying mosquito breeding areas in the hope of reducing the incidence of malaria, and I enjoyed the thirty minute flip, the first of many I was to make in the reliable old DH 82a.

11. *Convoy Leader*

After a spell of testing newly assembled Blenheims and Hurricanes, it was time to get back on to the route, this time as a convoy leader. I was crewed up with Flight Sergeant Carr, Navigator, and Sgt. Gregory, Radio Operator. For the convoy, all aircraft had white wash paint over their perspex canopies, to give some protection from the African sun, and the Hurricanes each had a number whitewashed on the sides, to help the leader keep track of his flock. I note that we left on the 6th February 1942, and arrived at Wadi Sidina on the 8th, having night stopped at Kano, and El Fasher. We were to leave the aircraft, my Blenheim and eight Hurricanes I think, at Khartoum. We completed the journey to Cairo in a Pan-Am DC 3, and after two days in Cairo were returned to Takoradi in an aircraft of the same type. Another spell of testing followed and on 3rd March we were off again with a convoy of Hurricanes. Myself and crew were in Blenheim IV V5956. We flew direct from Takoradi to Oshogbo on this occasion, due I think to some trouble with the runway at Lagos. We were at the time using the airfield at Apapja next to Lagos harbour, but the runway was very short, only about 900 yards. A new airfield was being built at Ekega, some miles inland from Lagos. We night stopped at Kano, as usual, and all went well until we reached El Geneina our next night stop. Here we lost one of our Hurricanes. He didn't crash or have engine failure, he simply lost sight of the rest of the convoy and the airfield while in the circuit preparing to land!

When we were en route, we flew in a shallow vic, four Hurricanes on each side of the leading Blenheim, far enough away to avoid constant throttle adjustments which would waste fuel, but close enough to keep the outside men comfortably in visual touch with the leader. When we approached the airfield for a landing at about five miles distant, the leader would 'waggle' his wings and the Hurricanes on his port side would cross over, passing under the rest of the convoy and forming echelon starboard. The leader would then fly over the airfield at circuit height and break to port, followed in turn by the rest of his convoy, which would then be in long line astern, ready for the circuit and landing.

We carried out this drill at El Geneina on that day, but for some reason or other one of the Hurricanes lost touch with the aircraft ahead, and all the rest of the convoy. He also lost sight of the airfield as well, and when I had landed he was circling away in the distance getting further and further from the airfield. We stood watching him for a few moments and then I ran to one of the Hurricane IIs – BM984 – in the hope of catching him and leading him back to the airfield. By this time people were firing Very lights to try and attract his attention, but to no avail. I rushed into the air and shot off to chase the lost aircraft. I was mindful that if I was not careful I could get lost too, so I set the compass grid ring, red on red, knowing that I had only to turn on to the reciprocal to get back. After a few minutes with no sign of the lost sheep, I turned back and was soon relieved to see the airfield ahead.

Now the question was what to do about the missing Hurricane. After about fifteen more minutes we knew that it must be on the ground somewhere out of fuel, so as soon as my Blenheim was refuelled, we took off to search. Of course we knew, or we thought we knew, roughly where to look, and for an hour carried a systematic creeping line a head search. We had with us the O.C Staging Post, as an extra pair of eyes and because he would have to get to the aircraft on the ground if we found it. He was an interesting cove who had once attempted to take off in a Gloucester Gladiator with no previous flying experience; of course he 'pranged' it. It happened like this. He was stationed at Khartoum as a junior Engineer Officer when a Gladiator force landed out of fuel some 50 or 60 miles into the desert. The aircraft was undamaged and the pilot was lucky enough to get picked up by some Arabs. Our friend went out with a jeep and a salvage party to see if they could bring the aircraft in. They found it, but realised that the terrain between the aircraft and their base was such that recovery would be impossible. Accordingly he decided to try and take off and fly back. They cleared a sort of runway into wind and started the engine. In he climbed on board and off he went. Of course with no flying experience he had no chance. He quickly swung off the prepared runway and the aircraft finished up on its back. The intrepid pilot was physically unhurt, though I expect his pride was somewhat dented. Perhaps the Gladiator is still there.

Anyway, back to our search. After about an hour we decided that we would never find our missing Hurricane, and in any case it was getting dark, so we turned for home some 30 miles away. We had not been going five minutes when a shout went up from Carr. There, not half a mile away on our port bow, a Very light was climbing into the sky. We turned towards it and saw a khaki clad figure waving madly, and the Hurricane in a ditch by the side of a dirt track. I turned and with wheels and flaps down made a low slow run past the stranded aircraft. It appeared to be undamaged except for a collapsed undercarriage leg. Then we made for home and arrived just as the sun was sinking below the horizon. The O.C. got his jeep and after a bite to eat, off we went to pick up our lost pilot. It was of course, quite dark by now, and luckily there was a rough dirt road leading in the right direction. We saw no wild animals, but in the light of the head-lights we saw many pairs of eyes, some extraordinarily wide apart! We found the errant pilot. He could not explain how he had become lost, but said that he had relaxed for a few seconds when in the aerodrome circuit and when he looked round again the other aircraft, and airfield, were gone. "I think", he said, "I must have been looking out of the wrong side of the cockpit!"

The next morning we continued our flight arriving at Fayoum Road without further incident. P/O Groves, the pilot of the lost Hurricane, came with me as passenger. From now onwards he was known, for obvious reasons, as 'Finger Groves'. Since early in the New Year the Ferry Unit had been busy delivering aircraft, mainly Blenheims, to our hard pressed Air Force in the Far East. I was now teamed up with a new crew, Navigator, W/O Warren and Radio Operator, Sergeant Smith, and we were standing by for a Far East delivery flight. On 20th March 1942 we picked up a Mark IV Blenheim V5998, at Fayoum Road, and positioned it at Kilo 8 ready for an early start on the following day.

We were off just after dawn on 21st March, with six Hurri-canes in tow. After landing for refuelling at Akir in Palestine we set off across the Syrian Desert bound for Habbaniya. I had some problems keeping my flock together as I climbed through some fairly extensive cumulous cloud over the high ground on the Palestine/Jordan border. We were under orders not to fly in cloud unless it was completely unavoidable. We, after all, lacked the precision and practice needed for successful cloud penetration in formation. In this case I was able to find a way round the clouds and soon we were heading eastwards over the route that had been followed by so many aircraft before us.

Because of the featureless nature of this region, it had long been the custom to use the oil pipelines as navigation aids in much the same way as pilots in other parts of the world used railways. This also had the advantage that as surface transport also did this, in an emergency landing, one would have help near at hand. Also there were emergency landing grounds at the pumping stations along the line. Our pipeline took us as far as Rutba Wells in the heart of the desert, and then disappeared North West, leaving us to make the last 200 miles with only the Damascus-Habbaniya 'road' for a guide. RAF Habbaniya must have been unique. It was in effect a self-contained city, isolated by 70 miles of desert from the nearest civilisation, the City of Baghdad! It had, not long before our arrival, demonstrated its self sufficiency by, against all the odds, defeating attacks by dissident Iraqui forces under the influence of Rachid Ali, their pro-German Premier. I say 'against all the odds', as not only were the defending forces heavily outnumbered, but the attackers were in possession of high ground, from which they could not only observe every movement, but also bombard the station with guns, kindly supplied, of course, by the British Government. There were also, it was said, German bombers standing by at Baghdad ready to intervene to ensure their protégé's success.

In the event, due to heroic efforts by the defenders, supported by a handful of obsolete aircraft, the attackers lost heart and the only service that the Luftwaffe could perform for Rachid Ali was to lift him to the doubtful sanctuary of Axis held territory. (By the way, was this the only occasion in W.W.II that Hawker Hart type aircraft were in action?). Anyway, by the time of our arrival this was all in the past and Iraq was firmly back in the Allied camp, though Habbaniya still bore the scars of her ordeal.

Soon after landing it became evident that the weather would prevent us from going on to our next stop, Shibah near Basra. At this time of the year in Iraq visibility is often very poor, due to rising dust. This is especially the case in the latter part of the day. In any case, in Egypt we had only been briefed for our flight as far as 'Hab', and as we were now officially under the aegis of Air Headquarters India, we were to be briefed here for the flight to Karachi. By the time this had been completed the visibility had become really bad, the sun was completely obscured and the light had taken on an unnatural orange hue. It was clear that we were due for a full scale dust storm and this shortly arrived, accompanied by hail and thunder of quite frightening proportions. In fact, the weather did not clear sufficiently for us to take off for two days.

During this enforced pause we were able to spend a day in Baghdad. After a 2 hour taxi ride across the desert, we were crossing the great bridge over the Tigeris and taking in the sights of the legendary city. I say 'sights', but anyone who has experienced a large Eastern city knows that tropical temperatures, plus the absence of organised refuse disposal and a satisfactory sewage system, ensures that the main impact is olfactory rather than visual. It would also be an unnerving experience for those who nowadays relentlessly pursue a single house fly, aerosol in hand, to be unable to distinguish a butcher's stall from a fishmonger's, until the black cloak of flies has been waved off the goods on offer. But however unsavoury the reality, it must be a thrill for a Westerner to be in the city of Aladdin and Ali Baba. It was the 24th March before we could take off for Shaibah. It was still very dusty and from 4,000 ft. there was no downward visibility except when the reflection of the sun caught one of the numerous patches of water. This meant that I was flying on instruments from just after take off until the top of the dust layer was reached at about 10,000 ft. The following aircraft could, of course, fly on the leader just as in cloud.

The flight to Shaibah took just under two hours, and although I did not realise it at the time, took us over territory infamous in the annals of British Armies. The names Mespot and Kut al

Imara would not have evoked pleasant memories in survivors of the 1915 campaign. We covered in an hour or so a route that, in reverse direction, it took a British Army many weary months to traverse at the cost of many casualties. Shaibah had of course, been immortalised in the RAF parody of the well-known Irish song. Shaibah Blues went like this:

A little bit of mufti fell from out the sky one day
And it landed in the desert so many miles away
And when the Air Force saw it there
It looked so effing bare
They said, "That's what we're looking for
We'll put our Air Force there".
So they sent a River Gunboat,
armoured cars and SHQ…

…and so on.[7]

Well, as far as we were concerned, the place lived up to its reputation. We only spent one night there, but could understand the despair of those there for months or even years. We night stopped at Shaibah because of the ever present dust haze and were happy to be off at dawn in the morning. It was a pleasant flight down the west coast of the Persian Gulf to Bahrein Island. Kuwait looked very peaceful away to port; this of course, was long before its emergence as an oil rich plutocracy.

The airfield at Bahrein is on a small isle to the north east of the main island, and is joined to it by a small causeway. The surface made an ideal natural landing area, marked out with black oil stains on the sand. After refuelling we pushed on to

---

[7] *Bawdy Ballads & Dirty Ditties of the RAF* (published by Woodfield in 2002) contains a large collection of similar rhymes and parodies.

Sharjah A glance at the map will show that, after crossing the Qatar Peninsula, the direct route is entirely over water. This did not worry us in our Blenheim, but the Hurricane pilots were wont to look down at the clear waters of the Gulf in which sharks of frightening size could clearly be seen. It is quite surprising but this had the effect of making a hitherto smooth running Merlin sound like a bag of nails! As a concession to the single engine pilots we were briefed to make a dog-leg to the south, overflying Yas Island, thus giving them a brief period when an engine failure might not mean complete catastrophe. I understand from friends who have since been to what is now The United Arab Emirates, but in those days was Trucial Oman, that Sharjah and Dubai are now thriving cities with skyscrapers and (nearly) all mod cons, whose bright lights at night can be seen for miles. In 1942 Sharjah was a fort, protecting a desert landing ground, and Dubai's main claim to fame was as a staging post for BOAC's flying-boat route to India.

Yes, at Sharjah one felt oneself to be in Beau Geste country, albeit in the wrong Continent. The landing ground was the usual flat sandy area, marked out by 40 gallon oil drums and, the fort was a traditional mud walled affair with a barbed wire enclosure nearby where the aircraft could be kept overnight under guard. This sort of security was necessary because the local tribesmen, while not actually hostile, had not been brought up with the Western ideals of honesty and fair play. So a Blenheim, unguarded overnight might well be found in the morning resting on is axles, while its wheels graced some local worthy's camel cart. More seriously, there were probably gentlemen in the nearby mountains who would give a fortune in goats, in exchange for a Browning machine gun.

There was one interesting local inhabitant of Sharjah Fort, a small gazelle type of animal with an insatiable appetite for ciga-

rettes, which it would eat. It wandered freely about the court-
yard, demanding its favourite goodies from visiting airmen. If
one happened to be a non-smoker and therefore unable to oblige,
it would become aggressively bad tempered. As it was equipped
with a pair of short very pointed horns and was about the height
of a large Labrador dog, it will be seen that this put one in danger of being maimed in a most unfortunate manner. The only
defence was to grab the horns and hold on, hoping that someone
would soon offer to share his packet of Victory V's with the
beast.

Dawn saw us airborne for Karachi. This was a four-hour
flight, passing the Peninsula and the Gulf of Oman, then following the Persian and Beluchistan coasts to Karachi. An emergency
landing ground was available at Jiwani close to Gwadar, the
B.O.A.C. Flying Boat Staging Post near the Persian/Baluch
border. There was also an airfield at Jask on the Persian coast of
the Gulf of Oman, but this was not manned by the RAF. It was
said that the tribes inhabiting the East Coast of the Oman Peninsula were among the least friendly of any on the route. In fact an
old RAF song seemed to apply:

> *"If you land to the East of the Bahrain Pass*
> *Might as well stuff your Lewis gun right up your arse*
> *You'll have no balls at all!*
> *No balls at all!*
> *If your engine cuts out you'll have no balls at all!"*

This I imagine emanated from the N.W. Frontier of India, but
luckily I know no one in a position to say whether it also applied
to Oman.

After taking off at Sharjah it was necessary to climb quickly to
clear the coastal mountain range fifty miles away and reaching
10,000 ft. in places. After crossing the fifty-mile wide Gulf it was

a simple coast crawl to Karachi. Simple that is, in fair weather. Very often the route is masked by stratus cloud. This however presents no problem as the coast line is indicated faithfully by cumulus forming over the land. It is quite possible to map read using the cloud. Worse than this though is the dust haze, limiting visibility to less than a mile, and rendering the ground invisible from more than about 3,000 ft.

Two convoys had spent the night at Sharjah. Mine was one and the other a convoy of Blenheims led by veteran pilot Joe King. I got away first and although the haze was very thick as we approached Karachi, my Hurricanes closed up nicely and stuck to me like glue. We caught a glimpse of the City as we passed over and soon the huge airship hangar at the civil airport loomed out of the haze. This hangar had been built for the ill-fated R.101, which of course did not survive to use it. After a tight circuit we were stepping onto Indian soil for the first time. Joe King's convoy had been due to take off from Sharjah half an hour after us. About three quarters of an hour after we had landed at Karachi he arrived, by himself. When he climbed down from his aircraft, it was clear that he was none too pleased. It appeared that his Blenheims had failed to close up on him when it was time to duck down into the murk on approaching Karachi. As a result the convoy had become dispersed and of course, Joe was the only one with a Navigator and a W/T Operator. The exact details escape me, but I think one or two of the lost sheep eventually made it to the airport, but a number did not.

The flight from Sharjah had taken four hours, so it was not long before we knew that the missing aircraft were on the ground somewhere. It was too late in the afternoon to do anything that day, but early next morning Warren, Smith and I were in our Blenheim heading westwards to search for the missing aircraft. We had decided that they would probably be near the sea as the narrow coastal strip provided just about the only possible crash landing area. We had searched up and down the coast as far as Jiwani, in case one of them had turned back, trying to reach that airfield. We eventually found one Blenheim lying wheels up on a sandbank. There was no sign of the pilot. However all the missing men turned up at Karachi eventually, mainly I think by dhow; but as may be imagined, there were several days of uncertainty until they were all accounted for, and a number of questions to be answered.

We found at Karachi that my Hurricanes were allotted to the training school at Risalpur (Raipur). Here No. I (F) Squadron I.A.F., the first Indian Unit to be equipped with modern fighters, would do their conversion. Risalpur is situated right at the mouth of the Khyber Pass on the North West Frontier, and the obvious route from Karachi was to follow the Indus to the point where the tributary from Kabul joins in and then follow that to Risalpur. The Hurricanes of course, would have to refuel en route, and there was an airfield at Khanpur where the right fuel was available, and although there was no RAF presence there, it was considered that we could manage. So the following morning we were away, heading north/north/east to hit the river. It soon became clear that India is just about the ideal country for pilot navigation by map reading. The most useful landmarks, rivers, railways, roads and large towns, are present in adequate numbers, but are infrequent enough to be instantly identifiable. Any stranger who has flown over say, the West Yorkshire industrial region, will know the railways, roads and towns are virtually useless as map reading aids because of their very profusion. In India they are usually present in exactly the right quantities.

Khanpur was a two hour flight up the Indus with the high ground of Baluchistan visible away to port for most of the time. The airfield was a sandy patch, no runways and a couple of small sheds. We landed in the normal manner and at the end of my run I turned my Blenheim 90 degrees to port and watched the Hurricanes as they made their approaches. All landed safely except one, which hit the ground heavily, wiping off both under-carriage legs. When the dust had cleared we could see the pilot, unhurt climbing from his cockpit.

As was normal on airfields of this type in India, apart from a *chowkidar* or caretaker, the man in charge was the Burmah Oil 'wallah', an 'Anglo' Eurasian and a very helpful fellow. He sent his driver out to pick up the pilot of the stricken Hurricane, and bring in his parachute and personal kit. I told him I ought to put a call through to Karachi to let them know what had happened. He said that there was no 'phone at the airfield, and the best thing to do was to go into town and send a telegram from the Post Office. So while he supervised the refuelling, Warren, Smith and I rode into town on a Tonga, a small two-wheeled cart rather like an Irish jaunting car, to find the Post Office and to get our first experience of India in the raw.

Coming from the Middle East we were used to the heat and the smells - though India did seem to be hotter and smellier even than Baghdad - but what first struck me was the amount of spitting that went on. Known we later found out, as 'the war cry' the average Indian brings it right up from his boots. At first I thought that they were spitting at us as despised Britishers, but soon realised that it was just a national habit, connected I believe, with the chewing of betel nut. Having sent our telegram the next job was to arrange for the local police to guard the crashed Hurricane, there being no Army in the vicinity. This done, we returned to the airfield to find our aircraft refuelled and ready to go. I now had an extra passenger, the unfortunate Hurricane pilot, and I think we all enjoyed the flight up the Indus and into the majestic scenery of the foothills of the Afghanistan Mountains, past Kohat and Peshawar and so to Risalpur. The features that stick in my mind are the settlements perched high on ridges or peaks, seemingly inaccessible to anything but a mountain goat.

We were received with some interest at Risalpur, bringing as we did the first 'modern' fighters to be seen in that part of India. We also found out an interesting thing about the area. Here it was possible to get unlimited quantities of very acceptable Indian beer, brewed at the nearby Murree brewery. So a jolly evening was had by all and we all got to bed in good order, I think. In the morning I was asked to take an engineer officer down to Khanpur to look at the crashed Hurricane, and the flight there and back was a pleasant way of spending the day, prior to another evening on the Murree beer!

My Blenheim, having carried out its convoy leading duties was due to be delivered to Lahore, so the next day we made the short flight, only just over the hour, to the famous old city. The northern cities of the Indian sub-continent I find very much more pleasant than those in the south. They enjoy of course, a cool (for India) climate from about November to March. Frost at night is not unknown in December and January and therefore the people have to find shelter of some sort, and it is not possible to sleep in the streets all the year round as it is in Bombay, Calcutta or Madras. This makes the city a much cleaner more orderly place, and the more rigorous climate has its effect on the character of the people.

We were to return to Karachi from Lahore by rail and as the train was not leaving until late afternoon, we went to a hotel for a few hours relaxation. The best Indian hotels at the time of the British Raj (and to this day I imagine) were impressive places. Cool and dimly lit, with marble floors and wide stone staircases, massive pillars and large airy rooms, they would seem to have been modelled on the palaces that the Maharajas had been wont to build for themselves for a thousand years or more. The only noise to be heard was the rhythmic beat of the electric punkahs (no air conditioning in those days), and the subdued conversations of turbaned servants - bearers to the initiated. Most of these would be men in their late 30's or 40's, often being retired soldiers from the Indian Army, as their campaign medals showed. Somehow the Indian bearer brought to his calling a dignity which shames those in the West, who think that to serve is to be demeaned.

Our train for Karachi was due to leave in the afternoon and we left the hotel in good time to get a drink or two at the station refreshment room. Surprisingly enough, to those used to English station buffets, with their plastic ham sandwiches and tea come coffee (anyone's guess which is which), Indian station refreshment rooms were an Aladdin's cave of treasure. In the first place, unheard of luxuries like real Scotch whisky was available, and could be bought by the bottle for something like 20 rupees (£1.50). Normally these were of the rather less common brands, Bell's, rare even at home, Queen Anne or Cranford's say. I suppose that the war had not interrupted the long established chain of supply. Add to this a cool quiet room where the 'Sahibs' could enjoy their meal while the train awaited their pleasure, for this is what often happened, as we were soon to find out. Contrast this with the chaos on the platform outside. The Indian peasant, when he needs to travel, and to judge by the congestion on stations and trains, a high percentage of the population were constantly on the move, does not go to catch a train. He goes to the station and waits until a train arrives that is going in his direction. This in much the same way as a Londoner catches the tube from Earls Court to Piccadilly, except that the Indian may be embarking on a three-day journey from Bombay to Dehli. He may, therefore, have to wait a day or two days or a week, for his train. So the station platform assumes the character of Blackpool beach during Bradford wakes week. Hundreds of people cooking, eating, sleeping, making love and in some cases dying, while packed together like sardines. The story of the London clubman who had been dead in his chair for three days before anyone realised; except for the three days, can become grim reality at an Indian railway station with temperatures at 90 degrees F.

When the train at last arrives there would be a concerted rush to climb on. I say 'on' advisedly, as all room inside the 3rd class coaches was soon taken up and the unlucky passengers proceeded to climb on to the carriage roofs or cling on to the buffers. I wonder how many Indians have been killed by falling under the wheels of trains, or being swept off the carriage roofs by low bridges or tunnels.

Our first class compartment was not air-conditioned (we were to experience this luxury on later journeys) but seemed very comfortable. It was arranged so that the two -bench seat could double as beds at night. Two other bunks folded against the bulkheads during daytime, were let down to form a top tier at night. This being very much like the old British Rail 3rd Class sleeper. There was a difference however, Indian express trains had no corridor, but each first class compartment had its own cubicle with W.C. and wash basin. Before we left Lahore an assistant Station Master walked down the train asking how many of the Sahibs were intending to take dinner at - I forget where, it could have been Multan - and after about four hours we trooped off the train and into the Station Refreshment room. The meal was excellent and a certain amount of drink flowed with it. So much in fact that when the train guard came and requested that the Sahibs entrained once more, so that the journey might recommence, he was greeted with a great deal of ribaldry. As a result he retreated to enlist the help of the Station Master who, almost in tears, begged us to board our train, which was already considerably late. Eventually we were persuaded to re-embark and the train started again on its journey southwards to Karachi. Bunks were rigged and we settled down for the night. The properly equipped Sahib travelling in India would have with him his bearer and a bed roll. The former would lay out the latter at the appropriate time in the appropriate place. We of course, had neither bearer nor bed roll and had to manage as best we could without.

As the journey progressed, various other snags manifested themselves. Much of the route traversed the Sind Desert, and even with all windows and shutters closed, a fine brown dust pervaded everything. In this state, moreover, the compartment was uncomfortably hot and stuffy. One had the choice therefore either of being roasted, but subjected to only a thin layer of dust, or of getting some 'cool' air and suffering a veritable dust storm, augmented by a generous ration of smuts and cinder from the locomotive. As always in such cases, one strove unsuccessfully to find an acceptable compromise.

On arrival at Karachi we found that we had been booked to return to Egypt by flying boat, but had four days to wait. These were spent pleasantly in Karachi drinking and swimming at the Gymkhana or the Boat Club - all transit officers being temporary members of both. In the early hours of April 4th we were taken down to Karachi harbour to join the Empire Flying Boat 'Cambria' for the flight to Cairo. The modern air traveller, used to Jumbo Jets carrying 300 or 400 passengers, will find it difficult to picture the quiet dignity of travel in these 'big' flying boats. For those used to the hassle of Heathrow or Gatwick, let me describe the journey.

In the half-light, just before dawn, the passengers, together with the crew (2 Pilots, Navigator, Radio Operator and a Steward) were taken out to the aircraft by launch, with their luggage. On embarking, they found a passenger cabin more akin to the size and shape of a modern living room than to the pressurised tube that is a modern jetliner's fuselage. A seat beside a large rectangular window gave a perfect downward view, unobstructed by the high wing. After a few minutes the four engines were started and the moorings cast off. During the taxi out to take off point, the engines were opened up in turn, to check Boost, R.P.M. and Mag Drop. The modern jet passenger would wonder what on earth was going on! Soon the aircraft was swung into wind and lined up with the water flare-path, whose lights were by now fighting a losing battle with the rapidly approaching dawn. Then came the thunder of all four Pegasus engines with the cabin windows obliterated by flying spray. The acceleration would seem mild by modern standards, but was adequate, as in many flying boat bases the available take off run was virtually unlimited. The spray increased, likewise the water noise, as the aircraft lifted onto the step, whilst both finally ceased as the boat rose off the water to climb away into the gathering daylight.

Our itinerary was Quada, Dubai, Bahrein, and Basrah for the night. My Log Book tells me that these legs were of 2hrs 35mins, 3hrs, 2hrs10mins and 2hrs 30mins respectively. A gruelling day's flying for the crew but quite pleasant for us, as we were taken ashore at each stop and given appropriate refreshments at the B.O.A.C. rest house. As we flew low, at only a few thousand feet unless forced up higher by mountains, there was always something to see out of the large windows. The only snag was that especially at the hottest part of the day, the air was bumpy, and pilots, when not actually handling their aircraft, are not entirely immune from airsickness!

Our night stop was at the Shatt-al-Arab Hotel at Basrah. This stood on the bank of the river serving the Airport on one side and the flying boat base on the other. The hotel seemed to us most luxurious, seemingly untouched by the austerity brought on by the war. The only snag was that we had a very early call in the morning. Chota Nagpur (strong Indian influence here) arrived at some unearthly hour around 5 a.m, and we were glad to settle down to doze in our flying boat seats as we headed North West for our first landing on the lake at Habbaninga. From there our route took us across the Syrian Desert to a landing on Lake Tiberius, and just before dusk we were down on the Nile at Cairo. So we had taken two days, with seven landings, to cover a distance that a modern jetliner would manage in about four hours, but it had all been most civilised. There must be many people who think that no airliners will ever compare with the old Imperial Airways Empire Flying boats.

Back in Cairo after a brief interlude on the houseboat 'Egypt', we were off to India again, this time leading a convoy of Blenheims, which meant that we could make Cairo–Habbaninga direct. I see from my Log Book that we changed aircraft at Habbaninga, and had a day's delay there, why I cannot now remember. This time the aircraft were to be left at Allahabad and the leg from Karachi was made direct in four and three quarter hours. This flight across the heart of India showed us again what an easy country India is for map reading from the air. There being no accommodation on the aerodrome, we spent one night in an Allahabad hotel before we boarded a train for Karachi, via Delhi. In India, as in England, railways tend to radiate from the Capital City. I think it was on this journey that we first experienced the joy of air conditioning. Not only was the temperature in the compartment kept down to a comfortable 75 degrees but the sealed windows kept out all dust. The one snag was on alighting from this cool odour free haven, one walked into what seemed like a wall of heat and smell. After a few days waiting at Karachi we were found seats on a West bound D.C.3, which, after a night stop at Basrah, delivered us safely to Almaza Airport, Cairo. On May 7th 1942, I was back at Almaza boarding a BOAC Lockheed Lodestar (a stretched Lockheed 14) for the trip back down the route to Takoradi, for what was to turn out to be a last visit.

The Lodestar night stopped at El Fasha and dropped us at Lagos, where we picked up a USAAF DC3 (we had not yet learnt to call them Dakotas). It took us to the American base at Accra (accent on the first syllable now) for the night and then on to Takoradi in the morning. Ten days at Takoradi and a convoy of short range Hurricanes was ready with a Blenheim V BA211 for me and a new Navigator, Flt/Sgt Smith in place of Warren, who had stayed in Cairo.

The Mk.V Blenheim differed from the IV in that it had a redesigned nose and a new type of rear turret. It also had Mercury XXX engines with constant speed fully feathering airscrews. The cooling gills were electrically operated, with a separate switch for each engine, unlike the Mk.IV where one manual control operated both sets. The snag with that was of course that if one engine was overheating, both sets of gills had to be opened. In the event of engine failure, this could be serious. The throttle controls were placed on a central console with their associate pitch levers and not tucked away to the pilot's left as in the older Mk. IV. The hydraulic controls for flaps and undercarriage were moved and re-designed, and altogether this made for a much neater and better cockpit. Unfortunately the weight was also increased and in spite of the extra power provided by the uprated Mercury engines, performance was not up to the standard even of the old Mk.IV. It was for this reason no doubt, that the Mk.V failed to distinguish itself as an operational aircraft.

This trip proved to be the longest that I made. Starting on 21st May, we did not arrive in Cairo until 1st June. Delays occurred at Lagos, one day and Kano five days. As we had to make stops at Oshogobo (between Lagos and Kano) and at Fort Lamy, this was a tedious trip. To add to my misfortunes an anopheles mosquito must have realise that this was her last chance to get me at Takoradi. As a result, soon after arrival at Cairo I was whipped off to hospital with a nasty bout of Malaria. To those who have not suffered I don't recommend Malaria. The effect of the fever on me was as if I had a continuous cinema performance going on inside my head, and as soon as my eyes were closed the pictures streamed away unasked and unwanted. Blessed relief came with some drug, I know not what, which gave me the feeling of floating one foot above the bed in perfect peace. The RAF hospital in Cairo took good care of me and after about two weeks I was considered fit enough to go to a pleasant convalescent hostel on the eastern seafront at Alexandria.

This was June 1942, and students of the history of WWII will know that during that month General Rommel was at the very gates of Alexandria – well almost. As can be imagined, we watched his progress with some anxiety and, as we were attached to no particular unit at the time, made our own tentative plans to move smartly eastward should the worst occur. The 'loyal' shopkeepers and bar owners of Alexandria were also closely watching events and it was said that pictures of Hitler and Rommel were kept at the ready under bars and counters to replace those of George VI and Churchill, in time for the arrival of the new customers. The story also went round that one such tradesman had in fact made the switch, acting on one of the many unfounded rumours, just as a party of Jolly Jacks appeared, enjoying their run ashore. The subsequent events are easily imagined.

In the event, as we all know, General Auckinleck stopped Rommel in his tracks at El Alamein and was promptly sacked for his pains, leaving the way clear for the little man in the black beret (although he did not wear it then) to get on with the serious business of winning the war.

Fit and well again, in early July I returned to Cairo and the houseboat. With the expansion of the war effort against the Japanese in India, the Aircraft Delivery Unit (Middle East), to which I belonged, were required to provide a nucleus of pilots to form a unit based at Karachi. I found that my name was on the list, so after a brief stay at a transit camp at Almaza a USAAF C-47 (Dakota) took us along the familiar route to Karachi.

12. *India*

At Karachi we were based at the Civil Airport, which we shared
with the US Air Force. We ate in the airport restaurant and our
living quarters were in a number of bungalows belonging to the
airport and presumably built for the use of civilian employees.
Most of the aircraft we dealt with were shipped in crates to
Karachi and assembled at the old established RAF base at Drigh
Road, a few miles on the Karachi side of the airport. After they
had been passed by the test pilot, at that time a most pleasant
S/L by the name of Dennis Mitchell, we went over by road and
flew the aircraft across to the airport, doing a brief acceptance
check on the way. At first most were Mk I Hurricanes, and we
took them up to Risalpur to the Fighter OTU. The route up the
Indus to Lahore had been abandoned, presumably because of the
lack of a suitable staging post en-route, so we used the rather
longer way round via Jodhpur and Delhi.

Jodhpur was, of course, one of the princely states and the Maharajah was at that time a young man intensely loyal to the
British Raj, as were most of his contemporaries. He had established a thriving flying club at Jodhpur Aerodrome in pre-war
days and on the outbreak of war this became the basis of No 2
EFTS, for training Indian Air Force pilots. The Maharajah had,
of course, learned to fly at his own flying club and held the
honorary rank of Air Commodore in the Indian Air Force.
Nevertheless, he insisted that he should earn his wings the hard
way and went up to Risalpur to do a full Service flying course.

The OC at Jodhpur was S/L Peter Bond (who we shall meet
again later in my story under less happy circumstances). He

achieved notoriety at Jodhpur in a rather unfortunate manner. When the Hurricanes first started to come through, though an experienced service pilot, he had not flown any 'modern' types, and was now restricted by his job to an occasional flight in a Tiger Moth. Naturally, he wanted very much to have a 'go' on a Hurricane, and he persuaded a Sergeant pilot from a convoy passing through to let him 'borrow' his Hurricane for a short flight. Well, all went well until Bond was back in the circuit wanting to land. Could he put the wheels down? He could not! The selector lever refused to move from neutral into the down position. However much he tried to force it, it would not budge. Eventually he was forced to belly land on the grass beside the runway. One can imagine the feelings of the unfortunate Ferry Pilot, and these were not improved when it became clear that there was nothing wrong with the undercarriage or its selector. Bond had simply omitted to lift the safety catch that prevented the undercarriage lever being moved accidentally. I do not imagine that AHQ India was overjoyed about the incident!

We organised our convoys after the pattern of those from Takoradi except that we had several Hudsons and crews allocated to us which led the convoys and ferried the pilots back to Karachi after the job was done. On my first flight from Karachi we night stopped at Jodhpur (2 nights), Delhi and Lahore. As this was the time of the southwest monsoon, I would imagine that it was the weather that delayed us. It was quite pleasant to be just a follower and not to have the responsibility of looking after a gaggle of radio-less Hurricanes.

Peter Rivington + Hurricane, en route to the North West Frontier, India 1942.

Back at Karachi we heard that a number of Mohawks were ready for collection at Drigh Road and I was quick to get over there and get my hands on one. I have always considered flying new types of aircraft to be one of the most enjoyable aviation experiences. This was especially so in those days, when a five minute cockpit check was all that was needed by way of ground preparation. The Curtis Hawk 75A, known to the US Army Air Corps as the P-38, had been ordered in large numbers by the French Armée de l'Air. After the defeat of 1940, the outstanding orders had been diverted to the RAF under the Lend/Lease arrangement, and the aircraft renamed Mohawk. It was pleasing to look at, and like the majority of American products, a delight to fly. However, it had been developed in the mid-1920s when American military aircraft tended to lag behind their European counterparts in performance. As a result the bulk of the Mohawks found their way to India, where I suppose the opposition was then considered to be somewhat less formidable than in Western Europe. No doubt the Air Ministry had noted that during the campaign in France the Hawk 75As had been outclassed by the Bf.109s, and with a top speed of just over 300 mph at 14,000ft was much inferior to the Mk.I Hurricane.

Although the Mohawk did sterling service against the Japanese and was operational until 1944, perhaps its greatest claim to fame is that it sired that great line of inline engined P-40 fighters, which included the Tomahawk, the Kittyhawk and the Warhawk. Unlike its more celebrated stablemates, the Mohawk was powered by the wonderful Wright Cyclone GR1820 radial engine, surely one of the most reliable ever built, and with its toe operated wheel brakes and steerable tailwheel, took me back to the old Harvard days at Grantham. Wheel retraction, flaps and propeller pitch change, were operated electrically. The Curtis Electric propeller was unique in my experience, in that it could be operated as a fully constant speed unit or in an infinitely variable fixed pitch mode. The main landing gear retracted backwards to fit into wells in the wings. The aircraft handled in that compact solid manner typical of its country of origin, and its ample fuel load (considerably greater than that of the Hurricane) made it a most excellent A to B aircraft as well as being most responsive and pleasant for aerobatics.

I took Mohawk AR690 up to Peshawar, via Jodhpur, Delhi and Lahore, and a second AR672 to Calcutta via Jodhpur, Delhi and Allahabad. On the last flight I had some trouble which made me turn back after take off at Allahabad. I can't recall the details, but it meant a night stop at Allahabad and an air test in the morning. All was well and I was ready to push on to Calcutta. However, the authorities at Allahabad insisted that single engined aircraft were not permitted to fly unescorted, why I cannot imagine, and so I would have to wait for a convoy to come through. However, there was an odd looking Beechcraft (the single engined bi-plane with the backward stagger) about to take off. It was going my way and I was allowed to go with that. Of course as soon as we were airborne it was obvious that the Beech was far too slow for me, so I waved good-bye and pushed on to Calcutta.

The drive from Dum Dum Airfield seemed even more malodorous than is usual when approaching a large Indian city, culminating in the usual mixture of Victorian magnificence and eastern squalor. At this time the Japanese had raided Calcutta by day on one or two occasions, and a Hurricane squadron had been stationed on the midden in the city centre, using the central roadway, the Red Road, as a runway. I can only imagine that this was done to reassure the population, as one would have thought that an airfield away from the city would have been as effective, and a great deal easier to operate from. As it was, a number of Hurricanes were damaged owing to the narrowness of the 'runway' they were using.

Around this time, news was coming through of the defeat of the Axis armies at El Alamein. This, coupled with the German disaster outside Stalingrad and the build-up of American strength that we could see around us, gave us a clear picture of how we were going to win the war, as opposed to just hanging on, Micawber like, as had been the case until then.

Back at Karachi (via a lift in a US Dakota, I think) there was some interesting news. Ferry Control, Middle East had requested help in moving some Blenheims to India and would we send some pilots? Would we? I'll say we would! Within a few days myself and crew (Sergeants Hurry and Allen) plus a number of Blenheim pilots, were setting off for Cairo. On this occasion we travelled in a BOAC Armstrong Whitworth Ensigns, at the time one of the largest aircraft in the world. However, coming from the same stable as the Whitley bomber and, like the Whitley, being built in the manner of the proverbial brick convenience, one could not expect too much of it in the way of performance. Our aircraft was one of the few fitted with four Pratt and Witney

Wasps in place of the original Armstrong Siddley Tigers, and I suppose this helped the performance as well as the reliability.

On arrival in Cairo we were told that our aircraft were waiting at Luxor, so after a day or so on the houseboats, a US Dakota took us there from Almaza. We had a day at Luxor, just time to test the aircraft and make a quick visit to the Valley of the Kings, before we were headed south for Khartoum, briefed to follow the southern route to India via Asmara, Aden and Masirah Island. There was some delay at Khartoum and I see that I swapped my Blenheim Mk IV Z7913 for a Mk V BA609. Then, on November 19th we were off for Asmara and points west. Asmara, some 7,000 feet above sea level, had been the capital of the Italian colony of Eritrea and we had heard tell of the comforts that the 'Ities' had provided for themselves, including, as we understood, a brothel with mirrors in the most unusual places. However, these pleasures were not for us, for duty called and after refuelling we were off to Aden (very much at sea level and devoid of all but the most primitive conveniences). Nevertheless an enjoyable evening was spent within the hospitable Mess at Sheikh Othman (Aden). Joe King (he who had had trouble with his Blenheim on the Beluchistan coast back in March) was among those present.

Taking off from Aden the next day we had a long haul along the South Arabian coast to Masirah Island, with a refuelling stop at Salala. This was nearly seven hours flying in all, following this not very inspiring coastline, and we were all glad to arrive at Masirah even though the R.A.F camp there consisted of just a few tents. The following day, 21st November, we crossed the Gulf of Oman, about an hour out of sight of land, to pick up the familiar Baluchistan coast and follow it to Karachi.

Taking my convoy in at Karachi Airport I made a silly mistake that could have had serious consequences. At Karachi the wind blows steadily from the west for much of the year but in November swings round for a short time to blow from the east. This means that for months on end aircraft are landing from east to west, and this had been the case when we left Karachi ten days or so earlier. Without looking at the windsock or landing tee – just pleased to be 'home' – I led my flock in to land east-west. But the wind was blowing some 15 mph from the east, so we were landing downwind (no voice radio contact with the tower of course and no runway caravan; unheard of in those days). Luckily, all the aircraft were able to pull up before the airfield boundary was reached, but my face was somewhat red when I faced the welcoming committee!

The CO and pilots of No.1 (Fighter) Squadron, Indian Air Force arrived at Karachi at about this time. They had completed their OTU at Risi or Peshawar, I forget which, and were down at Karachi to collect their Hurricane Mk. I aircraft and take them to their base in Eastern India, where they were to work up to full operation standard. The CO was a charming IAF Squadron Leader by name of Henry Ranganathan. Henry had been trained at Cranwell in pre-war days and his father was Indian High Commissioner in London throughout the war. As readers will perhaps have noted, Indian Officers trained in British Military Establishments tend to talk and act in a way that is more British than the British. Henry was no exception. His English accent was immaculate and his speech freely sprinkled with 'old boys' and 'don't you knows' and of course, the standard RAF slang of the day. Coming from southern India, Henry's skin was as black as your hat, but this did not inhibit him from referring to his fellow countrymen as "wogs", "black troops" or "our black brothers" etc.

A number of us spent the evening before the squadron was due to fly off as Henry's guests at the Karachi Club and a good time was had by all, enlivened by the host's practice of telling the most outrageously vulgar jokes in mixed company and getting away with it. The following morning we got up early to see the squadron off. As Henry was to stop off at Delhi for consultations, he elected to travel as a passenger in the Hudson we had provided as lead aircraft. It was flown by one of our most reliable crews. Also on board were two or three other passengers for Delhi, including, as far as I can remember a Wing Commander. The Hudson and the Hurricanes were able to take off in wide formation on the large Karachi airfield and formed up nicely to fly past and disappear eastwards, leaving us to return to a belated breakfast. About an hour later we were attracted onto the tarmac by a most extraordinary aircraft noise, a sort of "wuff wuff wuff". We looked up and saw an untidy gaggle of Hurricanes circling the airfield. The noise seemed to be coming from one of them. As it passed overhead, something appeared wrong with its propellers. One by one the Hurricanes landed and as the first taxied in we could see what seemed to be something very wrong with the pilot. As he took his helmet off, tears could be seen running down his face. Somebody climbed onto the wing.

"What's the matter? What's happened?"

"Oh, it was awful, it was horrible," came the answer.

"What was awful? What was horrible?"

No one seemed composed enough to tell as the other Hurricanes taxied in, leaving the noisy one 'wuff wuff wuffing' round the circuit. At last a young Anglo-Indian Pilot Officer climbed out of his aircraft. In a calm voice he told us what had happened.

It seemed that the damaged Hurricane had been in close formation with the Hudson, too close evidently, as a collision had taken place and the Hudson, its tail badly damaged, had dived straight into the Sind Desert some eighty miles from Karachi. They had been flying at about 6,000 feet and no parachutes had been seen. There was no possibility of survivors.

I do not recall what happened to the Hurricane pilot in question, but I suppose for a time he wished that his aircraft had dived into the desert alongside the Hudson – which 99 times out of 100 would have been the result of such a collision.

But all was not gloom at Karachi. By this time the Americans had been in the war for twelve months and they had established what the RAF would term an MU (Maintenance Unit). This was responsible for assembling a test flying aircraft brought in by sea, in much the same way as we were doing at Drigh Road. They used the big hangar built for the ill-fated R101. We made some good friends from among them. They also used 'our' hangar for maintenance work on heavy aircraft in transit to the Burma/China front. These were mainly Boeing Flying Fortresses and the occasional Liberator.

One afternoon one of the latter arrived from Habbaniyah. He circled and was clearly in trouble. We could see that one undercarriage leg was locked down while the other seemed to be jammed in the halfway position (the Liberator's undercarriage retracted outwards into the wing). After spending some time fruitlessly trying to get the wheels to lock down or retract fully, the pilot climbed the aircraft to about 3,000ft and baled out all his crew and passengers, except his co-pilot. He then made a faultless landing on one wheel, holding the aircraft level for as long as possible. It was a fine piece of airmanship and the damage done to the aircraft was minimal. It seems that the aircraft had become bogged in at Habbaniyah (its last stop) and while being pulled out, the undercarriage had evidently been damaged. It had retracted OK but failed to lower fully.

One lunchtime, one of our ground staff officers had been invited over to the American Officers Club for drinks. He had a great deal of work on his desk, so he telephoned to say that he would be late.

"Sorry Joe, but I'm up to my eyes here, so I'll be a little late. What I need is a clerk".

"What d'ya wanna a clock for?" came the American's reply. "Haven't you got a wristwatch?"

Sometimes it's easier if you don't speak the 'same' language!

One aspect of the American operators gave us endless amusement. They were supplying fighter aircraft to the Chinese Air Force – obsolete types for which the Americans had no use. I remember two types: a Republic P-43 Lancer, which looked like a scaled-down Thunderbolt, and a little fighter from the Seversky Aircraft Corporation that had a very wide spindly undercarriage. The Chinese pilots would come to Karachi to collect their aircraft and eventually fly off in a gaggle, heading eastwards for the war. This, however, never turned out to be as simple as it sounds. Firstly, when there were half a dozen or so aircraft ready for take off, no one seemed inclined to go first. They would circle round, jockeying for position, in a kind of "after you, Claude" fashion. The irreverent amongst us suggested that they were awaiting instructions from their ancestors, whose experience of kite flying hardly qualified them to give the advice required. Eventually one would pluck up courage and lead off, but the take-offs would rarely be completed without several ground-loops and a large number of kangaroo-hops. The entertainment was even better if one happened to be at one of their refuelling stops when they were landing. The antics reminded one of the 'crazy flying' acts in old fashioned air displays.

On return from our Middle East trip we found we had been allotted a couple of Harvards for training flying. These were not the curvaceous Mk.Is we had flown at Grantham, but the rather ugly angular Mk.IIs. Nevertheless it was good to fly a Harvard again, and it meant that we could convert our twin engine pilots back to singles in a fairly orderly fashion. Unfortunately a Cana-

dian Flight Sergeant parked our first Harvard on the mud flats
that form the coastline around Karachi. His story was that he was
doing aerobatics at a safe height when he got into a flat spin that
he couldn't recover from. Nobody believed him and it was fairly
obvious that he was indulging in a little unauthorised low flying
and dug a wing tip in the mud. He was very lucky to get away
with it. Unfortunately the incident led indirectly to a 'rocket' for
me, when a ferry pilot on rest from the Burma front chose to
'beat up' Mauripur airfield near Karachi just at the time when
the Group Captain, newly arrived to take over Ferry HQ, was
inspecting it. My fault was in not making it clear that low flying
was 'taboo'.

Another newcomer at about this time was the Vultee Vengeance, the RAFs first specialist dive-bomber. It had been ordered
in the summer of 1940, when this aircraft type was at the height
of its fame. But by the time the aircraft were beginning to arrive
it had become plain, after the failure of the Ju.87 in the Battle of
Britain, that there was little future for the dive-bomber in
Europe, so all Vengeance aircraft found their way out to India for
the Burma front. Here, carrying twice the bomb load of a Blenheim, it proved very effective when given adequate fighter cover.
It was pleasant enough to fly. The 1,700 hp double row Wright
Cyclone was, at that time, the most powerful engine I had handled, and a pilot certainly felt he had a man-size aircraft to deal
with. It had one or two odd characteristics. The fuel was held in
a number of self-sealing flexible bags contained in the wings.
Each of these bags, around eight in all, I believe, was fitted with
its own electrical fully immersed fuel pump. When one of these
pumps failed, as they quite frequently did, the fuel from that cell
was unobtainable. Aircraft were continually kept on the ground
because of fuel pump trouble. Another odd thing was the operation of the hydraulics. These operated the undercarriage

retraction mechanism, the wing flaps, the bomb doors and the dive brakes. The engine was fitted with an inertia starter. This was a common American system and the Harvard had one. It worked by spinning a small but heavy fly-wheel up to very high rpm using an electric motor and then engaging a clutch so that the energy, so stored, turned the engine sufficiently fast to start it. The engine started, therefore, with something of a kick and it seemed that the resultant shock to the hydraulic system was minimised if one of the services was set to operate as this happened. Normally the bomb doors were closed for this, so before starting, the selector was placed in either the 'open' or 'closed' position and as soon as the engine started, the bomb doors moved. On one occasion I failed to realise that the bomb doors had opened as I started and took off with them open. This was careless as, when sitting in the cockpit, if the pilot looked down between his legs when the bomb doors were open, he got a clear view of the ground below the aircraft. My take off therefore, was draughty, to say the least! This view downwards must have been handy on operations, as one could fly over the target until it could be seen directly below and then roll into the dive.

One afternoon while test flying a Blenheim from Karachi I found my route back to the airfield blocked by an odd looking cloud, something like a dust storm, reaching from ground level to several thousand feet. On flying through it, I realised it was an enormous swarm of locusts. It was like flying through a brown snow storm. (When flying through solid objects in the air, snowflakes, hailstorms or locusts, because of the relative speeds, they appear to approach the aircraft horizontally and at high speed. Makers of films about aircraft sometimes fail to realise this.) Very quickly the whole front of the aircraft became a mass of squashed locusts, making it difficult to see out of the windscreen. When we cleared the locust cloud I was able to regain some forward vision by opening the clear view panel and landed without trouble. The ground staff were not amused to see the mess the aircraft was in but from the engines came the most delightful smell of locusts cooking on the cylinders. I quite envied John the Baptist!

Early in January 1943 we started taking aircraft to the new MU at Jodhpur. This was just along the road, a mere 2 hours away. I went one morning with a convoy of Vengeances and a Hudson to bring us home. On arrival at Jodhpur I was number two to land in AN955, behind the first Vengeance. I settled into the approach, a comfortable distance behind number one, but as he touched down he flipped straight over on his back. Of course I opened up and went around again as the fire tender and ambulance came dashing across the airfield. The Jodhpur airfield had been extended to take heavier aircraft by building one runway that reached beyond the normal light aircraft landing area. This was now completely blocked by an aircraft upside down near the threshold. After about half an hour circling it became obvious that the crashed aircraft would not be moved for a long time, so I decided to land alongside the runway in the area normally used by Tiger Moths. Unfortunately, I didn't make a very good job of it. My approach was too fast and I should have opened up and had another shot, but foolishly I hung on and applied the brakes as soon as possible. It was by the grace of God we didn't have another Vengeance upside down on the airfield, for as I braked, the tail came up and we were nearly over. We were still doing about 30 mph when two 40 gallon oil drums flashed by on either side of the aircraft and we came to a bumpy halt, luckily with no damage done. It was thought that the crashed Vengeance had landed with the parking brake on. The pilot and the R/O were quite unhurt, which was very lucky, considering that they must have turned over at about 90 mph.

Around this time a fair number of aircraft, mainly Harvards and Hurricanes, were being moved into and out of Jodhpur. I went there as a test pilot to prepare the aircraft that had been in store. Jodhpur was being used as an overnight staging post, but as the unit was without experience in that line I gave the CO a paper drawing, mainly on my Takoradi route experience, showing how things could be improved for the aircrews. I intended to hand in a copy when I got back to Karachi but did not do so (a mistake, as will be seen later). Back at Karachi, a friend, Jack Strong, and I considered taking a short period of leave. He suggested that we wangle passages on a flying-boat to Cairo, stay on the houseboat 'Egypt' as 'ferry pilots' and, after a week or so, get ourselves an aircraft to ferry back to Karachi.

No sooner said than done. We requested passages for 'two ferry pilots' Karachi–Cairo and at the end of January 1943 were on our way. The trip proceeded as usual, except this time we alighted on the Dead Sea instead of Tiberius. Now this stretch of water is 1,200 feet below sea level and closely bordered on its western side by mountains more than 5,000 feet *above* sea level. Thus the ground drops away by about 6,000 feet over a distance of a mile or so. The flying-boat captain's way of approaching his Dead Sea alighting area was to follow a *wadi* (dried up river-bed) through the mountains, allowing his passengers to look the goats straight in the eye through the side windows. Then, when he came to the escarpment edge (which he could see but we couldn't) he chopped all four throttles and pushed the nose down to make his descent. To us, of course, it appeared as if all four engines had failed in the middle of the mountains. Incipient heart failure resulted amongst the passengers, especially those of us who were pilots.

The Dead Sea is very salty and as we took off again the aircraft was encrusted with the stuff.

In Cairo it was good to be in the houseboat Egypt again and we embarked on a very alcoholic few days, meeting old friends. Jack, being a New Zealander, introduced me to the wonderful chaps of the New Zealand Division (a number of whom were members of the Long Range Desert Group, who dashed around far behind enemy lines, shooting up camps and placing 'sticky bombs' on tanks and aircraft).

After a very enjoyable few days we called in at the Middle East Aircraft Delivery Unit and asked if they could find us an aircraft to fly back to Karachi. They obliged, but we had to go down to Khartoum by Dakota to pick up a Mk.V Blenheim which we took to Karachi via the South Arabian coast. We spent nights at Aden and Masirah Island. At Masirah we found no RAF at all – what had happened to the resident GR Squadron I can't remember. There was, however, a small unit of Arabian irregulars, who placed a guard on our aircraft and found a 'chowkidar' to unlock a primitive 'rest house' where we spent the night. We had to break into the aircraft's emergency ration pack for food, but luckily we were carrying a supply of whisky for our Karachi Mess, so we opened a bottle. This, combined with remarkably sweet cool water from a nearby well, gave us quite a memorable evening, sitting in the open under the Arabian stars.

The following day we had an uneventful three-hour flight to Karachi. While we had been away, changes had occurred there. A month or so earlier a Ferry Wing HQ had been formed in Karachi town. A Group Captain, newly out from the UK, had taken over and proceeded to build up a staff. Jack had always maintained that this was a 'bogus institution' and a prime example of empire building, and he found himself posted away to command the IAF EFTS at Secunderabad, near Hyderabad (Deccan). I was sucked into the new organisation as a staff officer, sitting behind a desk. I cannot remember that I achieved anything useful during my stay there, but one interesting experience did occur. With a Wing Commander and a Flight Lieutenant, both signal officers, the former a pilot, we took a Mk.IV Blenheim on a grand tour of India. I'm not quite sure what the object of the exercise was; many of the airfields we visited were unfinished, but we had a most enjoyable time. We called at Ahmadabad, Baragath, Nagpur (night stop), Raipur, Tilda, Jharsucra, Vizagaptam (N.S.) Cannavaram, Bangalore (N.S.), Madras, Colombo (N.S.), Trichinopoly, Cochin (N.S.), Bangalore (N.S.), Bombay and Karachi.

At some of the unoccupied airfields we had to fly low over the runways several times to clear them of people and animals. On landing we were often surrounded by an inquisitive crowd, and it was usually my job to stay with the aircraft to protect it, though sometimes there was the odd soldier or policeman to give a hand. At one stop an old man approached me.

"Why", he asked, speaking English in the Indian sing-song fashion, "do you need such big punkahs to keep you cool?" and pointed to the propellers.

At Colombo we landed at Ratmalana on a racecourse that had been turned into an aerodrome during the emergency. It was not long since it had been attacked by aircraft from a Japanese carrier force and it was still very much on a war footing. At Bangalore we used the Hindustan Aircraft Company's airfield. This was most interestingly camouflaged with tufts of some fabric-like material sprouting from the runway. Clearly they were expecting to suffer the same fate as had befallen Colombo. Incidentally, at Bangalore we used the most steeply undulating runway I have ever seen. From the take off position, one looked up a steep hill with only about 400 yards of runway visibility. What was happening over the brow was anyone's guess, and yours until you were doing 60-70 mph, when all was then revealed. Landing the other way, if one happened to reach the crest with rather too much speed, I imagine the chances of stopping were remote.

One day in the office at Karachi a fellow staff officer came in.

"I say…" he began, "we've had this jolly good report from W/C So-and-So at Jodhpur. He certainly knows how to run a staging post. The Groupie's very pleased with it."

He handed me a document. It was almost word for word the report I had handed in at Jodhpur, but this time it bore the OC Jodhpur's signature. I certainly had a lot to learn about the art of self advertisement!

By now a new airfield had opened at Mauripur, West of Karachi and the ferry unit moved there, now calling itself No.21 Ferry Control. I went back there in charge of training and spent a lot of time on Harvards, re-converting twin engine pilots onto single engine aircraft.

The first Beaufighters were starting to come through now and I was able to get a few flights in this most excellent aircraft. Using many parts from the earlier Beaufort, it had the much more powerful Hercules engines, which gave it the performance needed for its roles as night fighter, long-range day fighter and strike aircraft. It was very pleasant to fly, but the Mk.I had a tendency to swing on the landing run and could not always be completely held by brakes and rudder. Any tail wheel aircraft is unstable on the ground, the centre of gravity being aft of the main wheels. This means that once the aircraft has started to swing, without correction the situation rapidly deteriorates into a full ground loop. An aircraft of this type was best held straight on its landing run first by coarse application of rudder. If this was insufficient then brake was applied to the appropriate wheel. In most British aircraft of that time the brakes were pneumatic and worked differentially with the rudder controls, i.e. with the rudder, central brake pressure was fed equally to both main wheels; with full port rudder, the pressure was applied to the port wheel only. The amount of brake pressure applied was controlled by a hand lever on the control column. In most cases these pneumatic brakes were not over powerful, and it was possible to get into a situation, say when landing on a runway in a cross-wind, when after full rudder and brake had been applied, the aircraft still continued to swing. The only other corrective action available to the pilot in a twin engine aircraft was to open up the engine on the inside of the swing. This, of course, was not desirable as the object of the landing run is to kill an aircraft's speed, and opening up an engine has the opposite effect. In addition, large aero engines do not instantly respond when the throttle is advanced and it was easy for the pilot to over correct and find himself swinging in the opposite direction. This, in fact, happened to an unfortunate pilot at Karachi about this time. He found his Beaufighter swinging, applied full rudder, then brake, then engine. After a slight hesitation the power came on with a roar and the resultant opposite swing wiped off the under carriage. In later marks of Beaufighter greater stability was provided by giving the tail plane 12% of dihedral and extending the dorsal fin forward along the fuselage to form a fillet.

I also had the chance of getting in a few hours on the Dakota. As is well known, this famous aircraft was descended from the DC2s and DC3s that first flew in the early 1930s. Truly the ancestor of the modern airliner, this all-metal low-wing monoplane, with retractable undercarriage, wing flaps and constant speed propellers, set a pattern that was followed with the addition of the nose wheel undercarriage, until the introduction of the 'big jets' in the 1950s. Needless to say, the 'Dak' was a beautiful aircraft to fly and did fine work in South East Asia Command, as we were learning to call it, in general transport and supply dropping and flying cargo 'over the hump' to China. Of this an amusing story was told.

It was the habit of the defending Chinese fighters to look closely at Dakotas approaching from the West, as the Japs had, after their fashion, produced a copy of the DC3 for their own purposes. One US Dakota crew had adopted a small tame bear as a mascot and often used to take the animal flying. On one occasion, as they were approaching Chinese-held territory, they put the bear in the test pilot's seat of their 'Dak', engaged 'George' (the auto-pilot) and ducked down out of sight. An investigating fighter came alongside to take a close look and saw the US Dakota apparently being flown by a bear with no one else aboard. Presumably he swallowed his cigar and gave up the hard stuff for the duration!

In July 1943 I was sent to command the Ferry Unit at Asansol in Bengal. I flew there in a Mk.V Blenheim EH399 via Ahmedabad, Bophal and Allahabad. Asansol was, and probably is, a somewhat unattractive place. Take a large Indian city and add coal mining and heavy industry and you have a recipe for environmental disaster. We were in the local gymkhana club one evening and a visiting American was sounding off at the bar about the delights of Asansol.

"I guess," he said, "this must be the asshole of the world."

"Mmm…" responded a nearby urbane Englishman, "I suppose you're just passing through?"

This ranks high on my "I wish I'd said that" list.

My stay at Asansol was not a long one. I had been hoping for a posting to a Blenheim squadron and had been assured that, although I had not attended a Bomber OTU, with my experience on the aircraft, I had a good chance if I applied. Accordingly, some months previously I had done so. What I had forgotten was that before this, word had come down from Delhi that there was a shortage of flying instructors in India and asking for suitable names. Thinking, I suppose, that this might be a useful skill to acquire (correct), I allowed my name to go forward. This was the posting that came through, to an Instructor's Course at No.1 SFTS, Ambala.

I duly proceeded there by train.

13. *Instructors*

Ambala lies just over 100 miles north of Delhi in the Punjab, quite close to the foothills of the Himalayas. I did my course on Harvards and Tiger Moths. A pilot with 1,000 hours flying on 15 types of aircraft is very inclined to hold an inflated opinion of his ability. An instructor's course is an excellent way of providing much needed deflation. He is brought face to face with the fact that he is a pretty rough pilot with a number of bad habits. Ambala was an SFTS taking pupils from the two Indian EFTSs – No.1 at Secunderabad and No.2 at Jodhpur. The first real flying instructor's school was established by the legendary Smith-Barry at Gosport, towards the end of the First World War. Here a standard form of instruction was developed with a form of 'patter' that was first handed down by word of mouth and latterly, when the expansion of the RAF started in the later 1930s, was formalised and incorporated in *Air Publication 1732*. This was updated from time to time and in 1943 was established as the flying instructor's 'bible'. Perhaps it still is. I noticed at once that pre-flight briefing was an essential part of the teaching, and contrasted this with my experiences at Gatwick four years earlier.

One interesting experiment was carried out at Ambala while I was there. Ab initio pupils were taken and given instructions on Harvards at night only. Eventually they were sent solo, having never flown by day. There was, I suppose, little practical value in this experiment, except that pilots involved were not quite as prone to put day-flying and night-flying in separate mental compartments, as were the rest of us who had been trained more conventionally.

As a qualified flying instructor I was posted to No.1 EFTS at Secunderabad, where Jack Strong was CO. Secunderabad was the cantonment or military suburb of Hyderabad, the capital of India's principle princely state. The Nizam of Hyderabad was said at that time to be the richest man in the world. The story was told that earlier in the century, in the days of the 1943 Nizam's father, trouble arose in the state and it was thought advisable to load as much of the ruler's wealth as possible onto lorries in case the need to quickly evacuate arose. The trouble died down but these lorry loads of gold and jewels represented such a small proportion of the Nizam's wealth that they remained untouched in the Palace garages. This story was almost certainly apocryphal, but served to illustrate the Nizam's lofty financial status.

The EFTS was located at the civil airport, which had a small, quite handsome, whitewashed airport building. There was living accommodation for staff and pupils in this building, as well as a control tower that housed a small civilian air traffic control staff, employed by the state. The staff and pupils' mess was in a temporary building fifty yards from the tower and the two hangars. A small block provided administrative and technical offices. It was quite a compact set-up, forming part of the RAF Station, which also included a reception centre for recruits and a school for MT drivers. Our pupils were taken in as officer cadets and came to us after a short induction course at Poona. They were very much from the upper-crust of Indian society and included Hindus, Moslems, Sikhs, Parsees and Anglo-Indians. Only a minority of them were fired with a burning desire to get at the enemy, but they did like the idea of a commission, a smart uniform with wings on their breast and, if possible, a job in AHQ!

I remember meeting one of the Indian Officers I had known at Karachi and asking him how some of our mutual acquaintances among his countrymen were getting on. Oh, X was doing very well, a Squadron Leader in Delhi, and so was Y, he had the adjutant's job at Pindi.

"What about Z?" I ventured.

"Oh, he made a terrible mistake; he went to an operational squadron and got killed!"

I suppose one cannot blame them for their lack of enthusiasm for a cause that most of them thought of as only marginally their own. Exceptions to this were the Sikhs, a warlike lot who could not wait to get their hands on the Japs. Unfortunately, many of them found learning to fly very difficult. I remember one young Sikh, having broken a Tiger Moth on one of his early solo flights, begging his Flight Commander to allow him to stay on the course. His father, he said, had plenty of money and would pay for the aeroplane.

If my memory serves me right, in ascending order of ability, our pupils lined up something like this: Sikhs followed by Hindus, then Muslims, then Parsees and best of all, the Anglo-Indians (those of mixed European/Indian race). When I became a Flight Commander and could pick my own pupils from the course list, I notice that my log book is filled with names like Peters, Snell, Yardley, Springett, Cunningham and so on. The Anglos showed much the same aptitude as RAF pupils at home, but I suppose it is not surprising that the others, with their lack of a western-type of mechanical background, should have had more difficulty. Of course they all spoke English fluently and no doubt this language was in many cases the only common one amongst the pupils, coming as they did from all parts of India. Nevertheless, English was in some cases a second language to them, and pupils learning to fly have problems enough without language being one of them. I recall a passing out parade soon after I arrived at Secunderabad, where the CO had foolishly included, as a separate squad, a number of pupils who had not made the grade and were awaiting disposal instructions.

"Who are they?" demanded the AOC.

He was told.

"Give them another five hours in their mother tongue," he instructed.

Now two problems arose here. Firstly, did any of our instructors speak the 'mother tongues' involved, and secondly, if they did, could they translate the technical terms used in flying instruction? For example, it may be that the only translation of "open the throttle" would be "make the oxen go faster"! I don't remember the experiment achieving anything.

The training was divided into two stages, the 'ab initio' stage carried out in 'B' Flight, and the 'advanced' stage in 'A' Flight. I was concerned with the first stage during the whole of my time at Secunderabad and that suited me well, as my main interest lay in turning raw pupils (very raw in some cases) into safe Tiger Moth pilots. This process took about six weeks and then they went on to 'A' Flight for a further six weeks, for the polish to be applied.

'B' Flight flew from 7am until 9am and again from 5pm to 7pm. This was to enable the least experienced pupils to fly in the less turbulent part of the day. The advanced flight flew from 9am until 1pm. There was no work in the afternoons so we all retired to our charpoys (beds). When not flying, the pupils attended ground lectures. Flying was only rarely held up by bad weather and when it was, strong winds were most often the trouble. These could blow up very suddenly and, if there were a number of Tiger Moths airborne, with maybe some pupils solo, things could get quite exciting. The Tiger Moth stalls at around 45mph, so landing in winds of over 30mph could be quite a problem. The secret was to approach dead into wind, put the wheels on the ground with the power still on and keep the tail up until the wing tips had been grabbed by waiting ground staff.

I remember one evening, checking the windsock and taxiing to the take off point. On lining up, as I thought into wind, I noticed pieces of grass, paper etc. being blown past me in the direction I was facing. A sudden squall had turned the wind through 180 degrees and doubled its strength. I called to my pupil to get out and grab a wing tip and there I sat not daring to turn across wind until several more pairs of hands were available to help.

Of course the climax of an instructors work is sending his pupil on his first solo. We did not adopt the common practise of giving an independent check before solo unless the instructor was very inexperienced. When I considered a pupil was ready and the weather was satisfactory, wind not too strong and in a good direction, I would take him out and make him do two or three circuits and landings. I would place my hands on the crash pad at the front of my cockpit so that he could see that he was 'on his own'. If all went well and he made no mistakes, I would ask him to follow through on the controls while I did a couple of landings, and would instruct him to take over control if he thought all was not well. I would, say, hold off at 10 feet, or bounce the wheels and do a kangaroo hop, or again overshoot or undershoot. If the pupil took over confidently and smoothly and took the correct action, which for a beginner was, in every case to open the throttle fully and climb away to do another approach, then I would stop the aircraft at the up wind boundary, climb out, secure my straps and remove the front control column. A word of encouragement and off he would go to do one circuit and landing. We had long fabric streamers and these would be attached to the rear interplane struts to warn other aircraft that here was a first soloist, to be given a wide berth. It was quite a nerve-racking experience to watch your man as he took off, ("For God's sake keep the b---- thing straight"), and floated round the circuit, ("not too high you fool"), coming to the point across wind where he should close the throttle and start his glide approach. Then the phut, phut of the throttled back Gipsy and the swirl of the air past the struts and wires ("God he's got far too much speed"). Nine first solo's out of ten result in perfect landings and a mistake smoothly and confidently corrected is no disgrace, although it may play havoc with the instructor's nerves.

Our instructors were from both the RAF and the I.A.F. on about a 50/50 basis. The standard of the Indian instructors was very high. I particularly recall Arthur Chitumber, Chief Instructor of the Calcutta Flying Club in pre-war days I believe. It was Arthur who allowed his pupil to spin off his final gliding turn in, to land at 500ft. cooly recovering with 100 ft. or so to spare. The lad was reluctant to apply enough bank in the turn, handling the aircraft round with rudder and holding the nose up by pulling the stick back, thus allowing the airspeed to drop. So all the requirements for spinning were present and Arthur only had to apply a little more rudder and hold the stick back a little more firmly, and bingo, away she went. I do not suppose that pupil made the same mistake again, but I do know that the performance was a little hard on the nerves of those of us who were watching.

Our M.O. at Secunderabad was named Agit Singh, a Captain in the Indian Medical Service. He suggested that he could deal with our pupils more effectively if he did a bit of flying himself, so we put him through the complete course, solo flying and all, quite unofficially. About half way though my stay at Secunderabad, the Unit establishment was changed from a Squadron Leader C.O. who was also C.F.I., to a Wing Commander C.O. and a Squadron Leader C.F.I. Wing Commander Wilson came up from Lord Louis Mountbatten's H.Q. at Candy to take over. A month or two later a friend of the Wing Commander's, also from Candy, came on a visit while on leave, Surgeon Captain Birt R.N. He asked if he could do a bit of flying, so the C.O. agreed. "Give him dual but no, positively no solo". After a week or so, one quiet Sunday morning, Jack Strong, who had been flying with the Captain, said, "Give him a thorough check, and if he's O.K. send him solo, but not a word to the C.O." All went well and the Captain did a neat solo circuit and landing. We said nothing about it, and whether Birt ever told his friend, I never found out. By strange coincidence Captain Birt's father ran the chemist's shop in Devizes, where my father, a local G.P., obtained many of his drugs.

A group of EFTS instructors at Secunderabad in 1944.

Another visitor, also named Birt, was a friend of mine from Grantham days. Mike Birt, by now a Squadron Leader, wrote and asked if he could stay with us for a while whilst he was on sick leave. He was Flight Commander of a Beaufighter Squadron at the Burma front, and while returning from a sortie, had been badly wounded in the hand by fire from the ground. As he had several hundred miles still to go to clear enemy held territory, he asked his Wireless Operator to give him a shot of morphine from the aircraft's first aid kit, but the W/Op. was unable to operate the ampule properly, and the drug was not injected. "Luckily" said our M.O., as it would very likely have rendered Mike incapable of flying the aircraft, and that would have been that. As it was, he put up with the pain, and landed safely at base, minus a couple of fingers on his left hand. Although the hand was in plaster, we let Mike amuse himself in a Tiger when he felt inclined.

In addition to our Tiger Moths we had Anson LT151 to give the pupils navigation practice and Harvard FE317 to make life more interesting for us. We also used the Anson for general communication duties and I recall taking a soldier with a damaged eye to Madras for hospital treatment and the C.O. to Coimbatore for his leave in the Nilgiri Hills. On one occasion, a number of us piled in to the Anson and went to Bombay for a jolly weekend (no rubbish about prohibition in those days).

After a time our Harvard was taken away and replaced with Fairchild Cornell FZ372; an odd little aeroplane, very much on the lines of a Magister. We were asked to report on its suitability as a replacement for our Moths. Surprisingly, although fitted with a six-cylinder Ranger engine of 175/200hp, the performance was disappointing, in fact, with its big flaps lowered its rate of climb away from a baulked landing was dangerously poor. (I see from reference books that its performance was inferior to the Magister in almost every respect.) So we could not recommend 'the cornflake' as we dubbed it, for use on our airfield (admittedly 1,700 ft above sea level), although I understand that it was used in both Canada and Rhodesia, where the airfields must, in some cases, have been as high, but perhaps not as hot.

So life went on in our quiet backwater as the stirring events of 1943 and 1944 unfolded. I'm sure most of us felt the way I did, with a sense of frustration at being away from the real war, but I at any rate, had learned the futility of kicking against the pricks. We had a very pleasant little mess, with an Indian chef who was good at curry, and whose idea of writing a menu had us in fits. 'Fleds Beef' was fairly straight forward, but what about a savoury called 'Angels on arseback'! Our main drink was 'Parry's Navy Gin' made in Madras, quite passable, if a little scented, when made up with a 'John Collins' and fresh limes. There was also 'whisky' and 'brandy' made in Hyderabad. We understood that these consisted of the same alcohol base, mixed with flavouring and dye to give them their character. No one who wanted to retain his eyesight touched them. Australian beer was sometimes available at the little cafe in the hills, near the airfield, at six rupees a bottle, a sinful price for those days, nearly 50p.

In March 1944, Buck Taylor the burly Rhodesian 'B' Flight Commander left for home and I took over. He got on very well with the Indian instructors and they used to tell him that after the war they would come and visit him in Salisbury. "You know", Buck would say, "they're wonderful fellows, but I couldn't invite them into my house at home". In pre war days the colour bar in Rhodesia was as strong as it was to the South in the Union.

Some amusing incidents stuck in the mind. I remember a conversation with an I.A.F. Flying Officer who had come on our course. (A few pupils came to us from other branches of the I.A.F. and not straight from civilian life). "How", he asked on being shown round the aircraft on the first day, "does the aircraft move along the ground?" "Well", came the answer, "you open the throttle until it starts to move, and then throttle back slightly to stop it gathering speed too quickly". "Yes", he replied, "but as there is no driving shaft between the engine and the wheels, what makes the aircraft move?" Complete collapse of young flying instructor, as they used to put it in 'Punch'. On another occasion a young Sikh flying solo (not one of my pupils, I'm glad to say) was at the point in his landing when he should have checked the glide, to fly level with the ground. The main wheels and the nose cowling hit the ground at the same time. A somewhat shaken young Indian was extricated from the wreckage quite unhurt. "What on earth happened?" asked his instructor. "Oh!" replied the young man, "I knew I had either to move the stick back or push it forward, but I forgot which!"

After an engine failure on one occasion, a pupil made a very creditable forced landing on the midan near Hyderabad. He climbed out of the undamaged aircraft, found a policeman to stand guard, and went off to telephone the aerodrome. Quite naturally, he was feeling pleased with himself until, on looking back, he saw to his horror that his aircraft was in flames. He rushed back to it, but there was nothing he could do and it was totally destroyed. What on earth had happened? No one could make it out, until that is, an old man reported to the hospital with burns on his hands. How had he got them? Well, when the 'big bird' came down from the sky on to the midan, he took his young grandson to look at it. He noticed water dripping from a place under the front, so he went over to wash his hands. Suddenly everything caught fire and he ran away. Was he smoking at the time? No, he had taken the rolled up leaf out of his mouth and had thrown it in the wet patch under the big bird to put it out. The young man and the policeman had said "no smoking".

We used to send our pupils to an airfield at Bidar, about an hour's flight N.W. of Secunderabad for their cross country flight, and soon after my arrival I was asked to take an R.E. Captain there to check on some construction work that had been done. Like many other airfields in India at that time, Bidar had been built for the military, but was not actually in use. I suppose it was there in case of a Jap invasion of the Indian East Coast. So after landing we were on our own, and to get started again I had to swing the prop, after explaining to the Captain how to handle the throttle and switches. I slaved away swinging the propeller with out getting a kick from the engine. The Gypsy Major has an inertia system incorporated in the magnets, and as you turn the prop a spring coiled and released with an audible click, providing a spark at the critical moment. 'Nay click hi', as the Indian mechanics put it, then it was 'nay click engine start hi' as well. At Bidar that afternoon it was 'nay click hi' and no amount of bashing the relevant part of the mag. with a stone (standard corrective practise), would produce one. So we sent an interested onlooker for a gharry, went into town, rang Secunderabad and told them of our problem. It was too late to do anything that day, so they said they would send someone out in the morning. Next stop was the Government guest house which the chokidar was very pleased to open up for us. On then to the railway station where a bottle of Bell's was obtained from the buffet, and so back to the guest house for a shower, the Bell's, and a most excellent chicken curry. The guest house was most spectacularly situated on an escarpment, with a balcony looking out over the surrounding countryside. It was quite a memorable evening.

In the morning we breakfasted on the balcony. We watched the blue smoke rising from the villages far below. There dot like figures fanned out from their houses into the surrounding bush, to squat and answer their calls of nature, each with his little brass pot of water, a practise that must have remained unchanged for thousands of years. Our relief aircraft arrived that morning with an engineer on board. He soon produced a 'click' and we were off home.

As was standard practice in India, we each had our own bearer (or personal servant). Mine was Anthony, and I remember Jack Strong's was a magnificently moustached character called Sammy. These bearers became very attached to their Sahibs and were paid 30 rupees a month (about £2.25) which to them was a very good wage. One's bearer would act as a cross between a valet and a personal butler, and was in a position of considerable power, as he was able to hand out contracts for the Sahib's dhobi (laundry) and the supply of firewood for heating water, and of course, to take his cut. In large service Messes the bearers would line the walls of the dining room at meal times, waiting for their Sahib to appear. They would then serve him and him alone. This would seem to be a very great waste of manpower, but that has no meaning in India.

The RAF at this time laid down four years as the normal over-seas tour, but service in certain areas, West Africa for one, counted double. This meant that my six months in Takoradi counted as a year, and in November 1944 I was posted home. I was given a nicely alcoholic send-off, which finished on the station platform, with Anthony, my bearer, near to tears. As it happens, the railway line to Bombay passes close by the aero-drome at Begumpet, so they gave the train a mild 'beat up' with a formation of Tigers.

The transit camp at Bombay comprised a number of bunga-lows in a residential part of the city (commandeered for the purpose). We were quite comfortable there but not unnaturally, were chiefly interested in the harbour, watching the troopships with an eagle eye. If you had to spend a few days kicking your heels, you could do worse in those days than to be in Bombay. As an added bonus to those of us interested in cricket, a match was taking place while we were there, the Cricket Club of India XI (equivalent to our M.C.C.) v a Service XI. In the club side were both Nyadu brothers, C.K. and C.S. and several other well known names. The Services included D.C.S.Compton (no less), Peter Cranmer (Warwickshire C.C.C. Captain and England Rugby centre threequarters), and Peter Judge of Glamorgan. As Service officers we were accorded honorary membership of the C.C.I., and were able to watch this match at the Bradbourne Stadium in some comfort. There was for instance, a perfect view of the cricket while leaning on the bar, and ordering a 'John Collins'. It was while we were watching this match that the buzz went round that a troop convoy had entered the harbour, and very soon we were embarked on H.M.T. *Multan* bound for home. We disembarked at Suez; travelled overland to Port Said over the Christmas period 1944, and re embarked on the 'Cape-town Castle'.

Things were very different now from the dark days of 1941, when I had been travelling in the opposite direction. The Mediterranean was now cleared of Axis forces and the U-Boat menace in the Atlantic beaten. Victory was clearly in the air as we sailed into Liverpool Bay and home.

14. *Home Again*

After a short leave I received my posting instructions to No.53 OTU at Kirton-in-Lindsay, Lincolnshire. My previous experience had been so varied that I didn't know, until I saw the aircraft dispersed round the airfield, that I had been posted to fly Spitfires. This pleased me greatly. The OTU was based on two airfields; Hibaldstow and Kirton itself. The training was in three stages. Stage one, flying from Hibaldstow, comprised some twenty hours familiarisation on the Spitfire Mk.Vb. In stage two, also from Hibaldstow, another twenty hours were spent on gunnery and bombing, and the final twenty hours, from Kirton, covered formation flying, tactics and night flying. For the first stage we lived at Kirton and flew from Hibaldstow. For the second, we lived and flew from Hibaldstow, and for the third we lived and flew from Kirton.

Kirton Lindsey was a pre war 'expansion' type station. That is, it was built in the mid 1930s when it became clear that the 'war to end wars' had done no such thing, and the British Government was forced to take its collective head out of the sand. Most people who have served in the RAF will recall this type of station with some affection. Solidly built of red brick, once you had found your way around one, you knew them all. The Officers' Mess, Sergeants' Mess, Airmen's blocks, SHQ, Sick quarters, hangars, all dominated by a tall brick water tower, were a pleasant change from the wooden shacks and Nissen huts that proliferated during the war. The buildings were fine, the only snag was that such stations were sited in the dear old far-off days when Heyfords, Harts, Furies and Gauntlets rode the skies.

These needed a maximum of 1000 yards of well-drained grass to operate, so the best place for their airfields was on high ground. So the RAF's new airfields in Lincolnshire were built in the spine of high (well, high for Lincolnshire) ground running north and south through Lincoln. With the coming of the war and the need to operate much heavier aircraft in all weathers, 1,000 yards of grass would no longer do, 2,000 yards of concrete were now needed. In some cases (at Waddington and Scampton for instance) there was room for this expansion. In the case of Kirton there was not. So it remained a small grass airfield and its fine permanent buildings were largely wasted.

My fellow students on the course were a mixed bunch. Most were fairly experienced and from a variety of non-operational flying jobs. A number had spent the last year or so helping to train army glider pilots by towing their little Hotspurs with Miles Masters from Shobdon in the border country of Wales. Another group consisted of young Free French pilots completing the last phase of their training. After breakfast on the first morning at Kirton we were piled into one of those familiar RAF buses and driven the few miles to Hibaldstow. Here we were introduced to the legendary Supermarine Spitfire.

As all students of aviation history know, the Spitfire was the only allied aircraft to remain in front line service before, throughout, and after the war. Admittedly, the Griffon engined Mk.24 was a very different beast from the Mk.1 of 1936, nevertheless, the ancestry was clear for all to see. Our Spitfires were Mk.Vs, a version which first entered the service in 1941, to enable the RAF to compete on equal terms with the Luftwaffe's new Fw 190s and the Bf 109Fs and G's. By 1945 therefore, they were a bit long in the tooth, but I have heard it said that the Mark V was the most enjoyable of all the Spits to fly.

The first day was spent in learning the cockpit. I see in my Log Book a whole page of certificates of proficiency, a far cry from the 'quick cockpit check and off' that was the custom at Karachi. Then the next day there was a dual check on a Miles Master, with the emphasis on the curving approach to the runway advisable on the Spitfire, because of the poor visibility over the nose on the approach and landing. The Master had first appeared as an advanced trainer in 1938, powered by a Rolls Royce Kestral engine. This gave it the speed of 225 mph. The Mk. II appeared in 1939, with a Bristol Mercury, and in 1940 came the Mk. III with a Pratt and Witney Wasp. No.53 O.T.U. had Mks. II and III. After the brief thirty minutes dual in the Master came two blank days, and then on the 27th February 1945, my first flight in a Spitfire.

At Hibaldstow I had my first experience of WAAF Aircraft Mechanics. In 1941 there had been plenty of them as clerks in the Officers' Mess, but to find them around dispersal, looking after the aircraft, was a new experience. It was at Hibaldstow, a few weeks before our arrival that a W.A.A.F. was taken round the circuit on a Spitfire, and I say 'on' advisedly. It was well reported in the national press at the time and has been since. It was the custom for an airman (or airwoman) to ride on the tail of a Spitfire as it taxied out to the runway for take off. There had been cases of aircraft tipping onto their nose when taxiing, due to gusty conditions, aggravated perhaps, by harsh use of the brakes. The rider on the tail would, of course, slip off as the aircraft paused on the taxi track before turning onto the runway. On this occasion the tail riding W.A.A.F. failed to jump off, perhaps the pilot was in a hurry. Spitfire engines tended to overheat on the ground. Anyway, the aircraft was gathering speed on the runway with the girl still riding on the tail. She was now in the classical predicament of the man hanging on to a tethering rope of a rising airship - if he fails to let go before a certain height, he can no longer do so. By the time the girl realised that the aircraft was no longer taxiing, but was taking off, the speed was too high for her to drop off. She, therefore, had no alternative but to wrap herself around the fin and tail plane and hang on for dear life. Almost at once, the pilot must have realised that something was amiss. By the time he had got the throttle fully open he would have found that the tail was not coming up as usual. I suspect that the aircraft would have become airborne much too early in a tail down attitude. The pilot's first reaction would be that he had taken off with the tail trimmer wound fully back. By the time he had wound the wheel fully forward, and still found the aircraft very tail heavy, it would be too late to abandon his take off. I imagine he would probably have had to use two hands on the stick to hold it forward, to prevent the aircraft climbing and stalling. If the passenger had fallen off at this point, there is little doubt that the aircraft would have dived straight into the ground. It is remarkable that the Spitfire could fly at all, with the C of G so far back and the interference of the airflow over the tail surfaces, which must have reduced the effectiveness of the elevators. Anyway, one presumes that the pilot would by now have been told by the Control Tower what had happened, and a startled glance in his rear view mirror would have provided confirmation. There was now nothing for it but to fly round the circuit and make the smoothest landing possible. The aircraft was landed and brought to a stop with the, by now, extremely frozen W.A.A.F. (it was January or early February remember), still wrapped round the tail surfaces. The press reported that she simply jumped to the ground and suggested that they all go over to the N.A.F.F.I. wagon for a cup of tea. I imagine the pilot felt like something a good deal stronger!

Anyway, back to my first Spitfire flight. I had of course, experienced the rumble and thump of the Merlin engine while flying Hurricanes, so when the engine was started the effect was quite familiar. What was not quite so familiar was the long nose cowling stretching up and away and quite blocking any forward view. This made taxiing difficult, as the nose had to be swung from side to side to ensure that all was clear forward. Taxiing was not made any easier by the narrow track of the under carriage, made necessary by a retraction system which folded the wheels outwards into the wing (a feature also shared by the Bf 109). I had not used V.H.F. R.T. (Radio/ Telephone) before, so the experience of talking freely with the Control Tower was a new one for me. Permission obtained to line up on the runway, I slowly opened the throttle, feeling the familiar surge that takes over from rest to 100 mph in about ten seconds. There seemed to be no trouble keeping straight, and when the tail came up, the visibility over the long nose was just fine. She flew herself off the ground and then came the change hands bit. You see the lever operating the under-carriage retraction was on the right of the cockpit, and the throttle control was on the left. This meant taking the left hand off the throttle to hold the stick while the right hand operated the under-carriage lever. As the elevators on the Spitfire were very sensitive, it was common to see aircraft doing a porpoise act as the undercarriage started to retract.

First impressions were very favourable. The only single-seaters I had flown previously were Hurricanes and Mohawks. This was a very different experience. The only snag was the weather. Misty, with 8/8th cloud (I seem to remember we used to say 10/10th in those days), at about 1,500 ft. I flew up the canal past Brigg to the Humber, and then up and down the estuary for some time, getting used to the feel of the controls and just enjoying the Spitfire. Back at Hibaldstow, after about an hour, I joined the circuit, made the approved type of curving Spitfire approach and she settled herself on the runway like a thoroughbred. I do not recall ever making a bad landing in a Spitfire, everything seemed so 'right' all the time. Later the same day I had another flight, one and a half hours, marked in my log book as 'Sector Recco', which means, just having a look round the local area.

The next week or so was spent in becoming thoroughly familiar with the Spitfire, aerobatics, climbing to 30,000 ft., cross county navigation exercises and practice homeings. This enabled two or three ground stations to take a bearing on the aircraft. These bearings were passed to the tower, where they were plotted on a chart. The point where the bearings crossed was the aircraft's position. The controller could then pass a course for base. This system, clumsy though it seems compared with modern systems, worked quite well, but the number of aircraft that could be handled at one time was very limited.

Towards the end of this phase we practiced flight formation flying, led by an Instructor. These formation flights often finished with a 'tail chase'. This was an exciting exercise in which the aircraft formed 'long line astern' with say, 100 yards separation. The leader then climbed, dived, turned and carried out all kinds of aerobatics, to be repeated exactly by the following aircraft. After about two weeks we passed on to the second stage of training. We moved out of the comfortable Kirton Mess and into the Hibaldstow Nissen Huts. The Spitfires now were the clipped wing version of the Mk.V. On these aircraft the span was reduced by just over three feet, and the wing tips squared off. The object was, I believe, to improve the low-level performance, and the aircraft looked very business like, though perhaps not quite as handsome as the original.

We now turned to armament training, air to air and air to ground firing, dive bombing with practice bombs. The ranges for air to ground firing and bombing were just off Spern Head, while the air to air firing took place out to sea off the Point. We fired at the usual drogues, towed by a tug version of the Master, the Martinet. Some of the Spitfires were armed with the usual .303 Brownings. I can't recall how many, but not, I think, the full eight, while others had two 20 mm. cannons. I had one abortive detail on the latter type, abortive because one cannon jammed after about two rounds, and the yawing caused by firing the other one (they were of course mounted in the wings clear of the airscrew disc) made a steady aim impossible. Quite a number of our exercises were carried out with camera gun only, and one's films were then analysed and criticised by an Instructor. Anyone who has fired at a moving target knows it is necessary to allow deflection i.e. to aim ahead of the target so that it and the round(s) arrive at the same point in space at the same time. In this the gunner has been aided from the earliest days of air fighting by a bead and ring sight. The size of the ring would be governed by the speed at which the target could be expected to be travelling, and the velocity of the shot. This size was so arranged that in the case of a full deflection shot, (with the target travelling at 90 degrees to the attacker), a full ring's deflection was needed.

In the late 1930s a refinement to this simple ring and bead was introduced, the reflection-sight. In this, the ring and bead were projected in light on to a small glass screen, and could only be seen if the gunner's head was in the correct position. In addition, the diameter of the ring was adjustable to give an indication of correct firing range, according to the type of aircraft being attacked. This still left the gunner to judge the correct deflection, and some of the best pilots proved to be the worst shots and vice versa. The final refinement, introduced during the war, was the gyro gunsight. This was fitted to our Spitfires. Clearly, if a target is moving very fast across the sight, the gun must also move fast to hold the correct deflection. If the gun is fixed to an aircraft, then the aircraft must be held in a steep turn to achieve this. The steeper the turn the greater the 'G' force, so if the sight could be made sensitive to 'G', then it could automatically register the required reflection. As anyone who has done the simplest school-boy physics knows a spinning gyro will react to a turning movement in direct ratio to its magnitude. The sight, controlled by a gyro, could be made to register automatically the correct deflection. So, all the pilot had to do with the gyro gun sight was to hold the bead on the target and the sight took care of the deflection. All this scientific help did not make air to air firing a foolproof matter, and, as in many other things, 'there's many a slip!'

We also practiced dive bombing, using an off shore target. The Spitfire was not an ideal aircraft for this exercise, as with its clean lines and absence of dive rakes, it picked up speed very quickly when going down hill. I see from my Log Book that my best effort produced an average error of 97 yards for eight bombs, so I imagine a few fell quite a bit closer than that.

With the armament phase of the course completed, the final two or three weeks were spent once more at Kirton in tactical training, formation flying, in flights as a squadron, dog fighting and ground attacks. Following the pattern of the air war being waged on the Continent at that time, great stress was placed on the latter. In fact, we had to be warned off making our attacks on trains and motor traffic too realistic, as we were frightening the life out of people on the ground. It was at this time that I came within an ace of killing myself, and was only saved by the wonderfully safe flying characteristics of the Spitfire.

As I have said, the engine tended to over heat on the ground, so when waiting for a formation to get together, it was sometimes necessary to get airborne and wait in the air rather than on the ground. On this occasion we were lined up on the grass at Kirton for a formation take off, waiting for the last couple of aircraft to come out of dispersal. My rad. temperature was hovering around the 130 degrees C mark and little puffs of steam were coming from the vent on the engine cowling. I therefore decided to get airborne and wait up there. Wheels retracted, I was climbing away when looking back I saw the rest of the formation beginning to move across the grass on their take off run. Then I did the most idiotic thing. I throttled back at about 500 ft. to allow the others to catch up. Any pilot will know that this was a quite suicidal procedure. The aircraft, still in the climbing attitude, lost speed and approached the stall. At this point I owed my life to R.J. Mitchell, for instead of flicking over into a spin, the dear old Spit stayed on an even keel, losing height and vibrating violently. This may seem unbelievable but, for what seemed like an age and was probably only a few seconds, I sat wondering if the aircraft could be landed on the fields below in that condition. Sanity then returned and I slammed the throttle open, eased the stick forward and returned to the world of rational flying. People on the ground said that my aircraft actually disappeared below the level of the airfield (Kirton is, of course, on high ground), but I don't think I ever let on what had actually happened.

At the end of the course the posting lists were announced. Most of us were destined for 2nd Tactical Air Force (2nd T.A.F.), supporting the armies now pushing across the German border, but first we needed to go to Aston Down in Gloucestershire to convert to Hawker Typhoons. The Typhoon looked, and had been, a brute of an aircraft. Weighing nearly twice as much as the Hurricane, from the same stable, its Napier Sabre sleeve valve engine produced twice the power of the Hurricane's Merlin. The 'Tiffey' first flew in early 1940, but teething troubles delayed its introduction into the service, and it was not until late 1941 that it first saw action. Even then it was dogged by persistent engine airframe troubles. The Sabre engine was chronically unreliable, not a happy characteristic in an aircraft whose main operational task involved crossing and re-crossing the English Channel. However, in the event of engine failure over land, the pilot had the advantage of sitting behind a most effective bulldozer of an engine, capable of demolishing stone walls, or even houses, as if they were cardboard. However by 1945, after its early failure as a general purpose fighter, due to poor high altitude performance, the Typhoon had established itself in the role for which it became famous, as a most effective ground attack fighter. It carried up to 2,000 lbs of bombs (twice the load of the twin engined Blenheim, with which Bomber Command started the war), or most effectively of all, eight 60 lb rocket projectiles. It was said that even when these rockets missed a tank (which, after all, presented a very small target), they scared the living daylights out of the crews, so much so, that the sight of approaching Typhoons was often enough to make tank crews bale out wholesale. By the time I came upon the Typhoon, the engine and air frame problems were largely solved, and I enjoyed flying this most impressive aircraft.

This was my first experience of the cartridge starter for aero engines. The problem of engine starting had been approached in many ways since engines became too big to be turned over by hand by one man. There was the idea of the chain of men pulling on a rope attached to a bag over an airscrew blade. Then there was the 'Hucks' Starter'. This consisted of a Model 'T' Ford in similar chassis with a vertical drive shaft taken from the gearbox up to a horizontal shaft, projecting forward at airscrew level. A dog on this shaft engaged with a corresponding dog on the airscrew boss, and thus the starter's engine could be made to turn the aircraft engine. As may be imagined, this was a somewhat hazardous procedure, and I remember the accident digests being full of 'Hucks' Starter' mishaps even as late as 1939. Another way to solve the problem was to have a removable starting handle that turned the engine on (as in the Mk.I Anson). The Americans were fond of using a small fly-wheel which could be spun up to high R.P.M. either electrically or by hand, and then engaged with the engine, allowing the energy so stored to turn the engine (e.g. The Harvard).

The British system most commonly used early in the war was to turn the engine on directly by an electric motor, as in a car's self starter. The problem was that the battery carried in the aircraft was very quickly flattened by the load needed to turn the big engine. This meant that an outside battery had to be provided (the familiar trolley- acc.), with loss of flexibility of operation. A solution, as engines got bigger, was the cartridge starter. This used a cartridge not much larger than that for a 12 bore shot- gun. When fixed, the expanding gasses acted on a piston that provided the energy to turn the engine over, briefly but sharply. If conditions within the cylinders were right, the engine would fire and with luck, keep going. This was a once and for all operation. If the engine failed to start, another cartridge had to be selected (in most cases this could be done from the cockpit), and a fresh attempt made. The magazine carried five or six cartridges. The disadvantage of the system was that if the engine got over rich, it was not possible to correct this by churning the engine over with an electric starter until the situation corrected itself. The advantage was that a big engine was given a good sharp starting kick, by a light and simple starting mechanism.

I found sitting behind 2,000-plus hp of Napier Sabre engine an awe-inspiring experience, recalling my first Hurricane flight from Takoradi. Once in the air the impression was one of sheer brute force. This was the first aircraft I had flown which showed 300 mph on the airspeed indicator in level flight, but the reader may say, "both the Hurricane and the Spitfire had a maximum speed far above that. Why, the Mk.I Hurricane in 1938 could do 320 mph and that with its fixed pitch two bladed airscrew". Quite so, but that speed was achieved at nearly 20,000 feet where, due to the rarefied atmosphere, the airspeed indicator would read only about 230 mph even though the true airspeed was 320 mph.

I first flew the Typhoon on 4th May 1945, and four days later came V.E. Day. It was clear that we would not now be needed in 2nd T.A.F., but nevertheless, our course continued, and in seven flying days I achieved over fifteen hours, including several low flying sorties and some aerobatics. Aston Down was quite near my home area of Devizes, and I was able to visit a number of familiar spots at low level and high speed, and quite legally! The second phase of the course consisted of bombing and rocket firing. Our range was in the Severn Estuary, just where the Severn road bridge now stands. I see from my log book that I dropped my last four bombs with an average error of 27 yards, and my last four rockets with an average error of 18 yards - good enough, I imagine, to make most tank crews see the error of their ways! In all I flew just under twenty hours on the Typhoon. How did it compare with the Spitfire? Well, if the Spitfire was a ballet dancer, the Tiffy was an all-in wrestler! Certainly in many ways it was easier to handle, its massive wide tracked undercarriage giving far more stability on the ground than the dainty narrow landing gear of the Spitfire. The Typhoon hauled its enormously thick wing through the air mainly by brute force. It did a superb job towards winning the war, and with the end of the European conflict its task was finished (by the end of 1945 there were no

Typhoons left in front line service). Its direct descendants, the Tempest, and the Sea Fury, were to become, perhaps, the ultimate in single seater piston engined fighters.

The course at Aston Down was over and the posting to 2nd T.A.F. cancelled, but the war in the Far East still went on. My posting was changed to No.126 Squadron at Bentwaters, where I was delighted to find the squadron was equipped with the redoubtable North American Mustang. The Mustang, as is well known, was a prime example of Anglo-American co-operation. The early Marks, with the Allison engine, were not particularly successful, due to poor performance at altitude, but when the aircraft was fitted with the Rolls Royce Merlin, built under licence in America by Packard, it was transformed. Its maximum speed was nearly 450 mph at 25,000ft, its range 1,700 miles with drop tanks, and its six .50 Brownings packed a massive punch. When it is considered that in 1940 the best single engine German fighters could only spend about ten minutes over London when flying from bases in Northern France, and in 1944 Mustangs were able to spend twenty minutes over Berlin, flying from bases in Eastern England, it will be seen what great strides forward had been made. It is said that the sight of Mustangs over Berlin in 1944 (months before D-Day) first brought it home to the Germans that the war was lost. Goering tried at first to bluster and say that the fighters had been carried into the German heartland by strong westerly winds, and that they would never get back to their bases. He could not imagine how such stupendous range could be built into a fighter that had proved to be more than equal to the best that the Luftwaffe could offer.

No.126 Squadron had been mainly engaged in long-range escort work. This was now finished and the word was that we were to be part of Tiger Force, the British contributing to the final defeat of Japan in the Pacific. To this end we trained seriously and enthusiastically. Our Mustangs were the Mk.III version at first, and later we were equipped with the Mk.IV, P51D to the Americans.

It was good to be flying American aircraft again. I had always admired the neat layout of their instruments and controls, and the precise feeling they gave in the air, especially on the landing approach, which always seemed to me to be steady, as if the aircraft was on rails. Maybe this was my imagination, but later when I flew Lockheed 12 Skyraiders, Avengers and the Beech Expediter, the impression was confirmed. At this time we were able to fly over the Continent without getting special clearance, and many of our exercises involved crossing the Channel.

The Wing Leader at Bentwaters was a Belgian by the name of Donnet, who had been in the Belgian Air Force as a young Flying Officer when the war began. With the over-running of his country by the Germans and the destruction of the Belgian Air Force, he was able to slip into civilian clothes and avoid capture. Eventually, he and a friend located a light aircraft hidden in a shed in the grounds of a chateau used as a H.Q. by the Germans. They were able to get this aircraft into flying order and without any opportunity of testing it, take off at night and fly to England. Donnet joined the RAF and had a distinguished war career, later attaining high rank in his country's Air Force. It was not surprising, therefore, that when he was leading, his Wing often found themselves in the vicinity of Brussels!

Early in August I was at Old Sarum doing an Army Co-Operation Course when the Atom bombs were dropped on Japan, and of course this meant the end of any plans to send us to the Pacific. However work at the Squadron continued much as before. On my return I found that we had been re-equipped with the Mustang IV. This was the version with the tear drop pilot's canopy and dorsal fin extension. Early in September we started practising for a fly past over London to commemorate Fighter Command's victory in the 'Battle of Britain', five years earlier. Twenty-four Squadrons took part in this event staged on 15th September, and as can be imagined, it was quite a feat of organisation to get everyone over St. Paul's Cathedral and the Palace in good order. After this we did not land back at Bentwaters, but went to Bradwell Bay on the Essex coast for a fortnight's armament training.

Pilots of No.126 Sq. and a Mustang IV at Bradwell Bay Armament Training Camp in September 1945. Peter Rivington appears 3rd from the left in the rear row. The tear drop canopy of the Mustang can be seen behind him.

I understand that when the Armistice was signed at the end of the previous war, everything stopped as if chopped off with an axe, and men were pitch-forked back into civilian life in a chaotic manner. This time it was determined that the Forces would be run down in a more orderly fashion. At Bradwell Bay we carried out the usual Air to Air and Air to Ground firing, and low level bombing. Flying my Mustang IV, I see that I achieved 25% hits on the Air to Ground target and an average error of 6 yards in low level bombing - this latter seems to be almost too good to be true. Some of us were I think, a little over keen when shooting at the ground targets, bringing the aircraft back spotted with mud, kicked up by our own bullets.

I recall, on arrival at Bradwell Bay we were taken to the range for a demonstration of Air to Ground firing. The aircraft demonstrating was a Mosquito, and the pilot, clearly wishing to put on a 'good show' dived rather too steeply, coming in a little too low. After firing, and finding the ground approaching at an uncomfortable rate, he was forced to haul back sharply on the stick and then brought the aircraft to the verge of a high-speed stall, with a wing starting to drop. He corrected this by releasing the backward pressure, but in the panic of the moment, his hand must have clamped round the stick pressing on the trigger and sending an unwanted burst of fire out to sea. One knows just how he felt.

On leaving Bradwell we didn't return to Bentwaters, but went to a new base at Hethel, near Norwich, which became a factory and test track for Lotus cars, I believe. My Log Book indicates 'Squadron Formation, Bradwell Bay–Hethel, 20 mins.' I have no doubt we did our best to arrive in a spectacular manner. The routine was for the aircraft to fly low over the runway in echelon starboard, breaking port in pairs to turn down wind for landing. With about 300 yards separation between each pair, we would have all twelve aircraft on the runway at the same time, the last pair just touching down as the C.O. and his wing man started to turn off at the far end. I imagine that this sort of performance would cause a modern air traffic controller to have a stroke. And remember that these were propeller driven tail wheel aircraft, with very little forward visibility when on the ground.

It was at Hethel that I was again saved from disaster by sheer luck. Returning to the airfield after some exercise or other, I had just touched down on the runway when the engine cut dead. I realised at once what had happened. I had omitted to turn on to a full tank before joining the circuit, and if the fuel had run out just thirty seconds earlier! In piston engine aircraft, in those days, the pilot had to select manually his various fuel tanks, and it was quite normal practice to allow the engine to cut, at a safe altitude of course, on one tank before changing over in order to use fully the aircraft's fuel supply. One would naturally ensure that the selected tank had adequate fuel available for the circuit and landing. One's pre-landing checks should take care of this, should! Anyway in this case I was able quickly to select a full tank before the propeller had ground to a halt. I was the only one to know how near the crash crew had come to picking up the pieces of my aircraft in the fields short of the runway.

Early in November the Squadron lost its Mustangs. I suppose that these were 'lend-lease' material and were due for return to the United States. We were to be re-equipped with D.H.Hornets, the smaller single seat younger sister of the Mosquito. Everyone was looking forward to flying what was, I suppose, the fastest piston engined aircraft ever to serve in the RAF. However before this could occur I was posted away from the Squadron to a desk job. Squadron Leader Administration Lincolnshire Sector 12 Group. This might sound a high powered job, but in fact the Sector was a moribund Unit and my task was to close it down. The Sector H.Q. was in Blankney Hall, near RAF Digby, which acted as our parent station. One consolation was to be found on the airfield at Digby. An old colleague from pre-war Gatwick and Grantham days, Derek Ford, was sitting there twiddling his thumbs, I/C the Station Flight. This consisted of on Mark IV Mustang KM226, and in this I was able to blow the cobwebs away whenever I could escape from the office. Our quarters at Blankney Hall were not as salubrious as they sound, for the RAF had at some earlier stage contrived to burn down all but the servants quarters.

I was at Blankney Hall from just before Christmas 1945 until the spring of 1946, when I was posted to No.12 Group H.Q. at Watnall, Nottingham, as O/C the Aircraft Accident Section. Talking of accidents, a near accident at that time, I had acquired a car that was the apple of my eye, a 1931 International Aston Martin. This was a beautiful piece of machinery. I used to look at it in pub car parks and marvel that it actually was mine. But it had a drawback, common I imagine to most cars of this vintage. Although it would go like the wind and corner as if on rails, the means of stopping it were woefully inadequate. On one occasion when heading down south on the Fosseway I picked up a hitch hiking airman. A few miles further on, having worked up a fair speed, I came unexpectedly upon a crossroads. To my consternation a tractor pulling a long trailer, slowly crossed my path until the road was completely blocked. Maximum application of the anchors only seemed to increase our speed of closing and as the obstruction, oh so slowly, cleared away, I was just able to swerve round it. I shot a glance at my new passenger, white as a sheet, he was clearly wishing he had walked.

I had enjoyed my short stay at Lincolnshire Sector, where my Group Captain was Arthur Donaldson, younger of the two well known brothers. The other was Teddy, of world speed record fame and later to become *Daily Telegraph* Air Correspondent. A third brother had been killed earlier in the war when his Squadron was lost in the *Glorious* during the evacuation from Norway. His Wing Commander was 'Paddy' O'Neil, who I had last known at Wick in 1940. It was he who had tried to raise the morale of our troops in Norway by dropping newspapers and cigarettes, and had received two direct hits from 'friendly' 40 mm

Bofors shells, for his pains. Talbot Rothwell of Gatwick and Grantham had been his second pilot on that occasion.

No.12 Group H.Q. Fighter Command was located in a rather unattractive group of wooden huts in Watnall, a suburb of Nottingham. My work consisted mainly of accident investigation, although the other facet, accident prevention, was just coming to the fore. It might be thought that to be continually picking up the pieces after what, in many cases, were fatal accidents, was a somewhat depressing job. I did not find it so. In fact, going back to that first Court of Enquiry at Hooton Park in 1940, the investigation side of accident prevention had always interested me. I would have enjoyed making a speciality of it, but in order to do that, one would have needed additional qualifications.

We had a small Communications Flight based at the Rolls Royce Airfield at Hucknall. This consisted of a couple of Mk. XII Ansons and a Proctor. The Anson XII had a re-designed fuselage, giving greater headroom with a changed window layout, and most importantly, hydraulically operated flaps, undercarriage, and constant speed airscrews. I used one of the Ansons to visit Stations when there had been an accident requiring Group Investigation. These accidents varied from the tragic to the bizarre. In the first category came the case of the Mosquito from Middleton St. George, which according to eye-witnesses simply rolled over on its back and dived into the ground from about 1,500 ft. Before I went out to the site of this one, the Station Medical Officer asked me, in a most casual way, that if I found a head would I let him know, as there was one missing. This made me turn over the wreckage a mite gingerly. In an accident of this severity it is almost impossible to collect all the human remains, and this does not make the investigator's job any more pleasant. We never found out for certain what happened, but as there was no evidence of structural failure, and both engines were under power on impact, the most likely explanation was that the pilot was attempting an aerobatic manoeuvre that went badly wrong. There was some evidence that he was in the habit of carrying out aerobatics at a low level.

In the bizarre category came the case of the two old ladies in their Austin 10, who strayed on to the perimeter track at Keevil while night flying was in progress, thinking they were on the road to Devizes. They realised their mistake when they found their car being sliced up by a very large aircraft propeller. Their luck was in, and they escaped serious injury, although the same could not be said of their car.

While at Blankney I had filled in forms applying for a Permanent Commission in the Royal Air Force, and in the summer of 1946 I heard that I had been unsuccessful, but had been offered an Extended Service engagement. This I declined. As it happened, with the expansion that took place around the time of the Korean War, many officers returned to the Service, and I might have been well advised to accept the Medium Service Commission. However, I have had no reason to regret the course of action I took. So in September 1946, I was due to leave the Service. I had decided to continue flying in civilian life, and had obtained a place on a course run by Straight Aviation Training at Bush House, London, with a view to obtaining a 'B' Licence and 2nd Class Navigation Certificate. On the day before I was due to leave Watnall, I called in to see Group Captain Dickinson the S.A.S.O. and my immediate boss, to say goodbye. I entered his office.

"Ah Rivington," he said. "Just the chap I wanted to see. Bad news I'm afraid. You'll have to get down to Llandudno. Peter Bond has killed himself in a Hornet down there."

I explained that I couldn't go as I was due at the Uxbridge Release Centre the next day, so we shook hands and I departed. Peter Bond had taken over our Mustang Wing from Donnet not long before I left No.126 Squadron. He was the same Peter Bond who had commanded the E.F.T.S. at Jodhpur (remember the incident of the belly-landed Hurricane?). It seems that he had flown down to Llandudno in a Hornet (the Wing were re-equipping with them) for a friend's wedding. On taking off to return home he had flown into a cloud-covered mountain. I was glad that I escaped having to carry out that investigation. It would not have been a happy ending to my Service career.

15. *Civil Aviation*

So I became a student in London, living in an Earls Court hostel and commuting to Bush House every day. I think I obtained a small Government grant to cover course fees and living expenses, and in any case was cushioned by three months leave on full pay.

A 'B' Licence and 2nd Navigation Certificate (2nd N) were the required qualifications for a civil airline pilot in those days. The 'B' Licence enabled one to fly 'for hire and reward', and the 2nd N permitted one to fly over long routes, for which the pilot, without this qualification, had to carry a navigator. Never a great mathematician, I crammed myself with a great deal of esoteric navigational 'Gen', retained for the purpose of the exam and forgotten straight away afterwards.

We were now in 1947, and anyone who was older than about six years at that time will remember how that year started. There was the great freeze and the fuel shortage, candles flickering in the London shops and sooty snow cluttering the London streets for weeks on end. It so happened that we were due to take our exams in the middle of the black out, or freeze up. Naturally they were cancelled. With the coming of the thaw, the exams were arranged again and I passed the 'B' Licence but failed the navigation, not badly, 70% was the required mark I believe and I got something over 60%. Anyway I had to take it again, and this time I passed without trouble.

Before I could be issued with my 'B' Licence I had to take a Ministry of Civil Aviation General Flying Test. This had to be carried out on a Tiger Moth flying from Gatwick - yes, dear old Gatwick again. I also had to pass an Air Registration Board technical exam on the Tiger. Even the A.R.B. were unable to make this more than a formality and I took the exam on the Anson as well. I chose the Anson because of my previous experience on the aircraft. Another popular choice was the Consul (Airspeed Oxford in civilian dress), as this aircraft was used by many of the small charter companies, where most of us would look for employment. So by the middle of the glorious summer of 1947, I was ready and qualified to find an airline pilot's job. Of course, I applied to B.O.A.C. and B.E.A. and was horrified to find that at 27 I was 'too old'. Their maximum age was 26 and in any case, they gave priority to ex Bomber or Transport Command four engine pilots. So I applied to a number of charter companies and eventually got a job with Southampton Air Services Ltd., at Eastleigh. They had picked out my application because they had just acquired an Avro XIX. This was an Anson XIX in civilian dress. The one that S.A.S. had acquired was however, a bit of a hybrid in that it had the old wooden wings and not the metal main planes of the later Avro XIX's.

Southampton Air Services was fairly typical of the many charter companies that mushroomed around this time. B.E.A. had not been long formed and were flying a variety of ex-service aircraft, mainly Dakotas, but with a few Ju 52's, of all things. They were quite unable to satisfy the demand for air travel and the charter companies hoped to cash in. Southampton Air Services had used an old D.C.2, which they flogged backwards and forwards between the U.K. and Malta at a satisfactory profit. However its tired old undercarriage finally gave up the ghost on the Luqua runway, and a replacement aircraft had to be found. They obtained a Lockheed 14, G-AGBG, a Lockheed 12a, G-AGDT and the Avro XIX, G-AGNI. I was to fly the Avro XIX and the Lockheed 12a.

I see from my Log Book that I first flew for Southampton Air Services on 23rd July 1947, and that in August I flew more than one hundred hours on the Avro XIX. The modern passenger would be amazed at the air travel of 1947. The Avro XIX had eight seats and a crew of two, a pilot and radio operator. We had no voice radio, and our navigation was carried out by map reading, assisted by the occasional bearing obtained using Morse Code. We flew from Southampton to the Channel Islands, sometimes to Northern Ireland and often from Croydon to Zurich or Geneva.

Croydon in those days was the chief airport for non scheduled airliners serving London, and had carried on much as it left off on the outbreak of war. Heathrow, in the process of building, was used by B.O.A.C. while B.E.A. used Northolt. In those days it was not permissible to sell individual seats on a charter aircraft. The aircraft had to be chartered as a whole. But with the shortage of seats on the scheduled airlines, the charter firms found plenty of business.

I carried my first paying passengers as a civil pilot on July 26th 1947, on a round trip between Eastleigh and Jersey, and on the 29th I took the Avro XIX to Croydon to position for a Zurich trip the following day. Croydon to Zurich was a four hour flight and the one thing that worried me was the navigation. I had teamed up with an excellent radio operator named Bill Race, but the navigational aids were crude in the extreme, and I would mostly depend on map reading. In the event I had no trouble, helped of course by the wonderful weather that prevailed over the whole of Europe in that summer of 1947. A glance at an Atlas will show that the direct route between London and Zurich follows the line of the first war battle fields, evocative of the history of that period - Arras, St Quinten, Cambrai, Reims, Verdun. It was very noticeable that over this whole strip of countryside there were no old trees and no old buildings. This much was clearly visible from the three or four thousand feet at which I was able to fly. I did seven return trips to Zurich during my first five weeks with Southampton Air Services, and came to know the route well enough to dispense with my maps - well, almost. "Put the map away, I know where we are", are among an aviator's classical 'famous last words'.

To illustrate how busy a charter pilot's life could be in the height of the season, during that August, I flew:-

- 6 trips to Zurich
- 8 trips to the Channel Isles, usually calling at both Jersey and Guernsey
- 1 trip to Deauville
- 3 trips to Belfast
- 2 trips to Paris
- 2 trips to Geneva, once going on to Nice
- 1 trip to Milan via Lyons
- Many of these trips meant positioning at Croydon. On 10th August this was my programme:-
- Southampton - Guernsey
- Guernsey - Jersey
- Jersey - Croydon
- Croydon - Deauville
- Deauville - Guernsey
- Guernsey - Jersey
- Jersey - Southampton
- Southampton - Croydon
- Croydon - Southampton

Altogether 6 hours 45 minutes flying, and nine take offs and landings. If the average time on the ground was thirty minutes, that makes a working day of nearly eleven hours. Luckily they weren't all like that.

One job I enjoyed was to fly to Cardiff and pick up an Italian family and take them back to their native Milan, for the first time since the war. As we didn't fly at night and we could not get to Milan before dark, we night stopped at Lyons on the way out. The next day, having dropped our passengers at Milan, we returned to Southampton, again via Lyons. I was received with some surprise and rapture when I returned. It seems that certain other pilots employed by the firm (there were three) had become a little 'bolshie' and tended to take their time over jobs like this. The firm at the time employed three pilots. The youngest, after myself, Peter Hillwood, was about to leave to take a test pilot's job with Cunliffe Owen, who were at the time developing the Concordia (prophetic name) feeder airliner, and had their factory on the other side of the aerodrome at Southampton. One pilot was somewhat elderly, ex-Imperial Airways, I think. He appeared to have some problems in getting from 'A' to 'B'. For example, on one occasion when taking a film making party from Southampton to Croydon in the Lockheed 14, he arrived back at Southampton around midday, much to the delight of the Company Management. This delight turned to despair when the entire film crew plus stars, disembarked. They had apparently spent a number of hours floating around above cloud, and on seeing a gap in the overcast, the pilot had dived for it and landed at the nearest airfield, which happened to be Southampton.

On another occasion when returning from the Continent to Croydon, in poor weather, he had estimated that he was over Kent. Knowing that if he continued north he would strike the south coast of the Thames Estuary, he decided that he could then turn left until he spotted a clear landmark, and then set course for Croydon. He duly arrived at a coastline and followed it, looking for a familiar landmark. After a while a passenger tapped on the cockpit door and enquired if the pilot knew where he was.

"Certainly," came the answer, "we are following the Thames up to London."

"Oh no you're not," retorted the passenger. "You're flying round and round the island of Jersey ... and you've passed my house twice already!"

After that episode, the pilot in question flew no more for Southampton Air Services.

The third pilot was Bob Low, who had been flying 'since Pontius was a pilot' – as the phrase has it – and could fly anything, anywhere. He had a liking for the delights of the bar after duty hours, but this never affected his performance in the air, although it tended to get him into trouble on the ground. Bob normally flew our Lockheed 12, and one of our best customers was a London Merchant Banker, Edward Beddington Behrens, later to become Sir Edward. He considered the little Lockheed to be his personal aircraft, and with his partners, Major General Sir Colin McVean Gubbins (of SOE fame in WWII) and Hugh Leveson Gower (brother of 'Shrimp', the cricket patron), they would fly here and there on their various business journeys. On one occasion I took 'The Three Musketeers', as we called them, to Belfast in the Anson – I imagine the Lockheed was unavailable for one reason or another – where they had an interest in a carpet factory. We stayed comfortably in the Grand Central Hotel, in those happy days before the 'troubles'.

On another occasion I took the Musketeers from Croydon to Yeadon, near Leeds. It was November and the weather was poor, with many snow showers and much smoke haze shrouding the Northern Industrial areas. If I have said that India must be one of the best map-reading countries, then the Industrial North of England must be one of the worst. The last forty miles of the route from Croydon to Yeadon was over the heart of the West Riding coalfields, from Sheffield to Bradford. There, the multiplicity of railway lines, canals and built-up areas, makes map-reading in poor visibility a nightmare. I got hopelessly lost with, of course, no assistance available from Yeadon. When the high ground of the Pennines loomed up, it was obvious that we had missed the airfield, so rather than blunder about in the smog looking for a very small needle in a very large haystack, I turned east, heading for the Humber. Soon the smog was left behind and the silver streak that was the Humber came into view, I set a careful course for Yeadon and, much to my relief, the airfield appeared below, bang on ETA.

It was at Belfast (Sydenham) airfield that I got my first insight into trade union restrictive practices. I needed to refuel and was asked to taxi up to some fixed petrol pumps. A chap strolled over, climbed onto the wing and asked where the fuelling points were. I pointed out the filler caps covered by flaps, which had to be opened with a screwdriver.

"Oh, I can't do that," said our friend. "I'm not allowed to use a screwdriver. I'll have to get a fitter ... but they're all on dinner break".

I climbed onto the wing myself, and opened the flaps with a coin.

"OK?" I said.

"OK," said he, and got on with the refuelling.

By the middle of September, charter work was beginning to die down, and rumours were rife that Southampton Air Services was to be sold. The aircraft had, I understood, been on the market for some time, but I suppose no sufficiently high offer was forthcoming. Anyway, a firm called Universal Flying Services, based at Fair Oaks airfield, near Chobham, showed interest and finally bought the aircraft and took me on as well. The Lockheed 14 and the Avro XIX were disposed of, and the Lockheed 12 joined a motley bunch of Rapides, Aerovans, Gemini's and Proctors already owned by Universal, who operated a RAF Reserve Flying School and a Flying Club at Fair Oaks, in addition to the Charter business. I enjoyed flying the '12', which was a fine example of a 1939 American light commercial aircraft, with none of the vices of its larger stablemate, the '14'.

The Manager of Universal at Fair Oaks was Major Tommy Rose. Just where the 'Major' came from I'm not sure, anyway it disguised the well known figure of the Flt.Lt Tommy Rose, who had carried out many record breaking flights in the 1930's. Although a charming man, I'm not sure that Rose had the business acumen to run a charter firm in the face of cut throat competition for rare winter bookings. In any event by Christmas, Universal's charter operations had ceased. Perhaps a reason for this may be deduced from two visits I made to Blackbushe airfield from Southampton, flying the Lockheed. The plan was to position at Blackbushe to pick up a party for Malta. This I duly did on the 29th November1947, only to be told that the trip was now postponed, so I returned to Southampton. There I was told that I must position at Blackbushe on 30th, to take the party to Malta first thing on 1st December. This meant an overnight stay in a Camberley Hotel for Brian Spark my Radio Operator, and myself. Early in the morning we were at the airfield and ready to set off for Malta. No passengers were forthcoming. A 'phone call to the charter company elicited the information that although he had at one time considered flying to Malta, and had enquired about costs and dates, no firm booking had been made, and now he had no intention of proceeding with the charter. So we'd made two return trips from Southampton to Blackbushe (1 hours total flying time), plus landing and parking fees, plus a night in an hotel for the R.O. and myself, all for a charter that never was. Hardly the way to run a successful business.

I remember another occasion when a crew flew an Aerovan from Fair Oaks to Southampton to do a job on the following day. On arrival one of the crew found that he had left his razor at home in Woking, so he flew the Aerovan back to Fair Oaks to fetch it. Imagine how many razors could have been bought for just the cost of the fuel used.

In January 1948 I moved my base to Croydon. There I joined Air Taxi's, a firm which had belonged to Southampton Air Services, and had also been sold to Universal. Here I first flew the famous DH Rapide. This delicate looking biplane, with its sharply tapered wings was pleasant to fly and the pilot, sitting well forward in the blunt nose, had an unrivalled view. It did, however, need careful handling near the ground, having a marked tendency to drop a wing sharply at the stall. However, if one set it down on the main wheels, allowing the tail to come down as the speed decreased, there was no problem.

Air Taxi's was a tiny one aircraft, one pilot outfit, with a small office in the Airport building. Here also were the other charter firms which air travellers before, and immediately after the war will recall. There were Morton's Airways, Olly Airways and British Air Transport. The mainstay of all three was the Airspeed Consul, which any RAF pilot would have recognised as a 'de-mobbed' Oxford. An excellent little aeroplane which I later came to know well, the Oxford/Consul, had the same Cheetah engines as the Anson, and being smaller, had markedly better performance figures. Its snag from the operators' angle was that it could only carry six passengers. Olly and Morton ran a straight charter service, while BAT's main contract was the ferrying of English newspapers to the continent in the early morning.

Around this time, a high percentage of the civil airliners flying were Douglas DC3s (commonly known as Dakotas) which had been bought cheaply from war-surplus stocks. It followed, therefore, that a correspondingly large percentage of air crashes involved Dakotas, which gave this exceedingly safe aircraft a bad name in the press and with the general public.

An airline company was one day picking up a passenger load at Croydon. A spokesman for the passengers approached the handling agent at the airport building and enquired in what type of aircraft they would be flying.

"A Dakota, Sir," came the unsuspecting reply.

"Oh dear," said the passenger. "We're not going in one of those! Isn't there anything else?"

"Just a minute…" said the agent, and went to a phone. After a brief conversation he returned, all smiles. "I've been able to get you onto a DC3 Sir, will that be alright?"

"That's fine," said the passenger. "We'd all agreed that we wouldn't fly in one of those Dakota things."

My one and only trip with Air Taxis was to fly four passengers – two married couples – to Paris and then on to Nice. The Air Taxis manager had persuaded these people that it was a good idea to escape from January in England to the Cote D'Azur, and that his DH Rapide was the ideal magic carpet to waft them there. So we spent a night in Paris and then set off for the sunshine. Unfortunately the weather was lousy; cloud from 1,000 feet up to about 20,000 feet and frequent snow. It was clear that I would have to find my way under the cloud so I chose to fly south to Orleans and then to follow the Loire to Nevers. If I could then hop over the 3000-ft ridge between there and the Rhone I would be in the clear all the way down to the Mediterranean. It was a rough ride and by the time Lyons was past my passengers had given up asking when we were going to find the sunshine and had resigned themselves to misery and air sickness. We landed at Nice after five hours in the air, by which time the passengers had decided that their return trip to Paris would be made by scheduled airline. After a day in Nice I flew to Paris via Lyons in better weather and picked up my passengers for the return trip to Croydon. I suspect that this trip was a bit of a 'fiddle', as I was asked to pay cash for all fuel and landing fees. Anyway, after this, Air Taxis folded and I remained at Croydon freelancing.

At the end of January I was able to fly the Air Taxis DH Dragon. This was the aircraft from which the Rapide was developed. It had Gipsy Major engines in place of the Rapide's Gypsy 6s and its wings were square-tipped after the fashion of a Tiger Moth. It flew rather like a twin-engined Moth.

There was much activity at Croydon at this time with people buying surplus aircraft – mainly Rapides and Proctors – from the RAF. I did quite a lot of work flying buyers and engineers to places like Little Rissington, Dumfries, Portsmouth, Ringway and Tollerton, to view aircraft or to prepare them for flight. This was mainly done in a Proctor belonging to Rollasons Engineering, another well-known pre-war Croydon name, but I also fetched a few Rapides from Dumfries, travelling up overnight by train.

Early in June, the General Manager of Rollasons asked me if I would be interested in an overseas job. Of course, there was only one answer when he told me that he had already sold one Anson Mk. I (yes, with hand wind-up undercarriage and all) to people called SATA in Tangier, and another aircraft was due to go soon. A pilot and R/O were needed to fly it out and operate it. The main route operated would be between Tangier and Nice and the aircraft would be based in Tangier. SATA, I discovered, stood for Societe Anomie de Transports Aeriers, registered, I presume, in Tangier.

16. S.A. T.A.

My first job was to get the Anson I endorsed on my licence. I visited the Air Registration Board H.Q. in London to arrange to take the exam. The chap I saw told me that I could take it there and then, but I pointed out that I would have to look up a few points first, such as the C of G limits, as laid down in the Certificate of Airworthiness. I may have remarked that it seemed pointless to memorise all these things, but it had to be done.

"Ah!" he remarked, "but you need to know the figures on the C of A. What would you do, for instance, if an engine fell off in the air?" This was typical of the thinking of some non-flying civil servants in the Ministry. To have answered, that the one thing which would *not* help would be a knowledge of C of A figures, would not have been understood. Anyhow, I took the exam the next day and passed without trouble. By now Rollasons had got the aircraft ready for test and I was pleased to find that Brian Spark (what an appropriate name), later of SAS, had been engaged as my R/O. We took the Anson on a couple of test flights from Croydon on June 30th and the next day was ready to set off, not for Tangier, but for Nice.

The Anson I, civil version, looked very much like its RAF counterpart, without the turret, of course. The long, glasshouse windows had been modified to give more of an airliner look and the inside was tarted up a bit with some soundproofing and padding. There were seats for six passengers. On 1st July we flew down to Nice with a refuelling stop at Lyons. I always enjoyed the leg from Lyons to Nice, about 1 hr 30 mins in the Anson. We followed the Rhone down to Montelemar, then past the unmistakable bulk of Mount Ventoux, over the Alpes Maritimes and on to Nice. The modern jet traveller, used to Le Var Airport at Nice, would not recognise the 1948 airport. The old runway can probably still be seen, but looks like a disused taxi track near the seashore, while a single wooden hut did service for an airport building. The control tower was also a temporary looking affair, inherited from either the Luftwaffe or the USAAF. It was a far cry from the plush modern airport. We were met by a suave, cosmopolitan multi-lingual Englishman, who I shall call Hoskins. He was he said, in charge of the French end of the operation, and took us to the Hotel Rhul, on the Promenade des Anglais, probably at the time, the second best hotel in Nice, after the Negresco.

In the Rhul bar, Hoskins, who was living in the hotel with his attractive French wife and young son, painted for us a very rosy picture of the SATA operation. It seemed that people were clamouring to fly between the South of France and Tangier. There was no direct scheduled service they could use and we would have no difficulty in keeping two aircraft fully employed. After a day in Nice we set off with a full passenger load for Tangier. The route from Nice took us along the Cote d'Azure to the Toulon/Marseille area and then across the Gulf of Lyon to Cape Creus on the French/Spanish border. After that, it was a question of following the Costa Brava past Barcelona to Valencia for refuelling. At Valencia it was safer to land on the taxi track than on the 'runway', where fist-sized stones threatened the Anson's wood and fabric construction. The Airport building was small and friendly, and the staff could not have been more helpful, although it was better we found, not to present the bureaucrats with anything remotely out of the ordinary if one wished to avoid endless telephone calls to Madrid and much delay.

After Valencia we were flying over the barren Spanish country-side with many odd-looking hills and mountains that were to become so familiar to us. The 12,000ft Sierra Nevada appeared on the horizon at least half an hour before we came abreast of it, with Granada nestling in its shadow. Then the sea soon came into view again and we crossed the coast at Malaga, heading for Gibraltar, Africa and Tangier. Tangier (or Tanger) Airport had one long concrete runway and not much else. Chief Engineer Michlemore, who I had met previously at Croydon, drove us the few miles into town and found us accommodation at a small hotel near the sea front at the east end of the town. The Hotel Bristol, which was to be our base for the next few weeks, was unpretentious but comfortable and stood just across the road from the much larger Rif Hotel, still known to holiday visitors.

We found that the SATA management in Tangier was in the hands of a firm of general merchants called Martinez. The two Spanish brothers who ran this firm were answerable to a City of London company in which Hoskins's father was a partner. We gathered that Hoskins junior had sold the idea of starting SATA to his father's firm, who had in turn involved their Tangier agents. 1948 was of course before the days of the package holi-day, and Tangier's main preoccupation was the international port, with all that involved in the immediate post-war world of short-ages and black markets. Administration of the International zone was in the joint hands of Britain, France and Spain. The zone must have been a haven for every kind of international smuggler and shady dealer, and I don't suppose the business of many of the passengers we carried would bear much looking into.

After a couple of days rest at Tangier, we started flying over the route which was to become so familiar to us during the next few months – Tangier, Valencia, Marseille (sometimes) and Nice. We rarely encountered any weather problems in that Mediterranean summer, the conditions being excellent on all but one or two days a month. Hoskins had indicated that we should no longer stay in the Rhul (much later we understood the background to this) so at the Nice end we took to using a small hotel a few blocks back from the seafront, where the restaurant was excellent and the accommodation very adequate.

We were kept busy and the normal routine was to arrive at Nice in the evening and set off on the return to Tangier early the following morning. We would then have a day in Tangier before the next trip. Once or twice we took passengers from Nice and Marseille to Geneva. If starting from Nice it was prudent to skirt round the western edge of the Alps to Grenoble and then to follow the Rhone Valley up to Geneva – a glance at the map will explain why – the old Anson not being too happy at the 16,000ft altitude needed to clear Mont Blanc! Hoskins came with us on one Geneva trip and borrowed 30 Swiss francs from me, which I happened to have left over from a previous trip. I should have known better…

Towards the end of August when we arrived at Nice, Hoskins informed me that we were due to fly back to Croydon the following day in order to pick up a boxer dog he had purchased. We were in Croydon for six days and Brian Spark, who had become somewhat disenchanted with the job, decided to take the opportunity to leave, so I picked up a new R/O, Joe Siebert.

On 27th August, with the boxer safely on board, we returned to Nice via Lyon and then to Tangier via Marseilles, and Valencia the following day. The leg between Tangier and Valencia was normally just over three hours and that between Valencia and Nice something over four hours. Allowing 40 minutes on the ground at Valencia, this was quite a long day. If we were able to get off from Tangier at 8 o'clock, we would arrive at Nice at 5 o'clock in the afternoon or more like 6 o'clock if a stop had to be made at Marseilles. As we only had a very sketchy continental breakfast in Tangier and did not normally bother about food at Valencia, by about 8pm in Nice we were very ready to deal with a gargantuan dinner, always forthcoming in our favourite restaurant.

Peter Rivington flying out of Tangier in an Anson, bound for the U.K. in September 1948.

In the early days Hoskins would occasionally come with us to Tangier to talk business with the Martinez brothers. He would sometimes ask the R/O to pass a message to Valencia asking the airport restaurant to prepare paella for our lunch and came to be on excellent terms with the catering staff. On one visit they gave him a quite considerable sum of money to buy watches, jewellery and so on, unobtainable in Spain. It appeared that Hoskins' business talks with the agents in Tangier were not too satisfactory, and he returned with us to Nice a day or two later.

As time went by, when we were in Tangier, the Martinez's would frequently ask us about Hoskins and when he was coming back there. The boys at Valencia also asked about him every time we passed through. We had raised our eyebrows over the trip to Croydon to fetch the dog and it seemed that the Hoskins family's lavish standard of living in Nice – rooms at the Rhul and so on – was causing some disquiet in Tangier. We were gradually realising that all the money taken by the agent at the French end of the route was being appropriated by Hoskins, while all the fuel bills, landing fees and our expenses were being passed on to Tangier. This could not go on. The Martinez's were especially incensed when passengers were booked through to Casablanca, as happened on a number of occasions, as all this meant to them was more expense, while the extra revenue stayed at the Nice end. This trouble resulted in the second aircraft being sent home in October. Early in that month I set off from Tangier with only one passenger, who I knew as a friend of Hoskins in Nice. When we were near Granada an engine cut due to fuel starvation, although an immediate change of tanks started it up again. It was normal to run the outer tanks dry before changing over, they normally lasted for about two hours, but the first tank had run out, in this case, in less than two hours, making it doubtful that we could reach Valencia safely, especially as we had a strong headwind. We could only assume that the tanks had not been properly topped up at Tangier (there was no gauge for the outer tanks). Luckily, Granada airfield was not far away, so we made an emergency landing there for fuel.

As I have previously indicated, the Spanish administrative system does not easily cope with out-of-the-ordinary situations. Granada was a military airfield and on landing we found ourselves practically under arrest. Luckily, our passenger spoke fluent Spanish and was able to persuade the airfield authorities that we were not spies, but nevertheless they sent us into Granada under escort and it was not until some official had made several calls to Madrid that we were finally free to find a hotel for the night, for by now it was too late to get on to Valencia.

We stayed at the Alhambra Hotel, right next to the famous Moorish Palace. Our balcony looked across the valley to the Sierra Nevada Mountains and the hotel was magnificent. We went out on the town for dinner that evening and had a most delectable meal. Only after we had finished were we told that we had been eating one of the more unmentionable parts of a bull! The following day we flew on to Nice, but due to the strong headwinds, had to refuel at Perpignan as well as Valencia. We were met at Nice by Hoskins and as we drove away from the airfield he pointed out a parked Beech Expediter. Could I fly it? He wanted to know, as he had bought it.

"Of course," I said, "but as it has French registration, there might be some formalities before I can fly it on my British licence". However, I knew enough about Hoskins by now not to give the matter another thought. He had, for instance, some weeks before, awarded me a handsome pay rise, which of course never materialised.

The enquiries at Valencia and Tangier as to the whereabouts of Hoskins and when he could be expected down the route, became more and more urgent. I felt very sorry for the boys at Valencia, who plainly could not afford to lose the money they had entrusted to our wayward 'manager'. The Martinez brothers were also getting desperate, trying to keep SATA going while receiving only half the revenue.

Another user of Tangier Airport was Gibraltar Airways, a subsidiary of BEA, who flew a service between the Rock and Tangier. They used Rapides and we always felt that as a 'scheduled' airline they gave themselves airs. I remember passing Gib on one occasion and seeing a Gib Airways Rapide a mile or so ahead of me, also heading for Tangier. I was able to put the old Annie's nose down and pass him without difficulty. When I entered the Tangier circuit I was well ahead of him and was at my parking place by the time he touched down. The Gib Airways pilot came up to me in the airport building and indicated his displeasure at my landing ahead of him 'a scheduled airline captain'! I pointed out that I had not baulked him in any way, and as far as I was concerned, it was a question of 'first come first served'. I expect his bad temper was partly caused by the monotony of his job. Imagine spending all your days on the ten-minute hop between Tangier and Gib.

During October the SATA operation was clearly bleeding to death from the haemorrhage at the Nice end. I was sorry, as it had been an interesting job. We saw the Costa del Sol and the Costa Brava long before the package holiday boom transformed the little fishing villages into concrete horrors. Tangier and Nice, at either end of the route, were interesting and enjoyable places to rest. We ourselves indulged in a little mild smuggling on our trips. Crew's baggage was never examined, so we used to take two thousand American cigarettes from Tangier to Nice. Their sale brought a profit of about £20. I'm sure that the authorities expected us to do this, and all went well for a time. But then, as always, someone got greedy and filled the whole nose compartment of an Anson with cigarettes, twenty thousand or so. Customs got wind of this and confiscated the lot. We were following on the next day, and on landing at Marseille our baggage was whipped off the aircraft. Of course we declared the cigarettes at once and they were held for us to take back to Tangier. We were then taken into a private cubicle, officially for a body search. Amiable customs man chatted for a few minutes, and then we all emerged again. It was all very civilised, but it stopped our nice little racket. Someone always spoils these things.

Tangier was predominantly Spanish, but the French influence was also strong. Prices in the shops were marked in pesetas and in francs and almost everybody spoke both languages. One of the Martinez brothers, Pepe, was a very extrovert type and we often used to have a drink with him. He spoke no English, I spoke no

Spanish but had a certain amount of schoolboy French, which rapidly, I will not say improved, became more fluent. We would sit over a beer or three conversing volubly in a language that I'm sure no Frenchman would recognise. Pepe was strongly pro France, and with the trouble blowing up in Germany that resulted in the Berlin Air Lift, he would enthuse about the day when he would be my rear gunner flying against the Russians.

I have said that the weather was generally very good, but there were occasional exceptions. I recall an RAF York coming in to Nice in a dreadful condition. It had flown through a thunderstorm out over the Med. The pilot's windscreen was cracked and the astrodome broken. The rubber de-icing boots on the leading edges of the wings were hanging in tatters and the nose of the aircraft looked as if it had been attacked with a small round headed hammer. The four radiators seemed to have suffered the same treatment, causing serious engine overheating. The other problem that we encountered on a few occasions was the Mistral, the wind that blows down the Rhone valley at anything up to 70 or 80 mph. As this is roughly the landing speed of an Anson, one or two landings at Marseille were a bit hairy.

During the month of October it was becoming clear that SATA could not last much longer. The second Anson was sent home and, at the Tangier end of the operation, patience was rapidly running out. It was not that there was a shortage of business. I completed seven return trips to Marseille and Nice during the month, plus a couple of sorties down the coast to Casablanca – well over one hundred hours flying. There was no doubt that things could have gone on quite profitably if there had been proper management at the Nice end. However, early in November we heard, with regret, that the firm was closing down and said goodbye to Tangier and all the friends we had made there, and flew our faithful Anson back to Croydon via Madrid and a night stop at Bordeaux.

There was 8/8th cloud cover over the South of England when we arrived. We were on top, so when the bearings we were receiving from Croydon told us we had passed over land, I let down on a northerly heading, breaking cloud at something under 1,000ft. As we broke I saw the River Thames passing underneath, then the Houses of Parliament and Whitehall was under my wing tip. As I turned towards Croydon, Whitehall seemed rather crowded and then it dawned on me; it was Remembrance Sunday and the time was just after 11 o'clock. I would not advise anyone to carry out this procedure today. Not only would they violate any amount of controlled air space, they would also find themselves dodging around a number of tower blocks which were non existent back in 1948, not to mention the Crystal Palace television mast!

On landing at Croydon we handed the Anson over to Rollasons and went our various ways. Later that week, as a kind of finale to the SATA venture, we had a date at the London office of the firm backing SATA in the UK, of which Hoskins Snr was a director. There we collected our final salary cheques and expenses, the Martinez brothers having at last tired of paying all the bills, and fended off the rather pathetic enquiries of Hoskins père as to what had gone wrong and where was his son. So ended an interesting venture and one can only speculate what might have come of it with proper management.

As a postscript, I did meet Hoskins once more at Croydon. He was not his old debonair self and had the hunted look of a man who expects to meet a creditor round every corner.

I never did recover my thirty Swiss francs.

17. *The Air Lift*

Back home again and jobless, it seemed a good idea to fill in some time and earn a little money, doing my annual RAFRO training. With my connections at Universal Flying Services, the obvious place to do this was Fair Oaks, then the home of No.18 Reserve Flying School. Tiger Moths in December are not the most comfortable of aeroplanes, nevertheless, I got in twenty or so hours flying and enjoyed meeting old friends at Chobham.

Christmas over, I heard that Flight Refuelling Ltd were looking for crews to man their expanding fleet of Lancasters and Lancastrians, operating on the Berlin Air Lift. Having no previous four-engine experience, I applied for and obtained a job as a second pilot and duly reported to Tarrant Rushton early in January 1949. Flight Refuelling Ltd had billeted their new crews in a four-star Bournemouth hotel, and bussed them out to the airfield each day. I found myself crewed up with Ken Swann (Captain), Johnny Johnson (Navigator) and 'Bert' Harris (Radio Operator).

After a week at Tarrant Rushton, which included 2 hr 45 min familiarisation and a trip to Langley to collect an ex-BOAC Lancastrian, we were ferried out in Lancastrian G-AKJU to Wunstorf , an ex-Luftwaffe fighter base near Hanover. On arrival we were taken some ten miles by bus to a small town, a village really I suppose, called Bad Nendorf, and put up in the local hotel, taken over for Flight Refuelling Ltd by the Control Commission. The hotel was small but comfortable, about the standard of an English 'Trust House' in a small provincial town. The German staff was willing and helpful, and the townspeople generally seemed glad to see us. I suppose we brought welcome trade to the local shops and bars and we, in turn, were introduced to the German habit of organising celebrations and parties that seemed to go on for days rather than hours. Not that we were able to participate fully in this activity, as we had a serious job to do.

Flight Refuelling had nine Lancastrian tankers based at Wunstorf. These, together with five Avro Tudors (Air Flight & BSAA) also at Wunstorf, and thirteen Haltons, which were Civil registered Halifaxes mainly Lancashire Aircraft Corporation aircraft flying from Schleswigland, were responsible in January 1949 for supplying the entire liquid fuel requirements of Berlin. Unlike the other companies involved, the flying of tanker aircraft had always been the sole business of Flight Refuelling. They were involved in the immediate post war experiments for in-flight refuelling, with BOAC's Empire Flying Boats on the North Atlantic route. Before the war, they had experimented with a Bombay Tanker. Two of their aircraft at Wunstorf were in fact Lancasters, not Lancastrians, with all the in-flight refuelling equipment still on board, and without the phased in nose and tail sections that characterised the Lancastrian.

The Lancaster/Lancastrian was turned into a tanker by simply fitting a large fuel tank in the bomb bay and connecting this to the two outer fuel tanks in the wings. The aircraft used the inner wing tanks in flight, and to dump the cargo fuel it was only necessary to open a single valve in the cabin, after a hose had been connected to the de-fuelling outlet protruding from the bomb bay. In the case of the two Lancasters equipped for in-flight refuelling, the operation was rather more complicated, as it involved unreeling the refuelling hose which was carried in the rear fuselage. We were able to carry 1,500 gallons of cargo fuel on each lift, and in Flight Refuelling's case, this was exclusively M.T. petrol.

There was much discussion in bars and crew rooms as to whether in an emergency, perhaps a long unexpected diversion, the M.T. fuel in the outer tanks could be used by the aircraft engines. The fuel cocks were of course, wired closed so that it was not possible, inadvertently to feed the engines with M.T. fuel. However the general contingency was that, provided low boost was used, the M.T. fuel could serve in an extreme emergency, to supplement the 500 or so gallons carried in the inner wing tanks.

Flying operations on the Air Lift were of course, continuous over the 24 hours, so in January two thirds of the flying was at night, and the crews working in a shift system. During each duty period a crew was expected to carry out two return trips to Berlin. Wunstorf to Gatow took about 1hr.30mins, and the return trip about 1hr.20mins. Allowing for 45 minutes on the ground at Gatow and 45 minutes at Wunstorf between trips, then the chock to chock time for the two trips comes to just under eight hours. The day was, therefore, divided into three eight hour shifts, and in theory each serviceable aircraft would carry out six round trips to Berlin in that time, under three different crews. I say in theory because the winter weather over the north German plain is not all that reliable. Bad weather, by which I mean the need for a GCA at either end of the route, meant an interval of five minutes between each aircraft, instead of the fair weather three minutes. If the weather was below GCA limits (say 300ft ceiling and 500 yards runway visibility) then flying was suspended altogether.

By a 1945 Agreement, all non-Russian air traffic between Berlin and the West had to use three twenty miles wide, 10,000ft high corridors. These led directly from Berlin to Hamburg, Hanover and Frankfurt respectively. As the Anglo/American Air

Lift used seven West German bases from Schleswigland up near the Danish border to Rhein/Main (Frankfurt) in the South, the complexity of the operation will be apparent. In the Air Lift, the North and South corridors were used for all flights into Berlin, and the centre corridor for all return trips, except that to Hamburg and Schleswigland, aircraft used the northern corridor both ways. Wundsdorf aircraft flew to Berlin via the northern and returned along the central corridor, which led almost directly to base. On the outward flight it was necessary to make a detour to the north to avoid two busy airfields, at Celle and Fassberg, both used on the Lift by the RAF and USAF.

With such a large number of aircraft using the corridors, it was obviously necessary to allocate to each base a height to fly but not always the same height both ways. In the case of the Wundsdorf aircraft, 3,500 feet was our allocated altitude both out and back. With a 10,000ft height limit and so many bases being used it was only possible to allow a 500ft vertical separation between aircraft. Luckily, only the southern corridor passed over high ground, the minimum safe height there being 4,500ft, whereas on the northern and central corridors, the safe heights were 1,000ft and 2,000ft respectively.

For our first trips to Berlin the new crews were split up, each member going as passenger with an experienced team. My Captain shrugged his shoulders when I introduced myself.

"You won't see anything except the runway lights at each end," he observed, and so it was. After take off we were in cloud at about 1,000ft and from then on simply flew the courses indicated by the navigator to take us over the various beacons. When twenty miles from the Frohnan (Berlin) beacon, we called Berlin Airways, announcing this fact, then using radar, broke cloud at about 1,000ft, well placed for the E/W Gatow runway. The return flight was even simpler, the Gatow runway being very nearly aligned with the central corridor out of the Russian zone. The British aircraft on the Lift were all fitted with a radar navigation/landing aid, BABS/Rebecca. When used as a landing aid this was turned into a Beacon at the end of the runway, and operated by the navigator, who gave range from the runway threshold and position in relation to the centre line. When used as a navigation aid and tuned to a 'Eureka' beacon on the ground, the aircraft could be guided to the beacon with a continuous indication of range. This enabled the British aircraft to pass to control their exact position in the corridors, e.g. 20 miles from a certain beacon.

The US aircraft did not carry radar and used MFDF beacons (also available to British aircraft) which gave them bearings but no range, and radio ranges that could also be used as a landing aid. They did not need to carry a navigator to use their system, but the drawback was that all aircraft flying a constant air speed between beacons could only obtain aircraft separation approximately.

The British aircraft also carried Gee, a navigational aid developed for Bomber Command in the late war by Decca. This was useful in the British zone, but the Berlin area was outside its range. Operated by the navigator, it gave a positive position on the ground. Using these aids it was possible for the navigator to guide the aircraft to Berlin and back without ever emerging from his office to look around him. After our initial trips to Berlin, we reformed as a crew and dropped into a steady routine, eight hours on duty, usually two round trips, and sixteen hours for sleep and recreation. It was January, so most of the flying was carried out at night, often in poor weather. The 24hour continuous operation was probably harder on the ground crews than on the flyers. For obvious reasons the latter had to have their set hours of duty and ample rest time. The maintenance crews on the other hand found themselves turning aircraft round and carrying out minor repairs for long periods our of doors in the bitter cold. Often there was snow on the ground and on the aircraft, which had to be cleared, and its no joke walking along the frozen wing of a Lancaster, brushing off the snow and applying a de-icing spray. A single false step could mean a crippling, perhaps fatal fall, on to the concrete apron some 15ft. below.

I remember one occasion when we refused to take an aircraft with an inch of fresh snow on the wings. It would "blow off as soon as we commenced our take off run" we were assured. Luckily we were well acquainted with the effect of snow and ice on aerofoils, not only adding many pounds of extra weight but also eroding the lift. A typical tour of duty would see us leaving the hotel at about 2.45 p.m. to be taken by coach to the airfield. A visit to the briefing room for weather reports and latest route instructions, and we would be taken out to the aircraft ready for a 4 o'clock take off. On receiving permission to taxi, we would join the queue of aircraft on the perimeter track waiting their turn to line up and take off. After the aircraft ahead was airborne, we would be given clearance to line up. Following a three minute interval (five minutes of a G.C.A. would be required at Gatow), we would be given permission to roll and would heave the heavy aircraft off the runway and climb away into the darkening sky en route for our first turning point.

Sometimes lights on the ground could be seen from our height of 3,500ft, also the brilliantly floodlit tarmac at Fassberg and Celle, where aircraft were being loaded with cargo for Berlin. More often nothing would be seen outside the aircraft except the red and green glow of air navigation lights reflected back off the cloud, enveloping the aircraft. From his curtained cell would come the navigator's disembodied voice giving us courses to steer and times at the beacons. Then our call "Berlin Airways, this is

Freddie Robert (Flight Refuelling) Jug Uncle (aircraft G-AGJU) Lancaster for Gatow with M.T. spirit, 20 miles Fronham". "Roger Jug Uncle, clear to Fronham". After the Fronham beacon we would call Gatow tower and be cleared to the Gatow beacon. After the Gatow beacon the lights of Berlin might be seen as we let down to 1,000ft and possibly the lights of Templehof on the port side as we turned toward the Gatow runway. On the final approach we passed a radio mast set on raised ground and festooned with red lights. It became customary to call "Christmas Tree" instead of "Finals'. If by any chance an aircraft was baulked on its landing approach and had to overshoot, the orders were to climb straight ahead and return to Wunsdorf by the usual route. There was no room for 'second chances' in the traffic pattern around Berlin. This only happened to us once. I think the runway was obstructed for some reason or other.

Once on the ground it was a short taxi to the de-fuelling point, and the German crews were very proficient in coping with the various types of tanker aircraft. We had just about half an hour to get a cup of coffee or tea before taking off on the return flight. This always seemed a more light-hearted affair, with a lightly loaded aircraft and an almost direct flight home. After a second round trip it was back to the hotel and probably time for a drink or two before bed.

As spring approached, more and more of our flights were in daylight and we began to be familiar with the land-marks en route to Berlin. The inward route followed the line of the river Elbe, entering the northern corridor near Wittenberge. Several Russian airfields were nearby and their piston engined fighters were a familiar sight both on the ground and in the air. Some Airlift pilots reported aggressive action by Russian aircraft, but we never experienced this. The sight of Berlin on the approach to Gatow was never to be forgotten. It was like flying over a honeycomb. Thousands of houses had just walls and no roofs. There could be no better indication of the price the German people had paid for following Hitler into defeat. The irony was that the same aircraft that had caused much of the mayhem were now providing a lifeline for the Berliners.

In mid April Flight Refuelling were moved from Gatow to Hamburg, where we flew from the civil airport at Fuhlsbuttel into a new airfield in the French sector of Berlin, Tegel. Our heights were now 1,500ft inbound and 1,000ft home, both in the northern corridor. There were not many home comforts at Tegel, a NAAFI wagon instead of a warm canteen, but Spring was with us and the weather was better and our spirits were that much higher. At about this time, before one of our trips to Tegel, the firm's manager in Germany introduced us to a small, elderly, somewhat diffident gentleman who was to be our passenger to Berlin. This was Sir Alan Cobham who proved to be a charming passenger and we were honoured to have been chosen to fly him. Most polite and unassuming, he might have been having his first experience in the air instead of being one of the most famous pioneer flyers of all time.

Soon after the move, one of our Lancastrians forced landed in the Russian zone on the way back from Tegel. All four engines fouled in quick succession, and the Captain did a fine job in setting the aircraft down on its belly with only minor injuries to the crew. Luckily it happened in daylight. They were on their second trip and their total flying time for the three and a half legs completed was just what could be expected of an aircraft which had not been refuelled at Hamburg between trips. Perhaps there had been a change of ground crew shifts at this vital time, when the aircraft was being turned round, and somehow the crew failed to check their gauges. Tiredness and familiarity can lead to inexplicable mistakes. Anyway, the crew arrived back a day or two later and the aircraft some weeks afterwards on a 'Queen Mary' transporter. The lads reported that they had hastily evacuated the aircraft after it slid to a halt, and when there seemed no danger of fire, made to return to it to retrieve their belongings. However, by this time a Russian soldier had appeared and indicated with this 'Tommy' gun that such an action would be very unwise. I imagine he thought that they were about to destroy their aircraft after a landing in 'enemy' territory. However, after the arrival of more senior Russian officers, better relations were established, and the boys were well treated and returned to the British Sector without delay.

In Hamburg we were accommodated in a very comfortable hotel in a relatively undamaged part of the city. Much of the bomb damage had now been cleared, but as little rebuilding had begun, there were, especially near the docks, huge areas that were completely flat, devoid of any sort of building. However it was four years since the last bomb fell and it would be surprising if, in a city like Hamburg with a people such as the Germans, the signs of returning normality were not all around. We encountered no hostility from the Germans, and were surprised to see the mountains of cream cakes in the bakers' windows; unheard of in food rationed Britain. We enjoyed sailing on the lakes in the centre of the city, an easy walk from our hotel, and under the auspices of the Control Commission, were able to play golf over one of the beautiful courses near the city (recreational transport provided free). There was also the NAAFI Officers Club, the Four Seasons, and one could not be in Hamburg without a visit to the 'Winkle Strasse' purely as an observer of course!

It seemed as if the Air Lift would go on for ever, but of course it was bound to end, and early in July the Russians lifted the blockade on Berlin. The Air Lift from then on was progressively reduced and although not finally wound up until the Autumn, the Civil Lift was quickly run down. It was not until the middle of August that the 'wet lift' was finally ended, by which time Flight Refuelling were carrying only token loads to Berlin. The majority of Flight Refuelling Ltd's 'lift only' crews were flown back to Tarrant Rushton in the second week of July, after a memorable champagne party laid on by the firm, and that was that. Our crew had completed 135 round trips to Berlin delivering some 270,000 gallons of petrol. Flight Refuelling altogether delivered more than 27,000 tons of petrol, nearly one third of the total taken to the city during the lift. By any standards a job well done. In doing it they lost one aircraft, destroyed in a crash in Wiltshire, when returning from Germany to Tarrant Rushton at night in bad weather, and the Lancastrian damaged when crash-landed in Russian territory, with no casualties.[8]

---

[8] The crash in Wiltshire occurred on 23rd November 1948. Sir Alan Cobham's Flight Refuelling Ltd Lancaster G-AHJW came down at the rear of Conholt Manor House in the village of Chute. The aircraft was carrying personnel who were returning on leave, which is why there was such a heavy loss of life. The only survivor was the W/Op. B. Stanley and those killed were pilot Capt. Reginald M.W. Heath, Nav Alan J. Burton, Flt/Eng Kenneth A. Seaborne, Capt William Cusak, Capt Cyril Taylor, Rad/Off Dornford W. Robertson and Nav Michael E. Casey. [Ed]

18. *Shorts*

Back home and once more looking for a job. I decided that, after my experience in the charter company and minor airline businesses, it would be a good idea to find something a little more stable. From my association with Universal Flying Services and then RAF Reserve Flying Training School at Fairoaks, I knew that there were jobs to be had in the quasi service world, where my instructing experience would come in handy. I therefore wrote to a number of firms running these training schools, offering my services. In the meantime, it was now the autumn of 1949; I went once again to Fairoaks for my annual fortnight, asking if I could do an Instructor's refresher course. Results were soon forthcoming after my applications to RFTSs and early in November I was taken on by Short Brothers & Harland Ltd. based at Rochester, Kent. This suited me well as I was then living in Sussex and could drive to Rochester every day without too much trouble. The Flying Services Division of Shorts was the only remaining branch of the firm still based in England. Their aircraft manufacturing business had been moved to Belfast, and amalgamated with Harland & Wolfe the ship builders, to become Short Brothers & Harland Ltd.

The Rochester branch at the time I joined, ran two RFSs (one at Rochester itself and one across the river at Hornchurch) and a flying club at Rochester. They were in the market for various other flying tasks that the Air Ministry and Admiralty were from time to time putting out to private tender. At this time the Reserve Flying Schools were run on the same basis as the pre war E&RFTSs, except that the pupils were already qualified air crew, and there was no *ab initio* training for the regular Air Force. Navigators were catered for as well as pilots, and to this end most RFS's had a flight of Ansons. I was first sent to help out with the instructing on Tiger Moths at Hornchurch, and stayed there until after Christmas when I returned to Rochester to join the Anson flight. The Ansons were Mk XXIs, the ultimate Anson, very like the Avro XIX I had flown at Southampton, except for the internal furnishings and metal wings, a far cry from the Mk.Is I had flown over the Western Approaches ten years previously.

The work consisted of flying reserve navigators on cross county flights all over the southern half of England and Wales. It was concentrated mainly at weekends, when the Reservists could get away from their jobs, with some mid week flying for those in continuous training and the few who could find the time. It was not exciting but had the merit of being secure. As secure that is, as any flying job outside BOAC or BEA. Shorts also had a number of civil aircraft at Rochester, a couple of Rapides, a Proctor and a Magister fitted with a rather natty glass house over the two cockpits, a one off job I think. These aircraft were used occasionally for charter work, but mostly for Army Co-operation. The object of this was to fly up and down a given line for an hour or so, to provide a dummy target for anti-aircraft batteries. This work could be done by day or by night and much of it was over London. Only those pilots with a civil flying licence could do this and we were paid the princely sum of five shillings per hour extra for our pains.

Much of this Army Co-operation was dull and boring, but occasionally it was quite enjoyable. I recall an occasion over London in daylight when the weather must have been quite exceptional. From 12,000ft I could see Battersea Power Station, the big hangar at Rochester Airfield and Brighton Pier, all from the same position. This will not be possible on many occasions today and in 1950 it was even more remarkable as the clear air regulations had not begun to take effect, and London was almost always enshrouded in a thick blanket of 'smog'. Flying above and around the metropolis in those days one felt very sorry for the millions whose whole lives were spent under that nasty yellowish pall. One saw why airmen used to call it 'The Smoke'.

Much of the Army Co-operation took place at night. Naturally we only flew in clear weather, and to be over London at 10,000ft on a brilliantly clear night was a fantastic experience. The advertising neon lights were back to their pre-war brilliance, or better, and it was possible to pick out all the main London landmarks and streets. From a position over say Piccadilly Circus, one could see the outlying towns as far east as the Medway towns, west to Reading, south to Redhill and north to Luton. It was a remarkable sight.

One of our pilots had an unfortunate experience in a Proctor on returning from a day time Army Co-operation flight. Coming back to Rochester from the north of the Thames, he could see the airfield from some ten miles away. He throttled back and glided down from several thousand feet for a landing. When at about 500 ft. and half a mile from the airfield, he needed the engine to help him correct a slight under shoot. Unfortunately he had neglected to take the precaution drummed in to all student pilots to keep the engine warm by giving bursts of throttle on the way down. He under shot the airfield, seriously damaging the aircraft and worse, badly injuring a child on the ground.

Soon after my arrival at Shorts the firm obtained a new contract, this time from the Admiralty. Instrument flying becoming a 'must' for all service pilots, and while the newly trained had this aspect taken care of in their training, the old hands needed the help of a special course to obtain the coveted 'green card' instrument rating. Shorts were contracted to set up an Instrument Training Flight at Rochester, equipped with Air Speed Oxford aircraft, provided by the Admiralty. Every two weeks some fourteen naval pilots, varying in rank from NCO to Captain RN, would come up each day from Chatham Barracks to fly dual in the Oxfords, and to do what ground instruction they needed to pass the Service Green Card rating check. Pilots from the Navy Instrument Testing Flight would come from Lee-on-the-Solent at the end of each course to pass the pupils out. It was around Easter time 1950 that I was asked if I would join the Instrument Flight. After a considerable amount of hard practice I was considered fit to take an Oxford down to Lee-on-Solent and take the I.F. test at the hands of the Navy. This hurdle surmounted, I started the grinding job of day in day out I.F. Instruction.

In charge of the Flight was a genial ex-RN Lt/Cdr Dickie Forwood. He had commanded the Navy Beam Approach Training Unit, and prior to his release from the Service had been serving at the Admiralty in London. He was therefore well pleased to obtain the job at Shorts when they took over the Instrument Flight contract. He gathered around him a mixed crowd of ex RAF and RN pilots, some of whom had been with him in the Service. The Oxford, as many hundreds, probably thousands, of ex Service pilots will remember, was a hardy little aircraft to fly. With a cruising speed of 140kts and a safe endurance of four hours, it was a very useful 'A to B' aircraft, as the many civilian operators who flew it as the 'Consul' in the immediate post war years realised. Unlike its senior but near contemporary the Anson I, it had power operated hydraulic flaps and undercarriage, and electric starters for the motors. It never aspired to the dizzy heights of constant speed airscrews however. It was an interesting aircraft to fly. Although perfectly docile when handled properly, it would not tolerate the ham-handed. Like many tail wheel aircraft with a short wheel-base but a wide track, it could be unstable on the ground. The inexperienced pilot would do well to watch for the swing on take off, and land on the main wheels with the tail held up as long as possible. With experience, three point landings were easy, but one had to be one jump ahead of the Oxford and not vice versa.

Instructors of the Instrument Training Flight at Rochester in 1951. Peter Rivington on the right of the front row.

For instrument flying practice we used a device called 'two stage amber'. The pilots' cockpit was lined with removable perspex panels, tinted amber. For normal flying these could either be removed or left in place, in which case the pilots would have a perfectly adequate, if amber tinted view of the outside world. If however, one of the pilots donned blue goggles, then, while having an adequate view inside the cockpit, the view through the amber screens was completely blanked out. This system worked very well and was vastly superior to the cumbersome hoods and screens previously used. Its one drawback was that in really bright conditions, say above cloud, enough light penetrated both amber screens and blue goggles to give a more or less clear view outside. In normal conditions however, the view through the windscreen and side windows was as black as any night in winter.

The instrument flying exercises we taught were dismissed by many as 'trick flying', unrelated to reality, but they certainly ensured that by the end of the course the pilots really could handle the aircraft 'by reference to instruments alone'. The exercise most feared and talked about by the pupils was known as 'pattern Baker'. To perform this the aircraft was flown on a steady course with the directional gyro set on 0. Using a stop watch the pilot would then turn at Rate 1, (90 deg. in thirty seconds) to port, climbing 1,000 ft. and rolling out on 90 deg. taking just one and a half minutes. After one minute steady on 90 deg. he entered a descending turn to port, coming out on 180 deg. again after exactly one and a half minutes, and descending 1,000 ft. After one minute he turned port again on to 270 deg. climbing 1,000 ft, again taking one and a half minutes. The pattern was finished when after one minute level on 90 deg. he turned port on to 360 deg. descending 1,000 ft once more. This whole exercise had to be completed with a maximum error of 100 ft, 10 seconds and 10 knots either way, and for most pilots it was ten minutes sweating blood.

We also practiced limited panel instrument flying, that is, without the use of the directional gyro on the artificial horizon, take offs on instruments, simulated GCAs and homings using our antiquated equipment and the XG beacon provided at

Rochester for our use. This last was peculiar to the RN and was used on HM Ships and Air Stations. Its continuously revolving aerial divided the 360 deg. into segments of 30 deg. the first from 345 deg.-015 deg. and so on. During its passage through each segment a different letter was transmitted in the Morse code. Thus if one heard the letter 'A' being transmitted one knew that a course of 180 deg. would take one home. In peace time the letters for each segment were fixed, but they could be varied for security in war time. Every station with a YG beacon would have a published let down sector avoiding any high ground. Ours at Rochester was the sector 015 deg - 045 deg. This had us approaching the aerodrome from over the Medway and Chatham dockyard, with no obstructions above airfield level. We used the YG beacon continuously, and this meant that we could take off from Rochester with two pupils, one in the left-hand pilot's seat and the other waiting in a passenger seat. We would climb above the clouds and do a two hour I.F. stint, checking position on the beacon every ten minutes or so. The session would normally end with a YG let down, and after a simulated GCA, where the instructor's "I have control", would be followed a few seconds later by the wheels kissing the grass (no runways at Rochester).

It was in many ways monotonous work, enlivened by the characters of many of our students, most of who was old experienced Naval pilots needing practice to achieve modern standards. For one reason or another I was normally given the most senior course members, and the names in my Log Book would evoke memories in many an old naval aviator. Shattock, Place (Midget Sub VC[9] turned aviator), Empson and Cassidi (all to achieve flag rank), Sholto-Douglas, Williamson (shot down at Taranto), Fell, Sylvester, Clutton, Cambell, Coxon, Hopkins, Welham, Cock-

---

[9] Lt. Basil C.G. Place, VC – Victoria Cross awarded 22/9/43.

burn, Lamb, Turnbull, Groves, Black, Luckraft, MacIntyre, Gibson, Swanton, Carver, Carmichael (who later achieved fame in Korea by shooting down a Mig in his piston engined Fury), and many more too numerous to mention. We ran the I.F. flight from 1949 to 1955 and during that time well over 1,000 Royal Navy pilots passed through our hands.

After a 'probation' period, when examiners from the I.F. Examining Flight at Lee-on- the-Solent came to check out each course, Pete Harrison, a long time employee of Short's who had taken over from Dick Forwood, and I went to Little Rissington to be passed as I.F. examiners by CFS. We flew over in an Oxford and the visit turned out to be a very pleasant social occasion, the testing being very much of a formality. From then on we could test our own courses for their I.F. ratings.

We could not expect to do hundreds of hours per year without some mishaps. Among many minor incidents two serious ones come to mind, one humorous and one tragic. The tragic one first. Rochester airfield is only a few miles from the former RAF Station at West Malling. At this time the airfield was in full commission, being the home of No.500 (County of Kent) Squadron, Royal Auxiliary Air Force, equipped with Meteors and No.25 Squadron with Vampire Night Fighters. It was an area that any wandering aircraft would do well to avoid. However on this particular day an Oxford with our instructor 'Johnny' Johnson and two Naval Officer pilots aboard, strayed too near West Malling and collided with a Vampire letting down at high speed into the circuit. The Vampire hit the Oxford from slightly above and probably never saw it. Although damaged, it was able to carry on and belly land at West Malling. The Oxford crew was not so lucky, losing most of a mainplane outboard of the engine. They were too low for anyone to have a chance to get out, and all three were killed. This was the only fatal accident we suffered during my fourteen years flying with Shorts.

The other incident could well have had a tragic ending had it not been for the coolness and airmanship of 'Dinger' Bell. On I.F. practice with two RN officers, he lost an engine without any warning, and when I say 'lost', that is just what I mean. One minute all was well, the next, the port engine was hanging from a few strands prior to falling off completely a few seconds later, and crashing down on to the Kentish farmland. 'Dinger' had a few thousand feet in hand, and as he had no idea how the aircraft would handle, if indeed it could be handled at all, instructed his two pupils to abandon ship, which they did in good order. Both landing safely although one had a bloody nose where his parachute pack snapping open had slapped him in the face (a not unusual hazard with the chest type of clip on chute they were wearing). 'Dinger' was now alone and wondering just what would fall off next. He found that he had reasonable control of the aircraft, albeit with almost full left aileron to counter the lost weight of the missing engine. Easing back his one remaining workable throttle, he carried on straight ahead to belly-land in a large cabbage field that appeared at just the right moment.

It is the sequel to his incident that is the amusing part. Naturally the Air Accident Investigation Branch of the Admiralty were anxious to know why an engine had fallen off their Oxford. They found the engine in a ploughed field and intact, although the propeller was broken in two pieces, presumably on impact with the ground. There had clearly been a failure of the engine bearings and an accusing finger was pointed at Short's Maintenance Engineers at Rochester, who had changed the engine shortly before. Had they over tightened the bearings and strained them, causing the failure? Things looked nasty in the Rochester hangars and the Chief Engineer wore a very long face. Then a few days later, a bright young spark of an Investigating Officer looked again at the propeller - one blade still attached, the other sheared off, but found lying nearby.

"Who", he asked, "guarded the aircraft for the first few hours after the crash?"

"A party of sailors from Chatham Barracks, one group for the aircraft, one for the engine," was the answer.

He asked to interview the guard on the engine.

"What," he demanded, "happened during your guard duty? Did anyone come near the engine?"

"No," was the answer, "except, of course, the chap who brought back the propeller blade."

"The what?"

"The chap who brought back the propeller blade. He found it in a hedge about a quarter of a mile away and knew it was part of the crash so he brought it along. We just put it with the rest of the engine."

"And you didn't see fit to mention this to anybody?"

"No, was it important?"

So the problem was solved and the Rochester engineers could breathe again. The propeller had shed a blade and the out of balance forces had ripped the engine out of its mounting so quickly that it seemed to have just dropped off.

The two occupants of the pilot's seats were lucky. The broken propeller could have ripped into the cockpit with disastrous results for them. Had that happened, and with the aircraft out of control, it is unlikely that the third crew member would have been able to get out in time.

In addition to the Instrument Flight, we also ran 'The Admiralty Flight'. This consisted of a couple of Harvards, two Firefly Trainers (the dual control version with the raised rear cockpit) and a Sea Fury Trainer. The purpose of this Unit was to enable officers posted to the Admiralty in Whitehall, to keep in flying practice and log sufficient hours each year to retain their flying pay. As all our clients were experienced pilots, any dual checks that had to be given were in the nature of a formality. I was usually given this task, and of course we carried out a certain amount of practice flying to keep our hands in, which in the Sea Fury anyway, was very enjoyable.

Peter Rivington briefing a pilot before duel on a Seafury at Rochester.

In 1953 the Indian Navy bought ten Sealand Amphibians from Shorts to set up their own Fleet Air Arm. The contract included delivery to Cochin, and the firm called for volunteers from its pilots for this task. I was keen to see India again and naturally put my name down, and so at the end of April found myself paired with Geoff Lawson, (who had one previous delivery and was therefore nominated first pilot) flying Sealand INS 106 from Rochester to Lympne to clear customs. We were in company with a second Sealand flown by Ray Gough (an experienced Flying Boat Captain from RAF Coastal Command) and Jim Smith, and made our way to Nice for our first night stop, refuelling at Lyons on the way. The flight from Lyons to Nice over the Alps Maratimes was as pleasant as ever, and as the sea came in view I recalled my days with SATA Geoff and I flew alternate legs and my first landing was at Nice. It was none too tidy as the Sealand controls took some getting used to. It was as if the elevator control wires were made of rubber, so each movement of the control wheel was followed by an appreciable time lag before anything happened. This could result in the aircraft proceeding down the runway in a series of ungainly switch-backs without the wheels ever getting onto the ground. However, one got used to it in the end.

After a night at the Nepresco at Nice we took off the next day for Bari, a three and a half-hour leg. As the amphibian Sealand had normal tankage for only around three hours, we had a fuselage tank of 50 gallons fitted for the ferry flight. This gave a safe endurance of five hours, but involved the co-pilot in some energetic hand-pumping in the rear cabin, to transfer the overload fuel into the main tanks.

The flight from Nice to Bari was pleasant and took us past the northern tip of Corsica, near the Island of Elba, and so to the Italian coast, north of Rome. We then had to climb to about 10,000 ft. to clear the Apennines, which were largely free from cloud, and so down onto the eastern coastline plain and to Bari where we were met by a charming Italian who was to look after us. He drove us into town in his own car and a memorable journey it was. He appeared to be unduly influenced by his racing driver countrymen, and drove in a manner more suitable to Silverstone or Monza than to a public highway. Italian roads seem often to be straight and quite narrow. It is a stimulating experience to be coming up behind a large camion, with a closing speed of around 50 mph, when there is another car approaching from the opposite direction. This experience is made all the more piquant when one realises that one's driver has not the slightest intention of slackening speed. All three vehicles seemed likely to arrive at the same piece of narrow road at the same time. Having sustained a number of near misses of this sort, one realises what a safe occupation flying is.

Our hotel was a comfortable one on the sea front, and during the evening and night, judging from the squeals of tortured rubber coming from the road outside, our driver from the airport had a large number of like minded compatriots. The next day was 1st May, and I suppose we were lucky to get away from Bari on this continental public holiday. However, get away we did, and had a long day's flying to Cyprus via Athens. Our route took us down the Italian coast across the Gulf of Taranto and then past Corfu down the Greek Coast and up the Gulf of Corinth to Athens. We flew at low level along the Corinth Canal, a remarkable fete of engineering that joins the Gulf of Corinth with the Athenian Sea. It is quite steep sided and absolutely dead straight for about twenty miles, and quite capable of handling quite large ocean going ships. At Athens we had no time to leave the airport, but there could be no doubt where we were with the Acropolis standing out on its hill only a few miles away.

The flight from Athens to Cyprus took nearly four hours and initiated a great deal of fuel pumping. At the halfway point, somewhere near Rhodes, Ray Gough had trouble with an engine - plugs I think. Anyway it began running very rough and seemed likely to pack up at any moment. However, things were not too bad as the Turkish coast was in full view to port and he managed to nurse the aircraft into Nicosia. A comfortable night was spent at the Ledra Palace - it was before the troubles -and we were ready to hop across the last stretch of the Med. over the Lebanese

Mountains and on across the desert to Baghdad. A plug change had cured Ray's engine trouble and the long flight of 4hrs.15mins. went without a hitch. As was the custom in these parts, we used the oil pipeline as a navigation guide, only abandoning it for the last two hundred miles or so to Baghdad.

We passed some impressive ruins that must have dated back to Old Testament times, possibly they were the remains of the Palace of Nebuchadnezzar on the great Euphrates River "by the waters of Babylon".

Baghdad did not seem much changed from my visit twelve years earlier in 1941. We had intended to night stop and carry on the following day, but the 3rd May was the Coronation of the King and nobody was working so we stayed to watch. The procession passed our hotel and the sight of Churchill tanks driving at 20 mph through a narrow avenue in the crowd, barely kept open by the police using their staves, was an awe-inspiring sight. The next day, 4th May, we were at the aerodrome bright and early and ready to take off for Bahrain. Our port engine started at once, but the starboard would only run while the ki-gas priming pump was operated. Stop priming and the engine faded away. After a few minutes vainly trying to get the engine to run normally, we gave it up and got out to look for the trouble. There were engineers there very familiar with the Gipsy Queen engine, though not of course with the Mk.70 installed in the Sealand. However, they located the trouble quite quickly, the drive to the fuel pump had sheared, so no petrol could get to the engine except via the priming system. On the face of it this was quite a simple matter, but not so. Firstly, a new drive shaft would have to be sent from the U.K. and secondly, the installation was such that the engine had to be removed from its mounting in order to fit it. Now another complication arose. Geoff Lawson needed to be home within a reasonable time for personal reasons, so he and Ray Gough changed over aircraft, and we waved good bye to Geoff and Jim as they set off for Bahrain and points east.

So Ray and I settled down to wait at Baghdad. The city is a strange mixture of the old and the new with ancient markets instantly recognisable from the stories in the Arabian Nights. The faded trappings of Empire – the British Club in town, now deserted, and the Country Club surprisingly still going strong, swimming pool and all. Some of the hotels were modern; ours was the Regent's Palace that was barely completed, with brick dust and half finished masonry everywhere. Our spare parts were ordered by cable and arrived with gratifying promptness on a B.O.A.C. flight - thus by the 11th May we were able to test fly the Sealand and the next day set off for Bahrain. As we had been delayed at Baghdad by paper work and formalities, and the Baghdad-Bahrain leg was to take around four hours, a night stop would have to be made at Bahrain. I flew this leg to Basra and on past Kuwait, down the West Coast of the Gulf. I don't think we saw any more of the ground in Iraq than we used to all those years ago flying Blenheims out to India. The flying was no problem, however, as the hard line of the dust at about 10,000ft. made an excellent horizon.

Over the Gulf the visibility was good and after the four hour flight we let down for a straight approach on the now concrete runway, no more oiled sand. I managed a very smooth touch down. We were made very comfortable at the B.O.A.C. Rest House and were away early in the morning for Jiwani, Beluchistan, over flying Sharjah and Dubai. These last two were still minor settlements, but were shortly to become oil rich cities.

Ray flew the Bahrain-Jiwani leg and I the Jiwani-Karachi. It seemed odd to be landing at Mauripur again, now a teeming Pakistani Air Force Base. The Paki's received us very well, in spite of the fact that we were flying aircraft with 'Indian Navy' written on the fuselage. After all, the Indians were and are not exactly their favourite people. Anyway we had a jolly night stop. We now had to fly the length of the Indian Sub Continent down to Cochin, landing at Ahmedabad and Bombay en route. The flight from Karachi to Ahmedabad across the Kuck Desert was as boring as I remembered it to be, but with just the right number of towns and railway lines to ensure that navigation was no trouble at all. At Ahmedabad we had, of course, to clear customs into India. As an aircraft from Pakistan, we were treated to the full works of officialdom, and anyone who has been in India will know what that means. If an Indian Customs or Immigration Officer decides to be obstructive, then brother, watch out!

While we were struggling with petty officialdom (the fact that our aircraft bore I.N. markings counted for not a jot), I recognised in the airport building an Indian who had been one of the civilian Air Traffic Controllers at Karachi in 1942. He was now, so I was told, a high official in Indian Civil Aviation at Delhi, and was touring airfields in a light aircraft (a Puss Moth I fancy). This was the same Indian Parsee, whose son's 'Navjot', I had attended in Karachi ten years before, so naturally I introduced myself. I'm sorry to say I received a very off hand reception. Whether he wanted to establish a 'we are the masters now' attitude, whether he as Indian, was not comfortable at being reminded of his time in Karachi, or whether he was simply not enjoying being bumped over the hot Indian plains in a light aircraft, I will never know. I do know, however, that my friendly overtures were not reciprocated.

At Bombay we landed at Santa Cruz Airport, and were soon on our way to the big city by taxi, passing the inevitable shanty-towns with their overpowering smell. Just as one could not get into the centre of any British city without traversing a mile or so of Victorian and Edwardian back to back terraces, so you could not avoid the shanty- towns in India. Bombay is bad, but not so bad as Calcutta. Madras I hardly know. We stayed at a quite reasonable hotel in Bombay, 'The Airlines' or some such name. The city was 'dry' of course. We could I suppose, in view of our mission, have sought out the Indian Navy and had a drink in one of their wardrooms, but I don't remember that we bothered. The final leg on the next day was from Bombay down the coast to Cochin - four hours and fifteen minutes. I don't think we were higher than 500 ft. all the way and were usually a great deal lower. That long straight Malabar coastline with its almost unbroken sandy beaches and interesting looking fishing villages fringed by the pounding Indian Ocean surf, made a grand finale to our trip. I think that the Portuguese enclaves of Goa were still in existence at the time, and I suppose they could in theory, have objected to our violation of their territory, but I'm sure they didn't bother.

We were met and looked after by the CO at Cochin, an ex-RN officer, now Commander IN, a charming man with a very dark skin but very 'British' in behaviour and name. Our return flight had been booked on Deccan Airways and Air India International (from Bombay), and we had only one night in a comfortable Cochin hotel before leaving by Dakota for Coimbatore and Bangalore, where we stayed the night. The following day, 17th May, I was delighted to find that the Dakota was to take us to Bombay via Begumpet, my old EFTS stamping ground of ten years before. The airfield had hardly changed, the runways were a little more clearly marked, but the airport building was much as I remembered it. I found a number of Deccan Airways pilots there (Begumpet was their main base), and amongst them was a Captain Sarka, Flying Officer 'Prof' Sarka IAF, one of our staff navigation pilots at the EFTS. It was a pleasant reunion, but unfortunately the other 'Prof', (F.O. Huigol IAF), one of our talented group of Indian Instructors, was away. He now held the exalted post of Chief Pilot Deccan Airways.

I wandered round our old Mess hut, now shuttered and deserted, and looked for the remains of the grass lawn we had laid outside - Mashona Park - in honour of 'Buck' Taylor the Rhodesian Flight Commander. This needed the constant attention of our mali (gardener) with a hose pipe, so it was not surprising that little remained of it. To walk round those buildings made me realise that places are nothing, its people that make things what they are.

The flight to Bombay was routine and that same evening we boarded an Air India International Constellation bound for London. After stops at Basra, Cairo, Geneva and Paris we arrived at London Airport some 24 hours after leaving Bombay.

Back at Rochester and back into the routine of I.F. Instruction on the Oxfords, occasional dual trips or solo flips in the Admiralty Flight Sea Fury, Firefly or Harvard, and a little Army Co-operation flying, mainly on Rapides. Occasionally there was a flight in Oxfords that went up in pairs to give RAF ground Radar Operators practice interceptions. These aircraft were provided by the Air Ministry and were separate from the Naval aircraft. Things went on in this fashion for another two years and around another 1,000 flying hours (my total was now something over 5,000), when in May 1955 I was asked if I would join the Rochester Naval Ferry Flight, also run by Shorts of course.

19. *The Ferry Flight*

In the early 1950s the Royal Navy Fleet Air Arm had on strength a very large number of aircraft of many different types mostly of World War II vintage. If I list a few that come to mind the reader will see what I mean:

Anson, Attacker, Avenger, Barracuda, Devon, Dominie, Expediter, Sea Fury, Firefly, Firebrand, Gannet, Sea Hornet, Harvard, Hunter, Sea Hawk, Mosquito, Sea Otter, Oxford, Sea Prince, Seafire, Scimitar, Tiger Moth, Sea Vampire, Sea Venom, Wyvern.

They also had a large number of Naval Air Stations from Lossiemouth in the North of Scotland to Culdrose (Helston) and Eglinton near Londonderry in Northern Ireland.

The work of moving these aircraft, as required, between Air Stations, Repair Yards and Factories required a fair sized Ferry Unit, if a great deal of First Line Pilot time was not to be wasted. As was the fashion in those days, the task was put out to civilian tender, and Shorts obtained the contract. I can do no better to convey the flavour of work on the Ferry Flight than to reproduce, by kind permission of the M.O.D., an article I wrote for the Fleet Air Arm magazine 'Flight Deck' in 1962.

••

ROCHESTER TRANSIT

"Brown shoes and a moustache - calls 'isself Lieutenant-Commander - let 'im get away with that Scimitar and 'e'll be refuelling at Omsk before you can say 'Burgess and McLean'!"

Not a likely remark as Shorts' pilots have been ferrying Naval aircraft for longer than many members of the Fleet Air Arm can remember.

This is not the place to answer the question "Why are civilians flying Service aircraft?" Except to say that the Admiralty and the Air Ministry for many years, and more recently the War Office, have found it convenient, for reasons that are partly financial, to have certain non operational flying tasks carried out by civilian firms under contract.

Shorts obtained the Ferrying Contract in November 1950 and have been carrying on ever since. The task consists of providing pilots to fly aircraft on transfer from one Air Station to another, to and from contractors airfields, and operating taxi aircraft to position pilots as required. The aircraft handled, therefore, range from brand new shining monsters from factory airfields, to oil streaked, battered "heaps", passed fit for "one ferry flight only" and going for scrap.

The Beginning

The list of aircraft ferried in the first month reads like a page from the catalogue of the Shuttleworth collection:

Firefly, Firebrand, Seafire, Sea Otter, Barracuda, Anson, Sea Fury, Hornet, Mosquito, Oxford and Harvard.

Almost all the pilots were "ex-crabs" and when it is considered how strange the idea of having civilians delivering and collecting their aircraft must have seemed to the Service, it reflects great credit on both sides that things settled down to run smoothly. The foundations of eleven years successful co-operation were laid in those first few months.

The pilots soon became web-footed and could even be heard at the bar talking of "going ashore", when, apart from the odd trip across the Gosport Ferry, they were never anywhere else; deck landing not being part of the task. (One deck landing has been made - the aircraft a chopper and the ship in harbour!).

Nomads

The Ferry Pilot's life is a nomadic one, with several nights in different wardrooms and on trains each week. It is being in the proximity of the London rail centres that makes Rochester such a suitable a base for the Unit. Living out of a parachute bag is one of the draw-backs of the job. Flying a great variety of aircraft types is one of the attractions.

Although the introduction of more complex modern types has made a degree of specialisation necessary (in the old days everyone flew almost everything), it is still not unusual for a pilot to fly five or six different types in quick succession. This effectively prevents boredom and, of course, H.R.H's advice on fingers applies.

To paraphrase an earlier Ferry Flight Chronicler: It does not improve ground crew confidence if a cheery "Ready to start" sign is followed by a loud report and an airborne cockpit canopy. Nor is it good policy to be seen with the pilot's notes for an Avenger open on one's knee while trying to start a Vampire.

It is probably the case that the Ferry Pilot is not in as good flying practice on any given type; as a pilot who flys that type only; but he is, and expects to be, judged by the same high standards. It is a fact that over the eleven years of operation, while *12,770* aircraft have been ferried and *26,000* hours flown, there have been only five heavy accidents in which there has been any degree of pilot error. During this time, two pilots have been seriously injured.

Luck and Good Judgement

There have been, of course, a few exciting moments during all this flying. For instance, the pilot of a taxi Dominie loaded with Ferry Pilots who finds one engine uncontrollably on fire with flames playing on the fuel tank and streaming back from the trailing edge, needs more than skill and a cool head. If no one is to get hurt-he needs luck (he got it and no one was).

Equally, the pilot of a Firefly whose engine cuts at 3000' over the Lake District above 8/8ths cloud, needs a large slice of luck if he is to survive. He got it too, and a green endorsement. In this case a bizarre touch was added when the first person to greet him as he stepped from his belly-landed aircraft was a lady-friend from Essex who happened to be passing by. Her male companion was most suspicious on finding that the two knew each other, clearly thinking that it was disgraceful the lengths to which these pilots would go to spoil a chap's fun.

The Moderns

With the introduction of faster, heavier and more expensive aircraft, conversion to the new types presents more and more of a problem. Often in the early days of a new type the Ferry Pilot's services are in great demand as each aircraft is "hot" and requires to be moved at once. But aircraft are difficult to come by for familiarisation. Way back, any pilot qualified on jets could ferry a new type, say a Venom or a Sea Hawk, after a cockpit check and a couple of circuits. Now, a week or more has to be spent on a conversion course. This means that about three pilots only can be qualified on each new type.

Taxi Aircraft

In an imperfect world where aircraft often become available for ferrying only about 30 minutes before they go u/s, taxi aircraft are the lifeline of the unit. Dominies, Devons and Sea Princes (Brrr!) have all been used. One or two pilots usually specialise in this work. There is one snag - if they stay on it too long, they get so spoilt that they have to be restrained from making a "May Day" call if the Decca goes u/s.

Kalafrana, Here We Come!

Overseas trips provide the spice in a Ferry Pilot's life. Mostly they are to Malta, but occasionally an aircraft has to go to Gibraltar. 428 of these flights have been made since 1950.

In 1958 four Sea Hawks were flown to Aden (two by Ferry and two by Service Pilots), and in the Autumn of 1961 a Hunter was taken to Singapore in company with two RAF Hunters.

The R.N.R.

Some six years ago a number of officers appeared in various H.M. Ships to do their annual R.N.R. Training.

The faces seemed familiar and when the disguise of negative moustaches and unaccustomed dress was pierced, they turned out to be Ferry Pilots who had joined the newly formed Air Branch of the R.N.R.

From this stems the quite legal use of naval rank by Ferry Pilots when booking accommodation in wardrooms or obtaining transport from a hard-pressed Supervisor at what seems to him to be suspiciously like opening time.

Unfortunately, although the R.N.R. status remains, the requirement to do annual training does not (one more excuse for a jolly down the drain).

It is interesting that the only officers who still wear the "A" in the curl of the braid are those of the R.N.R. (A) Branch.

In conclusion, a Ferry Pilot was asked what he could say about his work. "We count ourselves among the luckiest of pilots," he said, "and enjoy the variety of the work".

"Yes, we have to maintain the same qualifications as a Service Pilot - Instrument Gradings and all that. We send a hostage to Yeovilton each year and they put him through the hoop. Then he comes back and puts us through it - spiteful I call it".

"Yes a few things do annoy - like trains. Also, we do not like being called Airwork Ferry Pilots. We mean no disrespect to our friends at Hurn, Yeovilton, Lee and elsewhere, but it has always been Shorts Ferry Flight, so please get it right".

"Yes, I think that when I picked up the 100th production..... at the factory, they might have given me a small token of their esteem - an engraved tankard.....or a cheque..... But do you know I had difficulty in borrowing a ballpoint pen! Still, the A.E.O. gave me a cigar when I landed. Pity I don't smoke".

"No, things haven't changed much since the Seafire, Firefly days. The agony is over much more quickly now, that's all".

"I remember one aircraft, the Attacker it was, I think. They said it was too complicated and expensive for Ferry Pilots to fly....we ferried nearly 500 of 'em".

"Please excuse me if I rush now, I've got a date with a Sea Vixen".

"No, things don't change much".

••

The title 'Rochester Transit' was the R.T. call sign used by pilots when flying ferry aircraft with the pilot's own number. I used 106 so whether I was ferrying a Venom or a Wessex, I was 'Rochester Transit One Zero Six'. Taxi aircraft used to position or pick up pilots, dropped the word 'transit'. We became very familiar with the routes between the various airfields, so much so that maps became largely superfluous. In any case, so much of the jet flying was done above clouds when maps were not a great help. Some flights were more often than not carried out at low level, usually those on propeller aircraft and later on helicopters. I remember one particular trip in a Gannet to Culdrose, probably from White Waltham. This involved staying over land until past Plymouth (there was a firing range in Lyme Bay), and then cutting across St. Austell Bay on the direct track to Culdrose (Helston). On this occasion I was amazed to see large numbers of the most enormous sharks basking near to the surface. They looked big even from 1,000 ft. up and must have been six to eight feet long. I suppose these are the first that were hunted from the South Cornish coast.

There were one or two things that would have been imprudent to say in an article twenty-odd years ago. Trains, for instance. I don't suppose that I shall be releasing any startling information when I say that many Ferry Pilots were quite pleased to return home or go out to a job by train. We were allowed first class travel, including sleepers. The reader will not be surprised to hear that pilots though claiming first class travel, did not always buy a first class ticket. I can't remember exactly what the rail fares were in those far off days – something absurd like Elgin (Lossiemouth) to Kings Cross £12 First Class and £8 Second Class plus sleeper at £4 1st Class and £2 2nd Class, thus it was possible to make £6 profit on the trip. Now I'm sure that everybody, including the Admiralty, must have guessed that this was going on, but it paid them to encourage pilots to use trains. To fly a Devon, say from Rochester to Lossiemouth to pick up a pilot and return, must have cost at least £200 in 1950/60, so it was far cheaper to encourage rail travel. Add the fact that the night sleeper from Scotland enabled a pilot to get back to Rochester by 10 o'clock in the morning, ready to go on another trip if need be, and it will be even clearer that rail travel was a good thing for the Admiralty. It was not, such a good thing for Shorts, as they made a small profit on hours flown by taxi aircraft, which were of course provided by the service for use on the contract. On our numerous trips to Northern Ireland we sometimes used the taxi aircraft, but most often it was train and boat. B.E.A. was sometimes used, the flight from Aldergrove to London Airport taking well under two hours.

The Ferry Flight was formed in November 1950 and Dick Forwood moved over from the I.F. Flight to run it. Late of the Admiralty in Whitehall, Dick knew the ropes and had even had a hand in formulating the contract from the service side of the fence. He gathered round him a group of experienced ex-Service pilots, whose average flying time probably exceeded 2,000 hours. They performed well and apart from a few hiccups early on, the cropping of a Seafire's prop at Gosport and a Vampire's overload tank scraping the runway at Lee come to mind, the operation was nearly accident free. One pilot was seriously injured at Sydenham (Belfast) and landed up in the Loch. Another had a hairy emergency landing at Abbotsinch when his Sea Hawk's controls jammed. A back injury finished his flying career. There were the two instances mentioned in the article, to the Dominie and the Firefly, no injury in either of these cases. I had a forced landing in a Dragonfly helicopter due to engine failure - more of that later.

There must have been other minor occurrences, but I can't call any to mind. Soon after I gave up flying, the first and only fatal accident occurred. Harry Proudlove, ex-RAF and very experienced, was flying a Gannet from Belfast, where it had been stored, to I think, Culdrose. Due probably to weather, he chose to cross the Irish Sea to the Chester area and fly south along the boarder country to the Bristol Channel. When in the region of Malvern, his engine bay fire warning light came on, and he got clear indication that this was not a false alarm. He operated the fire extinguisher to no avail and, too low to bail out, was lining up for a forced landing when the aircraft exploded. Due to his high standard of professionalism the ground station he was in touch with, (probably the RAF master airfield at Shawbury), was able to monitor exactly his emergency. When the wreckage was examined it was found that a main fuel pipe had sprung such a massive leak that no extinguisher would have coped with the ensuing fire. As that was the only fatal accident suffered by the Ferry Flight in fifteen years intensive flying, it says quite a lot for the high standards maintained by the Navy, and for the professionalism of the pilots involved.

A typical week in the life of a Ferry Pilot in the middle 1950's might have gone as follows:

Monday:
- Passenger in Devon from Rochester to Lee.
- Sea Hawk: Lee to Abbotsinch (Glasgow).
- Sky Raider: Abbotsinch to Culdrose (Helston, Cornwall).
- Back to Rochester by night train.

Tuesday:
- Passenger in Devon from Rochester to Ford.
- Firefly: Ford to Yeovilton.
- Gannet: Yeovilton to Culdrose.
- Sea Prince: Culdrose to Brawdy (nr St Davids, S.Wales).
- Overnight Brawdy.

Wednesday:
- Venom: Brawdy to Stretton (nr Warrington).
- Passenger in Devon: Stretton to Rochester.

- Home for night.

Thursday:
- Passenger in Devon from Rochester to Anthorn (Carlisle)
- Vampire: Anthorn to Lossiemouth.
- Tiger Moth: Lossiemouth to Arbroath.
- Home on night train from Edinburgh.

Friday:
- Pilot, taxi Dominie: Rochester to White Waltham.
- Lee to Yeovilton to Rochester.
- Home mid afternoon.

Ferry Pilots with bowler hats and umbrellas, arriving at RNAS Anthorn for a closing down party in 1957. Peter Rivington appears 3rd from left.

Obviously more could be done in the summer than in the winter. Not only was the weather better, but extra daylight enabled flying to continue until the Air Stations closed, usually at 6 p.m. (1800 hours). In the mid winter it was dark soon after 4pm in the south and at about 3.30pm up in Scotland. No ferry flying took place after dark and the airfields usually closed at sunset. In addition to the Naval Air Stations, frequent calls were made at contractors airfields, either to collect new aircraft or to return older ones for refurbishing. These included Faireys at White Waltham, Hamble and Ringway, Armstrong Whitworth at Bitteswell, Westlands at Yeovil, D.H. at Hatfield and Christchurch (Hawarden), Airspeeds at Portsmouth, Supermarines at South Marston (Swindon) plus various smaller contractors at Little Staughton, Tarrant Rushton, Bedford and Hurn. Later Blackburns at Holme-on-Spalding-Moor became a regular port of call. The Ferry Pilot's life was a very varied one as far as aircraft types were concerned. I can do little better than record my feelings about the aircraft I was lucky enough to fly.

First the piston engined types:

Hawker Sea Fury FB II, T20 (Centaurus 18)

Very much the king of piston engined fighters. Directly descended from the Typhoon and very nearly identical to the Tempest II. Its Centaurus engine was as smooth as silk. It was beautiful for aerobatics and in every way a thoroughbred. This aircraft took some flying, repaid finesse and punished clumsiness, unlike the nose wheeled toys that followed it. The Fury Trainer has a comfortable rear cockpit, but unable to raise it in Fairey fashion (See Firefly), the occupant of the rear cockpit had to rely on a periscope device in order to see forward. The Fury's five bladed airscrew needed to absorb the Centaurus' power, looked an awful lot of propeller, especially from the cockpit. It must have provided an embarrassing amount of drag after an engine failure. Luckily I never had occasion to test this out.

Fairey Firefly 1, 4, 6, 7. (RR Griffon) various

A pleasant hack if you didn't mind sitting behind an engine that sounded like a bag of nails. How did Rolls Royce ever produce an engine like the Griffon? Another aircraft that rewarded the pilot for his skill. Like so many previous aircraft, re-design and development resulted in a steady deterioration in performance and handling. The Mk.I with the chin radiator was best. Of the re-designed Mk.7, least said the better. (Shades of the Blenheim V). The Firefly Trainer had the rear cockpit raised, provided with a separate hood and windscreen, and with dual control and full instrumentation. This layout had been pioneered during the war by Faireys with the Battle Trainer, the 'Dromedery Battle' as it was called. Occasionally we had a Firefly V9 to fly. This was the drone, radio controlled aircraft, converted for the Firefly 5. As long as you made certain that all the radio control equipment was disconnected, these flew like a normal Firefly.

Boulton & Paul Balliol (Merlin 35)

A nondescript type. It somehow felt wrong sitting side by side behind a Merlin. Not an unpleasant A to B aircraft.

Grumman Avenger (Wright Cyclone R-2600-20)

What is one to say about an aircraft that proved itself to be a world-beater in its class? It would be churlish to say that it flew like an airborne cow, and that operating the ailerons felt like using a muscle building machine in a gym. The auto-pilot worked well and I'm sure there are old pilots all over the world who would rise up in fury if I said a word against the Avenger. One Wright Cyclone engine took Lindburg from New York to Paris and I'm sure another would have taken an Avenger round the world if need be. Did one ever have an engine failure?

Douglas Skyraider *(Wright Cyclone R-3350-26WA)*

The Royal Navy used only the Airborne Early Warning version of the Skyraider. That is, the one with the large radome under its belly, and a cabin aft of the pilot's cockpit for the Radio Operator. The Skyraider was a beautiful aircraft to fly, with excellent controls and a dream of an auto-pilot. I flew many of them and remember with particular pleasure a trip out to Malta. I had only one 'hairy' moment in a 'Sky', the last I flew as it happened. Taking WT952 from Culdrose to Abbotsinch I was just abreast of Prestwick in fine weather, with Ailsa Craig standing out over to port, when the engine noise level rose alarmingly. A quick scan of the instruments showed the R.P.M. below the red line. The only snag was that the aircraft would not maintain height at that power. Nevertheless, Abbotsinch was only thirty miles or so ahead and I had plenty of height, so calling them up and telling them of my predicament, I was able to make a steady descent into the circuit and drift down to a safe landing. There would of course have been no question of going round again. It was later found that there had been a complete failure of the constant speed unit, which left the propeller blades up against the fine pitch stops. In spite of this, I still have the happiest memories of the old 'Sky'.

North American Harvard II (Pratt and Whitney Wasp)

This was not the curved graceful Harvard I had flown twenty years earlier at Grantham, but the angular squared off one, changed I presume, to make war time mass production easier. There is not a great deal more to say about the Harvard, except that it spawned one of the better Ferry Flight stories.

I went with 'Pancho' Brandt to Arbroath to collect two Harvards, and take them down to Lee-on-Solent. They were the last of a batch being handed over to the Portuguese Air Force, who had stationed an Engineer Officer at Arbroath to supervise the preparation of the aircraft. His work finished, he hitched a lift down to Lee in the back of 'Pancho's' aircraft. 'Pancho' was a well known Ferry Flight character. One of the original members, he had ferried more aircraft than anyone else and collected an MBE in the process, to add to the DFC he had won during the war with the RAF, 'Pancho', as his nickname implies, was a swarthy character of Mediterranean appearance, well known to everyone in the Fleet Air Arm except, apparently, to one Petty Officer at Lee. After we had landed and were sorting out our kit on the tarmac, this Petty Officer wandered over to Pancho's aircraft and went up to the Portuguese Engineer Officer, who was, as it happened, blonde and fair skinned. Casting a suspicious glance at 'Pancho' and, out of the corner of his mouth, he asked "Ow d'you get on with these ruddy Portuguese then?"

DH Tiger Moth (Gipsy Major)

The R.N. had a number of these little aircraft and unfortunately for the Ferry Flight they seemed to be required alternately in Scotland and in Devon. Thus, a Tiger Moth for ferrying was usually at Robrough (Plymouth) to be taken to Arbroath, or vice versa. There is nothing more to say about them except that they were cold and draughty and for that reason not popular with ferry pilots.

Auster V (Lycoming 130 h.p)

I think perhaps the R.N. had only one of these aircraft, but it seemed to appear on the Ferry programme very frequently. I flew it once and found the Lycoming engine had the endearing habit of cutting dead for about ten seconds every hour of so. This was not good for the nerves and as I was never able to land an Auster without giving the impression of a Kangaroo, my performance was not improved by the idiosyncrasies of the power plant.

TWIN-ENGINED AIRCRAFT

DH Dominie D.H.89 (2 Gipsy Six)

The Service version of the old Rapide ten seater and a very handy taxi aircraft. The Dominie flew like a twin engined Tiger Moth as long as three point landings were not attempted. The aircraft was a natural for wheel landings, and was easily kept straight on the brakes after the tail was down. The snag with attempting three pointers was that with the very high aspect ratio (sharply pointed) wings, a nasty wing drop was liable to occur at the point of stall. As a three pointer requires the aircraft to be set down in a stalled condition, the Rapide pilot must judge his height exactly if a neat landing was to be achieved. One foot out either way and the result would be untidy or frightening, or both! At Secunderabad we used to gather to watch the Tatq Airways Rapide arrive from Poona when we knew a certain pilot was at the controls. With admirable tenacity he consistently attempted three pointers. This was especially hazardous on our bumpy grass airfield, as even if the initial landing was achieved satisfactorily, the aircraft was liable to be thrown back into the air again in a fully stalled condition. His efforts were almost always spectacular.

Our Rapides were popular for short hauls, especially in warmer weather.

DH Devon (2 Gipsy Queen 150)

A thoroughly popular aircraft, warm, comfortable and easy to fly. At a cruising speed of 150 knots, the longest U.K. taxi trips were possible. These were the luxury R.N. transport aircraft and we were lucky to get them, but not for long as they were soon replaced by Sea Princes.

Hunting Sea Prince (2 Leondides 125)

We had one C.I. Prince early on. This was the short nosed aircraft, designed for the passenger role. It was furnished to Admiral's Barge standards, and predictably we did not keep it for long before it was replaced by the T.I. This was designed for Navigator and Radar Operator training and was cold, uncomfortable and noisy. The Prince was faster on paper than the Devon, but without the range. A long trip in winter in a Prince equalled some unhappy ferry pilots. Both the Devons and the Princes were equipped with Decca Navigators, with a visual display map, most popular with taxi pilots, and made flying possible in all but the very worst weather. Although we had our specialist taxi pilots, most of us took a turn and I enjoyed the work occasionally, for one thing, it almost always meant getting home at night.

OTHER TWIN-ENGINED AIRCRAFT

Beech Expediter (2 Pratt & Whitney Wasp Juniors)

During the war the Navy acquired a number of these aircraft from America for communications flying. It was an excellent aircraft, fast and with a good range. In civilian garb it was known as the 'Twin Beech' to distinguish it, I suppose, from the single engined, back stagger Beech Traveller. I only flew one Expediter and that was on a Malta trip, my first in fact. So I did my familiarisation flight on the first leg, Lee - Istres. I'm sure that wouldn't be allowed nowadays. The Expediter gave me no trouble, and after a night at Istres, I took it on to Halfar, with a landing en route at Elmas.

Short Sturgeon (2 Merlin 140)

I flew both the original long nose version and the short nose one, as modified at Rochester. Apart from the Coffman starter, whose cartridges had to be loaded from outside, the Sturgeon was an excellent aircraft from the ferry point of view. We had one at Rochester which we flew for Elliot Aviation to test their instrumentation, so I had quite a few Sturgeon hours when I joined the Ferry Flight. The aircraft was unusual in that its Merlin 140's had contra rotating props (as on the Spitfire 21) and this took care of any tendency to swing on take off. Arriving too late for its intended role as a carrier borne strike aircraft, it was converted to a high-speed target tug and was mostly used by the Fleet Requirements Squadron in Malta.

Accordingly, I had the pleasure of flying one out there and bringing another back at a later date. The only snag was, as I have said, with the Coffman starter, so on overseas flights we had to carry a crewman to reload after each starting attempt. The

Merlins easily got over-rich, and sometimes starting a Sturgeon was like firing a 21 gun salute. I never liked the cartridge starter idea for piston engines. The mixture had to be just right for the engine to catch, and there was no second chance.

One further twin engine aircraft should be mentioned, although this was not a Ferry Flight matter, the Vickers Varsity (2 Bristol Hercules 264). We had one of these at Rochester, provided by the Ministry of Supply. It was used by Elliot Aviation to develop some of their airborne electronic devices. We were just expected to fly the aircraft and do as we were asked. Pete Harrison (who took over the Instrument Flight from Dick Forward) and myself did the flying.

The Varsity was a development of the Viking Airliner, but modified to have a nose wheel undercarriage. A quite delightful vice-less aircraft, when loaded it seemed to fly almost as well on one engine as on two. An amusing sidelight on the Elliot work: sometimes when we were flying straight and level, their boffin would ask us to "go down 10 feet!" That might have been possible with their instrumentation, it certainly was not with ours. Because of this Varsity flying, Pete and I came in for an enjoyable trip to Farnborough each year to be checked out as 'test pilots'. At Rochester we also had a contract for refurbishing Beaufighters TT 10 (2 Bristol Hercules). I enjoyed the reunion with this delightful aircraft, made possible by my 'test pilot' status.

TURBO PROP AIRCRAFT

Fairey Gannet A.S. 1, 2, 4, 5. (1 Armstrong Siddeley Double Mamba 100 or 101)

The Navy classed the Gannet as a twin engine aircraft, and they were right in so far as it could be flown with either half of its

Double Mamba shut down. But a pilot with only Gannet 'twin' hours, would be all at sea with a real twin engine aircraft, so I always entered Gannet hours in the single engine column of my Log Book. The Gannet was the first Turbo aircraft I flew, and I went up to Anthorn for a quick conversion. After a thorough briefing on the ground, I made a 2 minute familiarisation flight, and was then judged competent to take the aircraft across the Irish Sea to R.N.A.S. Eglinton (near Londonderry). Managing a Mamba was quite different from operating a piston engine. The engines, once started, ran at a constant rpm. The throttles controlled the fuel flow and therefore the power produced the constant speed units on the props, keeping the rpm at the required figure of 8,000 rpm with the throttles closed at the ground idle position. For take off, the throttles were moved through a gate to 'flight idle'. The engines then ran at a constant speed of 15,000 rpm. Opening up fully produced no increase in rpm but an increase in power absorbed by the coarsening of the propeller pitch. Power developed was shown on a Shaft Horse Power gauge for each engine (maximum about 1,200). An additional check on engine performance was provided by jet pipe temperature gauges, a vital factor in all turbo operations. In the Mamba, a spill valve cut the fuel supply, should the J.P.T. rise beyond its safe limit.

Normally the front engine (front propeller really - the turbines were placed side by side) was usually started first by cartridge which spun it up to self maintaining speed.

The rear propeller was started by windmilling, with the first engine at full power. Each engine had the usual High Pressure Fuel Cock, with a button incorporated that actuated the relight system with the cock on, and the propeller feathering motor and propeller brake with the cock closed. A snag with earlier propturbines had been that in the event of power failure the propeller went at once to the fully fine ground idle position. Called discing, this caused an unacceptable amount of drag. In the Mamba this fault was overcome by the provision of 'flight fine pitch' stops, in position when the undercarriage was raised, which limited the propellers to a fine pitch angle of 21 deg. (Ground idling fine pitch was 6 deg.). This was an anti submarine aircraft and needed the ability to 'loiter' using minimum fuel, so the engine was designed to operate one half at a time. In this way range was also increased as the loss of speed was amply compensated by lower fuel consumption. Some Ferry Pilots liked to belt along on two engines at max cruise and 300 kts. Even on a short journey I preferred to fly on one engine with the out of use propeller feathered. As the working propeller was invisible from the ground, it must have startled those unused to Gannets to see a 'Single Engine' aircraft flying by with the propeller stationary! The drill was to change engines every half hour to equalise wear, and on arrival the ground staff would want to know for how long each half of the engine had run. It goes without saying that the propellers were contra rotating, so there were no swing problems, and the nose wheel undercarriage made it very difficult to make an untidy arrival.

The Gannet Mk.3 A.E.W. (Airborne Early Warning)

This was really a different aircraft from the AS Gannets. The pilot's was the only cockpit, the fuselage was deepened to provide a radar operator's cabin, and there was the large ventral radome. The tail pipes for the more powerful Double Mamba 102 were located under the leading edge of a slightly changed centre section, instead of above the trailing edge, as in the A.S. aircraft. Ferrying Gannets meant frequent visits to Fairey's at White Waltham airfield, always an enjoyable experience. The Royal

Navy paid a bitter price for the decision carried out, in the 1970's, to do away with conventional aircraft carriers and with them its A.E.W. aircraft. How many ships and lives would have been saved around the Falklands, by a flight of A.E.W. Gannet 3's, never mind the two squadrons of Phantoms that would have accompanied them.

Westland Wyvern *(Armstrong Siddeley Python A.S.P.3)*

In the summer of 1957 a number of us went for a couple of days to the Armstrong Siddeley factory at Coventry to do a Python engine course, so that we could fly the Westland Wyvern, now coming up for ferrying. One of the earliest turbo prop's, the Python would I'm sure, be considered ridiculously crude by modern standards. Horror tales abounded of Wyverns disgorging a mixture of detached turbine blades and molton metal when taxiing due to engine mishandling. In fact when we went to Stretton to fly our first Wyverns, we were shown a handful of assorted blades picked up off the airfield. It was true that the Python needed careful handling if engine damage was to be avoided hence the delay in getting the Wyvern into service as a deck landing aircraft. The Wyvern was certainly a giant for a single seater. To put matters in perspective, its all up weight at over 24,000 pounds was twice that of the three seater Blenheim Bomber serving with Bomber Command in 1939. Its engine power was well over twice that of the total power of the Blenheims and its payload three times as great. If you remember also that the Wyvern was one of the last examples of tail wheel layout, with all the difficulties of handling that that entailed, it will be seen that we were well advised to approach it with dire humility.

In the event, the Wyvern was a pleasant aircraft in the air, if a bit of a handful on the ground. The Python drove two four bladed contra rotating propellers. With both of these in fine pitch, the effect was to blank off the rear control surfaces. Thus one was warned not to do a wheel landing in a crosswind, but to three point the aircraft and allow the locked tail wheel to keep the aircraft straight. Also in the event of engine failure in flight (gulp!), the drill was to feather the propellers at once. As the warning ran - elevator control would not be effective at less than 160 kts with the propellers idling in flight fine pitch and this speed might not be achieved <u>even in a steep dive.</u> Oh yes, one was given plenty to think about. But then, I ferried ten Wyverns and the engines behaved impeccably for me. Good old A.S. As a matter of interest, my research leads me to believe that the Wyvern at 24,000 lbs was the heaviest propeller driven single seater aircraft ever built. It beats the twin engine D.H. Hornet by 4,000 lbs.

PURE JETS

The first I flew was the Gloster Meteor T7. This was the dual control (2 R.R.Derwent 5 or 8) Meteor, and I went to St Davids airfield in West Wales to do a conversion with Airwork Ltd. About twelve hours flying with them (my instructor was Jimmy Duncan who had been my pupil at Rochester on an I.F.Course) and I was a jet pilot. It was quite refreshing to get into the simple Meteor cockpit after the complexities of piston engines, and especially of the turbo props. The jet engine had two simple controls:

A high-pressure cock for turning the fuel on and off, and a 'throttle' control for regulating its flow. The engine instruments were equally simple, a rev. counter, a jet pipe temperature gauge and probably, an oil pressure gauge. In the twin engined Meteor, these controls were duplicated. As to the flying, nothing could be simpler. One had to get used to the fact that movement did not give the immediate response one was used to with piston engines, and that the fuel consumption was very high at low levels. So all A to B flying was carried above 20,000, and probably nearer 30,000 ft. The aircraft was provided with drive brakes so that one could get down from these heights quickly and at a reasonable speed. One thing I could never really come to terms with, being an old piston engine pilot, was the small fuel reserve one had to work with. If one flew a jet from say Lee-on-Solent to Abbotsinch (Glasgow), the flight time was about one hour. You arrived overhead with about thirty minutes' fuel, provided you stayed at altitude, but once having let down, that thirty minutes had become ten minutes at circuit height. If the weather was poor and a G.C.A. was necessary, then there would only be fuel enough for one circuit after a missed approach. Once having let down there certainly would not have been enough fuel to divert to another airfield. And when you bear in mind that our navigation aids were dependent on one radio set, failure of this at the wrong time could have meant abandoning the aircraft. The younger pilots, having been brought up to this, took it in their stride, but I never did.

A few of the Meteors we flew were ex RAF N.F.II's, to be converted to target tugs by the Navy. These handled very like Meteor 7's, but had a lot more fuel, under wing tanks being fitted as standard - that pleased me. They were built by Armstrong Whitworth and in addition to the redesigned 'glass house', they had a long nose to house the radar, and a angular tail in common with the late marks of single seater Meteor.

Supermarine Attacker (Rolls Royce Nene 3)

The Attacker was the first jet aircraft in service with the Navy in 1951, and I was just in time to fly one when they were being withdrawn from the Airwork F.R.U. at Hurn, to Abbotsinch for scrap, in February 1957. Unique in being the only tail wheel jet aircraft to go into service, it was a bit of a hybrid, using main planes designed for the piston engined Spiteful. It was a bit of a brute to taxi as, with no slipstream over the rudder, and with tail wheel lack of directional stability, one was entirely dependent on the brakes for control. In addition, there was the tendency for blast from the low set jet pipe to damage the airfield surface. The experience of one flight hardly qualifies me to judge the Attacker, but I do remember that it inherited a fuel system from its piston engine forbears that required the pilot to select fuel tanks as required. (In all other jets the fuel was drawn from the tanks in turn automatically, to prevent inadvertent flame out). I therefore found myself in the circuit at Abbots, flying on a very nearly empty tank. Luckily I was able to change to a full one in time. (A flamed out jet engine cannot be restarted simply by turning to a full tank as in a piston engined aircraft. Rather lengthy re-light procedure at circuit height is just not on).

Hawker Sea Hawk (Rolls Royce Nene 101 or 103)

The Sea Hawk must have been one of the prettiest little aircraft ever made. It certainly rivalled the Spitfire, and handsome is as handsome does, it flew beautifully. I never heard a rude word said of a Sea Hawk. I did hear some said <u>near</u> one, by a grizzled P.O. when a young Naval Airman lent over the cockpit and emptied a pocket full of pencils, pens and small screwdrivers into the bowels of an aircraft I was about to ferry, but that's another story. I well remember an American Navy pilot walking round my Hawk at Bordeaux when I was on my way to Gibraltar - he had parked his C-47 nearby. "Gee", he said, "What a cute little ship. Everyone should have one". That just about sums it up.

I can find only one fault with the Sea Hawk. The main fuel tanks were in the fuselage, one just forward and one just aft of the C.of G. It was important that they emptied together and in the correct sequence. A gauge was provided for each tank, and an information plate in the cockpit showed the weight of fuel (the gauges were in lbs) that should be left in each tank to keep the C.of G. within limits. This system could be temperamental, and then it was necessary to control the flow from each tank by use of the low-pressure fuel cocks. I only had to resort to this once, on a trip back from Malta with a very 'clapped' aircraft. I remember landing at Yeovilton, luckily on a long runway, with just sufficient brake pressure to turn on to the taxi track. I had to wait there to be towed in.

De Havilland Vampire T.22 (D.H. Goblin 35)

This was the two-seater trainer version. It was a pleasant little aircraft, and with overload wing tanks fitted, had a very useful range. I took one out to Malta and enjoyed the trip.

De Havilland Sea Venom F.A.W. 22 (1 DH Ghost 105)

This aircraft was developed from the Vampire and the RAF's Venom NF2. I never felt really at home with the Venom, probably because I didn't fly many. When strapped in to the ejector seat with leg restrainers and so on, I always felt like a trussed fowl. The rather poor forward view over the long nose, housing the radar, accentuated this effect. I'm sure there must be many pilots who swore by the Venom. I was not one of them.

HELICOPTERS

Early in 1958 it was decided that the proportion of helicopters in the Fleet Air Arm had grown to such an extent that it was important that some Ferry Pilots should be able to fly them. So Jim Smith, myself and 'Pancho' Brandt were selected to go on consecutive, overlapping 'chopper' courses with 705 Squadron at Lee-on-Solent. Now, if you want to cut a pilot down to size, send him on a 'chopper' course. Very little of his past experience will help him in handling this alien beast. Of course he has a background of basic airmanship, height, judgement and so on, but actually controlling the thing, well! The basic principles of flight of the helicopter are well known. Revolving rotor blades provide the lift to keep the aircraft in the air, obviating the need to maintain forward speed. A tail rotor provides lateral thrust, counter acting the tendency for the helicopter fuselage to turn in the opposite direction to the main rotor. When the aircraft is moving forward, and the rotor can be tilted to achieve this, the forward moving rotor blades generate more lift than the rearward moving blades. The rotor head is designed to eliminate this by allowing the rearward moving blades to adopt a greater angle of attack than those moving forward. The aircraft is controlled in the rolling plane by lateral movements, and in the pitching plane by fore and aft movements of the cyclic pitch control. This takes the place of the control column in a fixed wing aircraft. In addition, there is a collective pitch lever, usually at the pilot's left hand. This controls the pitch of all the blades together; moving the lever upwards increases their lift and the aircraft climbs, lowering it decreases their pitch and the aircraft descends. Moving the collective pitch lever also controls the engine power, up to increase, down to reduce, to help keep the rotor RPM constant, but a twist grip throttle control is also provided on this lever, for fine adjustment. The engine is usually connected to the rotors by a centrifugal clutch, so on the ground opening the twist grip throttle engages the rotors. The 'rudder' controls alter the pitch of the tail rotor, controlling the aircraft in the yawing plane. It all sounds very simple until you try. Providing the aircraft is kept moving forward, the controls can be operated in much the same way as in a fixed wing aircraft, but at slow speeds and in the hover, its like learning to ride a bike, easy when you can do it, but until then you keep falling off!

705 Squadron was equipped with Whirlwind 3 (Sikorsky S 55 Wright Cyclone R-1300-3), Westland built aircraft. RN pilots started their courses on the much smaller Hiller helicopters, but we skipped that stage. The Whirlwind 3 with 700 hp had a reasonable margin of power in hand, but the Squadron had a few Whirlwind 1's with a 600 hp Pratt & Witney Wasp engine. Here the power was sometimes marginal. This is important. These helicopters had fully articulated rotors. This meant that the blades were free to move upwards in the vertical plane to any degree. (Their movement downwards on the ground was restricted by 'droop stops'). In flight the only thing that stopped the rotor blades moving upwards on their hinges was the centrifugal force, set up by their rotation. But, if this force became too great (i.e. the rotor R.P.M. exceeded safe limits), there was danger of blade failure. When I say that the normal rotor R.P.M. was 200, the maximum 213, and the minimum 135, it will be seen that a little extra power was most useful when increasing collective pitch. It would have been possible to get into a position where the high pitch of the blades was slowing down the rotor, the blades were rising on the hinges (coning), thus reducing the rotor's effective diameter, and therefore its total lift, and insufficient power was available to increase rotor speed, needing a higher blade pitch and......need I go on? I have seen a Whirlwind 1 stagger away with the rotor blades at a quite alarming

angle, and the engine sounding as if it was just about to 'bust its braces'.

To return to the 'Chopper' Course, I was lucky in having a most excellent instructor in Bill Stevens, an RAF Flight Lieutenant seconded to the Navy. He was a most experienced helicopter pilot, having flown them in Malaya and Bornio, but more important to me, he was a very understanding instructor. After about six hours dual and frequent periods when I thought I'd never get the hang of the thing, I went solo and gradually became a reasonably competent helicopter pilot.

As well as the Whirlwinds 1 and 3, we did an hour or two on the Mk.7. This was the Anti Submarine Whirlwind, and was powered by an Alvis Leonides Major (the twin banked one) with cartridge starter. In service there was a certain amount of trouble with these engines, and the 7's were withdrawn from serving time. The helicopter engine gets one hell of a beating, often under conditions when cooling is not too efficient. At the end of the Course we had a few hours on the Dragonfly (the S.1 with an Alvis Lionides 50). This was the aircraft that equipped the Navy's first all helicopter squadron, and I think, while not being unpleasant to fly, it showed its age.

One of the trials of the trade that had to be learned was landing after descending in auto rotation. This state is arrived at when, with the collective pitch lever fully down and the rotor clutch disengaged, airflow instead of being forced down by the rotor blades under power, passes up through the windmilling blades with the engine idling or inoperative. The aircraft then descends like a sycamore seed, and the surplus energy stored in the rotor is used to soften the landing by raising the collective pitch control at the critical moment. In the event of engine failure in a helicopter, it is important at once to lower the collective pitch fully, thus allowing the rotor to go into auto rotation.

20. *Helicopter Ferrying*

Having completed the 'chopper' course, we were now able to ferry the aircraft. This did not mean we were finished with fixed wing aircraft, and my Log Book shows plenty of Sea Hawks, Venoms and Gannets as well as Whirlwinds and Dragonflys. A regular job was to collect new aircraft from the Westlands factory at Yeovil and take them to Fleetlands Repair Yard, for acceptance by the Navy. At first there were Whirlwinds Mk.7, but later on the Wessex started to appear, but more of that later. We beat a track across Somerset, Dorset and Hampshire - Yeovil, Sherborne, north of Bournemouth, avoiding Hurn circuit, the New Forest and Southampton Water, and so to the little 'Chopper' landing pad at Fleetlands. Helicopter cross-country flying was a case of back to basics. It was much like flying a Tiger Moth as far as height and speed were concerned, but warm and with an unrivalled view all around. From the pilot's seat (on the right by the way, not the left as in other aircraft - presumably so that the left hand operated collective pitch lever can be in between the seats and out of the way), one can look vertically downwards and watch the chickens scattering in terror as this noisy threatening bird swoops over them. But the snags present in light aeroplane flight were there also. With this generation of helicopters, instrument flying was in its infancy, so it was a case of keeping in contact with the ground if at all possible. If not, then it was better not to fly.

Jet flying was often a case of seeing the airfield at either end and a lot of cloud tops in between, but in a 'chopper' one really got to know the country. Typical routes were from Scotland

(Lossiemouth or Donibristle) to the south coast; could one get across to the west coast or was it better to stick to the east coast? It depended on the weather. Two refuelling stops would probably be required, Acklington and perhaps Waddington? In good weather, what about Silloth and Shawbury? Another common route would be Fleetlands to Culdrose - this was one hop. So the sea front at Bournemouth, the Dorset hills, Lyme Bay, Dartmoor, Plymouth and the south Cornish coast all became familiar ground. In Northern Ireland the Air Station at Eglinton was in full operation. Mk. 7 Whirlwinds were their staple diet, flown from Fleetlands. The route here was across the Hampshire and Wiltshire Downs, the Cotswolds and up the Severn Valley to Shawbury to refuel. Then continuing across the coast to Rhyl, past the Isle of Man and on to Ireland. It was quite a long sea crossing on a single engine, especially as the Leonides was not proving too reliable. We didn't wear immersion suits even in winter (though of course we had Mae Wests and dinghys) so it was a case of 'fingers crossed'. In the event, no ferry pilot had any trouble. I only had two serious mechanical faults when flying 'choppers' and both were on Dragonflys. In the first instance I took off from Brawdy to take the aircraft to Lee. As I crossed the airfield boundary heading east, the engine coughed, faltered and then picked up. I continued but found I had to use more and more throttle even to keep the speed at 60 kts. I was just beginning to think that there was no future in this, when I noticed the oil pressure gauge falling rapidly to zero. I quickly lowered the collective pitch lever to set up auto rotation, and seeing a field ahead (I was flying into wind), made a couple of S turns and a reasonable landing. By this time the engine was completely defunct. From my position on the ground I was able to call up Brawdy and tell them what had happened. As I unstrapped and got down from the aircraft, a number of breathless farm workers arrived. They asked if I was all right. They had seen me flying by with the aircraft streaming blue smoke. What had happened was, as I left Brawdy, the engine dropped a valve and it punctured a hole in the top of a piston. This accounted for the loss of power. The blue smoke was the oil being burnt and vented through the exhaust. After a few minutes the oil pressure was lost, and as I landed, the engine seized up. It was quite a job to get the aircraft out, as a couple of stone walls had to be moved.

Peter Rivington's Dragonfly helicopter force-landed in a field after taking off from RNAS Brawdy on 23rd October 1958.

The second Dragonfly incident occurred when flying from Donibristle to Silloth (Anthorn was by then closed). About twenty miles north of the Solway Firth, I smelt burning rubber. Everything in the cockpit seemed O.K. so I carried on with only about twenty minutes to go to Silloth. I was looking over the side at a small farmyard dotted with white chickens, when the cyclic pitch control was all but wrenched out of my hand, and the aircraft was on its side. I pulled the Dragonfly back on an even keel and found that it was all I could do to control it against the vibration now occurring. I now saw that the pressure gauge for the servos, which operate the controls, was at 0. Now the cyclic control governs the movements of a heavy rotor which provides the aircraft's lift. Servo assistance is needed to make the control loads acceptable, and damp vibration. My servos had failed. I was faced with about a twenty-minute flight in which I had to control the aircraft manually. We had practiced manual control on our course, but only for a few moments - now it was 'for real'.

It is very difficult to bring the aircraft to the hover on manual, so I called up Silloth telling them of my trouble and that I would be landing on the runway. I was most relieved when Silloth appeared ahead and there, right in the middle of the runway, was a bloke waving bats at me. I asked the tower to get him out of the way, as I intended to run the aircraft on to its wheels at about 40 kts. Luckily he got the message and ran off in time. It was found that the servo hydraulic pump had seized. The burning rubber smell was the drive belt running over the stationary pulley of the seized pump. I said 'thank you very much' and went home by train. If I had been half an hour instead of twenty minutes from an airfield, I'm not sure that I could have managed. It was a Dragonfly I took from Fleetlands to Plymouth to make the first (and I think only) ferry flight deck landing, as mentioned in the 'Flight Deck' article. Likewise, I once struck fog over Morecombe Bay heading north in a Whirlwind. For some reason I had decided to go to Ireland via the short sea crossing, Stranraer - Larne. After passing Blackpool the visibility got worse and worse and over the Bay, with no proper visual reference, sand dunes and mud flats in misty weather do not make for easy flight, I was half on instruments and half on visual reference at about 100 ft.

That is a recipe for disaster. I was overjoyed when the north coast of the Bay appeared and I followed the shore round that long spit of land to the west of Barrow-in-Furness. By this time I had had enough and, seeing a farm house with telephone wires leading to it, landed nearby and rang Silloth. They told me that the weather was absolutely dank and that I'd better wait. After just over an hour, Silloth rang back and told me that the weather was a bit better and I could come on. The visibility was so bad that I dare not lose sight of the coast. Rather than cut across that little inlet by Millom, I had to follow the coast round and up past Calder Hall and Bees Head (in cloud), Maryport and Workington and finally Silloth, where I thankfully repaired to the local hotel for the night. The pubs in that part of Cumberland were then under State control, and not a good advertisement for Nationalisation. What were they like? Imagine buying beer at a post office! The next day was a Friday, and with the weather no better I had permission from Rochester to go home by train. I can't remember who picked the Whirlwind up. It wasn't me.

These few examples might give the reader an idea of the trials and tribulations of Chopper ferry flying. As I have hinted, instrument flying in the early generation of Choppers was 'iffish' in the extreme. The main problem was the lack of inherent stability in the aircraft. This stability makes flying on instruments possible, or even easy, in fixed wing aircraft. Even without an autopilot, when properly trimmed it will, in smooth conditions, fly 'hands off' for a time that might extend to minutes. This was not the case with the Choppers. The Dragonfly did not have blind flying instruments at all. They were provided in the Whirlwind, but in order to use them the aircraft had to be flown like a fixed wing aircraft with 50 or 60 knots forward speed. Then the attitude shown on the artificial horizon bore some rational relation to the performance of the aircraft, and the reading on the A.S.I. This situation was to change with the introduction of the Westland Wessex H.A.S.1 (1 Napier Gazelle 161 free turbine engine). This aircraft had a fully computerised auto control system, providing both feel and stability, enabling the pilot to fly it on instruments as easily as on a fixed wing aircraft.

Peter Rivington handing over the first Wessex H.A.S. Mk.1 XM841, to the Senior Pilot of 815 Sq. at RNAS Culdrose on 17th May 1961.

It was in April 1961 that Jim Smith, 'Pancho' and myself went to Napiers at Acton for a couple of days, to do a course on the Gazelle, and then to Yeovil to fly the Wessex with their Chopper expert John Fay, as instructor. The Gazelle 161 was interesting, a 'free turbine' engine. This meant that instead of the power turbine being connected by direct drive to the compresser, it was quite separate. It was said that should the transmission to the rotor fail with the engine under power, the revs of the power turbine would build up so quickly that it would disintegrate in seconds. As I have indicated, the modern systems on the Wessex took a lot of the hassle out of helicopter flying, and the big aircraft was a joy to handle. On 17th May 1961 I took the first Wessex XM841 away from Fleetlands and handed it over to 815 Squadron at Culdrose, to start re-equipping them. The Wessex 1 was the first turbine engined helicoptor to be used by the Navy (they did not get the Gnome engined Whirlwind until 1966), and its smoothness and ample reserve of power was a revelation.

Peter Rivington taking off from Fleetlands Air Yard in Wessex Mk.1 XM840 on 2nd June 1961.

21. *Overseas Trips*

I have written that overseas were the gilt on the ferry pilots' gingerbread. I flew twelve trips to Malta, eight from Malta to the U.K. and one out to Gib. The aircraft involved were a fair selection: Expediter, Sea Prince, Sturgeon (2), Firefly, Skyraider, Gannet (3), Meteor (3), Seahawk (4), Venom (2), Vampire and pride of place, Whirlwind. The RAF maintained a staging post in France, first at Istres and later at Orange. If Orange was not within range, we would call in at Dijon or Chateauroux. Between Orange and Malta we would either use Elmas in Sardinia or an airfield on the Italian mainland, Patrica-di-Mare near Rome, or Naples. I did one Gib trip in a Seahawk, via Bordeaux, and Barcelona. The leg from Barcelona to Gib. took one hour forty minutes. The same in a SATA Anson would have taken five hours. Landing at Gib. from east to west, I found out what is meant by 'wind sheer'. On finals at about 140 knots the airspeed suddenly dropped to below 100 without warning. A panic application of full power restored the situation, but it was a nasty moment. I'd heard talk of funny eddies round the Rock, now I'd experienced them first hand.

In early December 1959 a group of us, four I think, were flown out to Malta on a trooping flight, the normal mode of transport Viscounts, and quite comfortable. Flying back the next day, because of a late start we could only get as far as Patrica di Mare. After landing, one of our number, Geoff Lawson, could hardly climb down from his aircraft. He was very ill with what appeared to be food poisoning. We had had a fair 'do' in Valetta the previous night and Geoff had obviously picked up something nasty. We waited a day and then carried on to Orange and Dijon. The Weather was very, very poor in Northern Europe, so it was wise to refuel at Dijon. Leaving there we had flight planned to Manston, the only airfield within reach in the U.K. with reasonable weather. Climbing up through cloud we experienced engine icing. With a turbo prop engine, icing occurs under the same conditions as airframe icing. In this case the ice started to build up around the engine air intakes. The result is a fall off of power, opening the throttle makes no difference, just a steep rise in jet pipe temperature. The answer is to get out of cloud to stop the ice forming. As power is falling off it is not easy to climb. To descend was impossible, as the hills north of Dijon rose to over 4,000 ft. and would almost certainly be in cloud. Luckily we found a clear layer which allowed the ice to disperse, otherwise we might have been forced down, not a pleasant thought. We dumped the Gannets at Manston and went home for the weekend.

'Pancho' and I took two Firefly U9's (modified as pilotless target drones) to Malta via Orange and Naples. While we were refuelling at Naples an American sailor came up and asked what the aircraft were. When we told him he asked if we both flew in one aircraft and brought the other along with us! Honestly! But pride of place must go to my Whirlwind trip to Malta in December 1961. This was in the nature of an experiment to see if it was a feasible proposition to fly helicopters out to the Mediterranean. The aircraft chosen was a Whirlwind H.A.R. 21 WV205, American built and with a good five hours endurance, for which I was to be very grateful. First was the flight planning. This was going to be a 'contact' flight and the problem was to get over the spine of high ground running north east across France from the Massif Central and thus into the Rhone/Saone Valley. Once there the rest of the flight would be plain sailing, following the river or the coast. I decided to go to the east of Paris across Champagne to Dijon; on this route there would be very little ground over 1,000 ft. In summer this would have been a simple matter, but December in Europe was entirely different. I went down to Lee by train (London to Portsmouth Harbour, Gosport Ferry and R.N. car) on the 2nd December (a Sunday) and reported to Fleetlands the next day. Unfortunately the aircraft was not ready, nor was it ready on the 4th, so I whiled away the time taking a Whirlwind to Portland. The flight was somewhat marginal, with clouds down on the white Dorset cliffs, and my helicopter skimming the rough uninviting looking waves.

I returned to Lee by train and it appeared that the aircraft would be ready the next day, 4th December. By now I was getting somewhat worried as I naturally wanted to be home by Christmas. My fears were well justified, as the Chopper still was not ready on the 5th and it was not until the afternoon of the 6th that we were able to set out. I say we, as I had been provided with a most stalwart companion in Petty Officer 'Robbie' Robbins, whose chief task was to do the day to day servicing of the aircraft. In the event, he also acted most efficiently as a map reader, stick holder (flying straight and level) and generally was a most welcome companion. As we did not get away until around 2 p.m. it was obviously out of the question to get further that day than our first stop, the French Air Force Base at Cambrai. The short winter days and the fact that we were working our way steadily eastwards, meant that at no time during the flight were we able to fly more than two legs a day. We flew eastwards along the south coast and headed out into the English Channel from Beachy Head. Crossing into France north of Abbeville, an hour and forty minutes total flying, brought us to Cambrai. The Frenchmen could not have been more hospitable and the next morning we were ready to carry on to our next stop, Dijon -

except for the weather. Heavy snow and low cloud over the high ground between Cambrai and Dijon put flying out of the question, so we settled down to another 24 hours of French hospitality. We were taken in to Cambrai town for lunch and the drive there was through rolling pasture land. I noticed that there was no even ground anywhere. Otherwise, flat fields, were a mass of shallow dish like depressions. Then I understood; even after nearly fifty years this ground, heavily fought over in 1914-1918, still bore the scars of the shell craters that had covered it in those days. Cambrai itself was a smart clean looking town. Although some of the buildings were of historic design, they were clearly less than forty years old and rebuilt from the destruction of the Great War, and there were no old trees. We are used in Britain to seeing trees aged 100 to 150 years. In that part of France in 1961, no trees were more than 42 years old.

The following day, the 8th, the weather relented and we were able to take off for Dijon. It was cloudy but fair, but there was a strong headwind. I estimated a flight time of three hours for the two hundred nautical miles. In fact it took four hours and our ground speed could not have been more that fifty knots, giving a headwind of forty knots (nearly 50 mph). The ground was snow covered, making map reading difficult and after passing St. Quenten I could recognise little on the ground. With my unexpectedly slow ground speed and no help from the radio, I was lost for about two hours. When within striking distance of Dijon I began calling them, to no avail. The weather was clear ahead, I could see the snow covered Juras quite plainly, but low cloud was beginning to form below and to port. Knowing that I must be somewhere near Dijon, I started to turn starboard away from the cloudy area. At that moment Dijon came through loud and clear and their instructions showed I was turning the wrong way. From then on it was a simple matter of letting down through the cloud on Q.D.M's and very soon the runway lights were ahead. Four hours was quite long enough.

We were barely half an hour on the ground at Dijon and then it was a quick dash south to the Saone, and on down past the vineyards of Nuits St Georges to Lyon, and a landing at Orange as dusk was falling. Another two hours forty minutes made it six hours forty minutes for the day. This was quite enough in a chopper. We always enjoyed our stops at Orange with the RAF and this one was no exception, so I suspect that Robbie and I were not feeling quite one hundred per cent when we set off again the next morning. One of the problems we had to solve was finding refuelling points. Of course we needed petrol (100 octane) not the more usual Avcat (paraffin). This meant that we were probably better off at the smaller airfields. So from Orange we made for Cannes, rather than the large airport at Nice. The weather was good and we were very nearly able to make the flight direct with only a slight detour to starboard to avoid the highest of the Alpes Maritimes. At Cannes we were held up for nearly two hours, firstly waiting for a bowser and then for the paper work.

Taking off from Cannes we started the long Mediterranean coast crawl that was to take us nearly all the way to Malta. We were making for Pisa, but providence dictated that we kept within sight of the coast, so we struck out north eastwards passing Antibes, Nice and Monaco, and so into Italian waters off San Remo. Now we were in the Gulf of Genoa and the cranes and buildings of Genoa itself were just visible away to port. Then came La Spezia and so to the airport at Pisa. Robbie secured and locked the aircraft, while I ordered weather reports and arranged clearances for the morning. We seemed to be parked rather a long way from the terminal building, but had to go where we were put.

We stayed at the Hotel Costa Mediterranean and were most comfortably looked after. After dinner we took a stroll to look at the flood-lit Leaning Tower and, although we had eaten well, Robbie, in true Navy style, could not resist a large slice of the fresh cooked pizza that the Italians sell in much the same way as we sell fish and chips. In the morning we found that there had been an attempt to break in to the aircraft. The cabin door had been removed by pulling the emergency jettison handle but as nothing else appeared to have been touched, we presumed that the clatter caused by the falling door had scared the intruder off.

It was now Sunday and it was a little difficult to get the airport people moving, but eventually, after Robbie had re-fitted the door, done his work with a grease gun on the rotor head and completed his D.I., we were able to get off for Rome. The coast bulges out south of Leghorn, and it was most direct to fly a few miles inland for the first two thirds of the leg. This gave us a chance to enjoy the unrivalled view of the landscape to be had from a chopper's cockpit. We saw many more bullocks pulling ploughs than we saw tractors, and the long straight roads clearly had their origin more than 2,000 years ago when they echoed to the tramp of the legions. These roads would have fascinated an aerial visitor from Mars. He would see the road, ruler straight for ten or more miles, then, a few miles apart, two brightly coloured objects, rapidly approaching one another. Just when it seemed there would be a catastrophic crash, they would flash past each other, seemingly with millimetres to spare. It looked for all the world like the most spectacular suicide pact, and I suspect, having experienced Italian driving, it must have felt like that to a passenger in the car.

Two hours thirty minutes from Pisa to Rome. Here we wasted time going to Patricia di Mare (our usual staging post), but not only was it closed, it being Sunday lunch time, but there was no

100 Octane petrol anyway. So we veered off to Champino Airport in Rome, where we got the fuel we needed. Champino to Naples was only one hour thirty minutes, but the coast of south west Italy, as so many holiday makers know, is an absolute gem, with mountains coming right down to the sea and little fishing villages and resorts tucked away in coves and inlets. Even in December it looked marvellous. On a coastal trip like this in good visibility one does not hug the shoreline, but rather aims a series of straight legs between visible headlands. If the visibility is poor then one tends to stay much closer in shore.

At Naples we were able to leave the aircraft in the capable hands of the U.S. Navy, but I cannot say that it is my favourite city, there is too much begging and poverty, and corruption too if the stories told are to be believed. Certainly one does well to keep ones wallet buttoned up in an inside pocket. To counter this, the great brooding hulk of Vesuvius, smoking and sulking, makes an impressive backdrop. Monday morning at Naples and we sensed we were on the last lap. Down round the instep of Italy and across the Messina Straits, and so past Catania to the American Base at Singonella. This is a fine country if you like volcanoes, with Stromboli smoking away twenty miles out to sea, and Etna, queen of them all, rising to over 10,000 feet on the east of the island.

We had planned to refuel at Reggio di Calabria, but could get no reply from them, so we pressed on to the U.S.Airfield at Signoella. There we took on fuel and were away as soon as possible on the last leg to Malta, one hour and twenty eight minutes. As always the flat shape of Malta appearing on the horizon was a most welcome sight, and the clipped RAF voice from 'Malta Airways' a most welcome sound. Flying has something in common with beating one's head against a wall, its best when you leave off. It was good to be amongst friends at Halfar, and to be told there was a Sea Prince WF934 to take home, but not we said, until Wednesday. On Wednesday we set off in the Prince for home, myself, Robbie and three passengers, spending the night at Orange and arriving at Yeovilton, via Chateauroux on the 14th December 1961, just in time to ferry a Gannet XP198 and a Dragonfly WG750 before Christmas leave.

So we have come to the end of the story. The last page of my Log Book reads:

- Meteor T7 WL353 to Malta
- Meteor T7 WL332 Malta to U.K.
- Dragonfly WG718 Lossiemouth to Fleetlands (via Leuchars, Acklington and Waddington).
- Wessex XP151 Yeovil to Fleetlands
- Varsity WL681 local flying at Rochester
- Wessex XP146 Fleetlands to Portland
- Percival Sea Prince WF129 Brawdy to Belfast

and on 26th October 1962 – Wessex to Portland

- … follow the railway to Dorchester then 90 deg. port and squeeze between the Downs and the cloud, and down over Weymouth with Portland looking for all the world like a miniature Gibraltar at the end of its shingle spit. There's the heliport and the yellow bats of the marshaller. Touch down on to landing spot number 8. Cut the engine, brake the rotor, all cocks and switches off. Climb down, walk away, don't look back.

Don't look back? How could I avoid looking back on a most rewarding twenty four years traversing Wilbur Wright's 'Infinite Highway'.

~ E N D ~

Appendix 1 – Aircraft Flown

Single Engine Types (Piston)

- Miles Magister (Gypsy Major)
- North American Harvard I & II (Pratt & Whitney Wasp Junior)
- De Havilland Hornet Moth (Gypsy Major)
- Avro Tutor (Armstrong Siddeley Lynx)
- Hawker Hurricane Mk I (Merlin III), Mk II B, C, & D (Merlin XX)
- Curtiss Mohawk (Wright Cyclone GR 1820 G-205A)
- Vultee Vengeance (Wright Double Cyclone GR 2600-A5-B5)
- Fairey Battle (Merlin III)
- De Havilland Tiger Moth (Gypsy Major)
- Fairchild Cornell (Ranger 6)
- Supermarine Spitfire V (Merlin 45)
- Hawker Typhoon 18 (Napier Sabre IIB)
- Miles Master II (Pratt & Whitney Wasp), III (Bristol Mercury XX)
- North American Mustang III & IV (Packard Merlin V1650-7)
- Taylorcraft Auster (Cirrus Minor) (Lycoming 0-290-3)
- Percival Proctor (Gypsy 6)
- D.H.Chipmunk (Gypsy Major 8)
- Percival Prentice (Gypsy 6)
- Fairey Firefly (T1.5.6.7.U9)(Rolls Royce Griffon 12 & 74), Mk.7 (Griffon 59)
- Hawker Sea Fury FB1 (Bristol Centauras 1B) T.20 18
- Bolton & Paul Balliol (Merlin 35)
- Grumman Avenger AS.4 (Wright Cyclone R 2600-20)
- Douglas Skyraider AEW 1 (R 3350-26 WA)
- Beech Tri-pacer (Lycoming)

Multi engined types (piston)

- Avro Anson 1 (2 Cheetah IX), XIX (2 Cheetah 15), T21 (2 Cheetah 17)
- Bristol Blenheim I (2 Mercury XII), IV (2 Mercury XV), V (2 Mercury XX)
- Bristol Beaufighter I (2 Hercules XVI), TT10 (2 Hercules XVII)
- Douglas Dakota (2 Pratt & Whitney Twin Wasps)
- Lockheed 12A (2 Pratt & Whitney Wasps)
- D.H. Dragon (2 Gypsy Major)
- D.H.Rapide (2 Gypsy 6)
- Avro Lancaster & Lancasterian (4 R.R.Merlins 24)
- Airspeed Oxford (2 A.S.Cheetah X)
- Short Sealand (2 D.H. Gypsy Queen 70)
- De Havilland Devon (2 Gypsy Queen 150)
- Beechcraft Expediter (2 Pratt & Whitney Wasps)
- Short Sturgeon (2 R.R.Merlin 140)
- Vickers Varsity (2 Bristol Hercules 264)

Propeller Turbine Aircraft

- Fairey Gannet (I Armstrong Siddeley Double Mamba 100 or 101)
- Fairey Gannet A.E.W. Mk.3 (1 Double Mamba 112)
- Westland Wyvern (A.S. Python A.S.P.3.)

Jet Aircraft

- Gloucester Meteor T7 (2 R.R. Derwent 8)
- Hawker Sea Hawk Mk's 1,3,5,6 (R.R. Nene 2,4,10)
- Supermarine Attacker (R.R. Nene 3)
- D.H.Vampire T 22 (D.H. Goblin 35)
- D.H. Venom F.A.W. 22 (D.H.Ghost 105)
- Armstrong Whitworth Meteor N.F.II (2 Derwent 8)

Helicopters

- Westland Whirlwind I (Wright Cyclone), 3 (P & W Wasp), 22 (P & W Wasp),
- 7 (A.S.Double Leonidies)
- Westland Dragonfly (A.S. Leonidies 50)
- Westland Wessex I (Napier Gazelle 161)

Appendix 2 – Glossary of Terms & Abbreviations

AA	:	Anti-aircraft
AEO	:	Aircraft Establishment Officer
AEW	:	Airborne Early Warning
AHQ	:	Air Headquarters
AOC	:	Air Officer Commanding
APO	:	Acting Pilot Officer
ARB	:	Air Registration Board
AS	:	Anti-submarine
ASI	:	Air Speed Indicator
ATC	:	Air Traffic Control
ATS	:	Advanced Training School
AVM	:	Air Vice-Marshal
BABS	:	Blind Approach Beacon System
BAT	:	British Air Transport
BEA	:	British European Airways
BOAC	:	British Overseas Airways Corporation
BSAA	:	British South American Airways
CAMB	:	Central Air Medical Board
CCI	:	Cricket Club of India
CFI	:	Chief Flying Instructor
CFS	:	Central Flying School
CGI	:	Chief Ground Instructor
CO	:	Commanding Officer
C of G	:	Centre of Gravity
CPF	:	Coastal Patrol Flight
CSE	:	Course Setting Compass
DFC	:	Distinguished Flying Cross
DI	:	Daily Inspection
DP	:	Duty Pilot
EFTS	:	Elementary Flying Training School
E&RFTS	:	Elementary & Reserve Flying Training School

ETA	:	Estimated Time of Arrival
Flt/Lt	:	Flight Lieutenant
FO	:	Flying Officer
FRU	:	Fleet Requirements Unit
GCA	:	Ground Controlled Approach
GP	:	General Practitioner
GR	:	General Reconnaissance
HQ	:	Headquarters
HMAMC	:	His Majesty's Armed Merchant Cruiser
HMS	:	His Majesty's Ship
HMT	:	His Majesty's Transport
HRH	:	His Royal Highness
IAF	:	Indian Air Force
IF	:	Instrument Flight
IN	:	Indian Navy
ITS	:	Initial Training School
JPT	:	Jet Pipe Temperature
LAC	:	Leading Aircraftman
LNER	:	London & North Eastern Railway
Lt/Cdr	:	Lieutenant Commander
MBE	:	Member (of the Order) of the British Empire
MFDF	:	Medium Frequency Direction Finding
MO	:	Medical Officer
MoD	:	Ministry of Defence
MT	:	Motor Transport
MTB	:	Motor Torpedo Boat
MU	:	Maintenance Unit
NAAFI	:	Navy, Army & Air Force Institutes
NCO	:	Non Commissioned Officer
OC	:	Officer Commanding
OD	:	Old Dauntsien
OTU	:	Operational Training Unit
PO	:	Pilot Officer
PT	:	Physical Training
QDM	:	Course to steer magnetic

RADA	:	Royal Academy of Dramatic Art
RAF	:	Royal Air Force
RAFO	:	Reserve of Air Force Officers
RAFRO	:	Royal Air Force Reserve Officers
RE	:	Royal Engineers
RFC	:	Royal Flying Corps/Rugby Football Club
RFTS	:	Reserve Flying Training School
RN	:	Royal Navy
RNAS	:	Royal Naval Air Station
RNR	:	Royal Navy Reserve
RNR(A)	:	Royal Navy Reserve Air Branch
R/O	:	Radio Operator
RPM	:	Revolutions Per Minute
RT	:	Radio/Telephone
SAS	:	Scandinavian/Southampton Air Services
SASO	:	Senior Air Staff Officer
SATA	:	Societie Anomie de Transports Aeriers
SFTS	:	Service Flying Training School
SHQ	:	Station Headquarters
S/L	:	Squadron Leader
SOE	:	Special Operations Executive
Trolly Acc.	:	Trolly Accumulator
UK	:	United Kingdom
USAAC	:	United States Army Air Corps
USAAF	:	United States Army Air Force
USAF	:	United States Air Force
VHF	:	Very High Frequency
W/C	:	Wing Commander
W/O	:	Warrant Officer
W/Op.	:	Wireless Operator
W.Op/AG	:	Wireless Operator/Airgunner
W/T	:	Wireless Transmission
WW2	:	World War 2